D1201655

The Governance of
Anglo-Saxon England
500–1087

The Governance of England

1 The Governance of Anglo-Saxon England 500–1087
   H.R. Loyn
2 The Governance of Early Medieval England 1087–1272*
   W.L. Warren
3 The Governance of Late Medieval England 1272–1461*
   A.L. Brown

*Publication 1985

The Governance of Anglo-Saxon England 500–1087

H.R. Loyn

Stanford University Press
Stanford, California
1984

For my mother, my wife and my sons

Stanford University Press
Stanford, California
© 1984 H. R. Loyn
Originating publisher: Edward Arnold Ltd
First published in the U.S.A. by Stanford University Press, 1984
Printed in the United States of America
ISBN 0-8047-1217-4
LC 83-50797

Contents

List of Kings   vii
List of Maps   viii
Abbreviations   ix
Acknowledgements   xi
Introduction   xiii

Part I   The Early Anglo-Saxon Kingdoms   1

1 The Kingdoms and their Kings to 871   3
2 Kingship and the Ranks of Men   30
  Leadership in War   31
  Control of Wealth   34
  The King and Law   41
  Ealdormen, Gesiths and Thegns   47
  Freemen and the Unfree   50
  Territorial Divisions   53
  The Church   56
3 The Reign of Alfred 871–899   61

Part II   The Later Anglo-Saxon Kingdoms 899–1066 79

4 Kingship and the Kings   81
  The Theory of Kingship   82
  The Succession   90
5 Government at the Centre   94
  The Household   95
  The Witenagemot   100
  The Secretariat   106
  Financial Organization–Treasury, Taxes and Coinage 118
  The King and the Administration of Justice   126

6 Government in the Localities   131
    The Shire   133
    The Hundred and the Tithing   140
    The Boroughs   148
    The Church   154
    Private Jurisdiction   161
    Military Organization   163
    Conclusion   169

Part III   The Norman Conquest   173

7 Norman Government in the Early Stages of
  Conquest and Settlement   175

Bibliography   198
Index   210

List of Kings

West-Saxon Kings

Edward the Elder	899–924
Athelstan	924–939
Edmund	939–946
Eadred [Edred]	946–955

Kings of England

Eadwig [Edwig *or* Edwy]		955–959
Edgar	(957)	959–975
Edward the Martyr		975–978
Ethelred [Æthelred]		978–1016
Sweyn Forkbeard		1013–1014
Edmund Ironside		1016
Cnut		1016–1035
Harold I, Harefoot		1035/7–1040
Harthacnut [Hardicnut]		1035/7–1042
Edward the Confessor		1042–1066
Harold II, Godwinson		1066

Alternative spellings are given of some of the Anglo-Saxon or Scandinavian names. Familiar names such as Alfred, Edward, Edgar or Ethelred have been kept in their modern spelling. *The Handbook of British Chronology* (2nd edn, Royal Historical Society, London, 1961) provides useful basic information on these and earlier kings.

List of Maps

1	The early kingdoms	11
2	The England of the Tribal Hidage	37
3	The Burghal Hidage	70
4	Meeting places of witenagemots in late Anglo-Saxon England	105
5	Anglo-Saxon mints	124
6	Anglo-Scandinavian England in the eleventh century	134
7	The dioceses of late Anglo-Saxon England	156
8	The Norman settlement	184

The maps in this book have been drawn using information from many of the available sources, particularly:

David Hill, *Atlas of Anglo-Saxon England*, Oxford 1981

Wendy Davies and H. Vierck, The Contexts of the Tribal Hidage: Social aggregates and Settlement Patterns', *Frühmittelalterliche Studien* 8, 1974, pp. 223–93

Simon Keynes, *Diplomas of King Ælthelred 'the Unready'*, Cambridge, 1980

Henry Loyn, *Anglo-Saxon England and the Norman Conquest*, London, 1962 and *The Norman Conquest*, London, 1965, 3rd edn 1983

D. Whitelock, *English Historical Documents* i, London, 1955

Abbreviations

ASCh	*Anglo-Saxon Chronicle.* Normally consulted in the edition of J. Earle and C. Plummer, *Two Saxon Chronicles Parallel* (Oxford, 1892 and 1899), and in the translation ed. D. Whitelock (London, 1961).
Asser, *Life of Alfred*	Asser's *Life of King Alfred,* ed. W.H. Stevenson (Oxford, 1904, reprinted with an article by D. Whitelock on recent work on Asser, 1959).
BAR	*British Archaeological Reports*
Bede, *HE*	*Bede's Ecclesiastical History of the English People.* Normally consulted in the edition by B. Colgrave and R.A.B. Mynors (Oxford, 1969).
BIHR	*Bulletin of the Institute of Historical Research*
BNJ	*British Numismatic Journal*
Beowulf	Normally consulted in the edition of A.J. Wyatt and R.W. Chambers (Cambridge, 1925). A good prose translation is the revised edition of J.R. Clark Hall by C.L. Wrenn and J.R.R. Tolkien (London, 1940)
CCCC	Corpus Christi College, Cambridge
CS	*Cartularium Saxonicum,* ed.W. de Gray Birch, 3 vols, and index (London, 1885–93).
DB	Domesday Book. Normally consulted in the Record Commission edition (4 vols., A. Farley and H. Ellis, 1783–1816) and in the appropriate volume of the Victoria County History
Econ.HR	*Economic History Review*
EHD	*English Historical Documents.* References to the first volume (ed. D. Whitelock 1955, 2nd edn 1979) are by number of document and page reference to the second edition. References to volume ii are to the edition of 1953 (ed. D.C. Douglas and G.W. Greenaway).
EHR	*English Historical Review*
EPNS	English Place Name Society

Haddan and Stubbs	*Councils and Ecclesiastical Documents,* ed. A.W. Haddan and W. Stubbs (3 vols, Oxford, 1869–71, reprinted 1964)
J.Soc. Archivists	*Journal of the Society of Archivists*
Lieb	F. Liebermann, *Die Gesetze der Angelsachsen* (3 vols., Halle, 1903–16). Where references are given to the laws by reign and number of clause only, reference should be made to this authoritative edition.
MGH	*Monumenta Germaniae Historica*
MHB	*Monumenta Historica Britannica,* ed. H. Petrie (London, 1848)
RHS	Royal Historical Society
RS	*Rolls Series*
s.a.	*sub anno*
TRHS	*Transactions of the Royal Historical Society*
WAM	Wiltshire Archaeological and Natural History Magazine
WHR	Welsh History Review
Wilkins, *Concilia*	*Concilia Magnae Britanniae et Hiberniae,* ed. D. Wilkins (London, 1737)
VCH	Victoria History of the Counties of England

Acknowledgements

My debt is great to many people for help in writing this book and I acknowledge here especially the contribution of Professor A.L. Brown, general editor of the series, who read two complete drafts of the book in typescript, making many valuable and constructive suggestions for improvement both in detail and in general arrangement, and also the contribution of the house staff of the publishers who guided a particularly complicated script safely through the proof and printing processes. It has been a pleasure to work in a field where so much active research is in progress, and I am grateful for help received not only from many friends and established scholars (and they will forgive me if I mention by name only the late Professor Whitelock and the late Professor Dolley to whom all interested in the field owe so much) but also from many young researchers, notably those working on charters and coins. A special word of thanks, as always, goes to my wife for preparing the index, a particularly fearsome task in such a complicated period.

Introduction

There was a strong tendency a generation or so ago to warn young scholars off the Anglo-Saxon period. Sir Frank Stenton's masterpiece in the Oxford History of England had appeared in 1943 and there seemed little more that needed to be said or written. Stenton himself did not share this belief. He knew well from his own experience how much needed to be done with the help of the growing and maturing disciplines of archaeology, place-name study, numismatics and linguistics. He also recognized fully the need for the historian's picture to be brought firmly into line with knowledge of developments among other European communities, Scandinavian, Celtic, and above all Frankish. The volume of work that has been produced over the last thirty or forty years bears proper testimony to the accuracy of his judgement. An attempt is made in the following pages to look at one of the most traditional of all aspects of the discipline, that which concerns government and administration, in the light of modern investigation.

A word of explanation first about method and approach might be helpful. Anglo-Saxon history raises some special methodological problems that must be grappled with before advance in understanding can be achieved. There is a surprising quantity of written evidence, if one takes the remoteness of the period, the chance of survival, and the lack of a powerful central archive into account. Judgement enters into the question when we come to assess the difficulties of survival. Some put heavy emphasis on all survivals, placing an almost mystic reverence on even the minutest fragment. Others treat the chance element in survival as the dominant and therefore are inclined to discount the fragments and to concentrate rather on what one must term recognizable bodies of material – laws, charters, lives of saints – material big enough in itself to generate its own critical criteria. To steer a course between what may be termed the tip of the iceberg school and the down to earth quantitatively critical school is no easy task. The further complication that the overwhelming preponderance of written material to survive comes from royal or ecclesiastical sources presents yet further difficulty. To give one example, letters in the vernacular are excessively rare, but there is plentiful evidence to show that they were by no means uncommon from the days of the conversion of the English to Christianity to the very end of the Anglo-Saxon period, Their scarcity is a function of survival not of production. My own methodological approach inclines me slightly towards the tip of the iceberg school, an inclination corrected in part by the intrinsic nature of the material demanded by a concentration on government and administration, where records were overwhelmingly royal and ecclesiastical throughout the period.

Recognition of the simple fact that permanent government was predominantly the creation of the kings and of the Church has determined the shape of the book. The early centuries are treated essentially as a preparatory period when the implications of the settlement and conversion are slowly worked out. Every effort has been made to avoid giving an impression of inevitability to the process of the making of England and yet there is a sense in which the welding together of peoples of the same economic background, social structure and language seems a natural outcome of settlement and even more so of conversion. Christianity was a literate civilized religion drawing sustenance from its deep roots in the experience of the Near East and Mediterranean world. As a literate religion it was also an educative force in the full Roman tradition. Men were made aware of their group unity in the religious and linguistic fields long before the political. Sharing in a common enterprise of European importance English missionaries to Germany in the eighth century conveyed this sentiment of oneness powerfully back to their kinsfolk at home in Wessex, Mercia, East Anglia, Kent and Northumbria. Even so, political groupings, dependent perhaps more than we used to appreciate on communications and access to economic surplus, remained small. The first two chapters of Part I aim at no more than pointing to the way in which the idea of belonging to a territorial community that was part of England came to replace the more primitive notions of tribal society. Special prominence is thus given to the final chapter of Part I, the Reign of Alfred, read as the true watershed of the whole period. Put in its simplest terms Alfred's reign represents the time when the loyalties and native governmental expertise of the Anglo-Saxons gathered around the one surviving ancient Christian dynasty. Even at the very end of his life and after his successful campaigns against the great Danish army of the 890s Alfred was no king of England. In terms of sheer acreage pagan or newly-converted Danish rulers governed more of historic England than Alfred. The potential remained. It is no accident that we have such a comparative wealth of information about the last quarter or so of the ninth century. The Chronicle, Alfred's Laws, his translations, Asser's *Life of Alfred*, remind us in their bulk of a phase in English history that was truly decisive. Alfred's reign can be read accurately as a culmination of past trends and as a critical take-off point from which could grow the new powerful Christian kingdom of England.

The themes of Part II are less abstract and more clear-cut than those that we have tried to disentangle in the first part of the book. The nature of the story and the nature of the evidence ensure that this should be so. Material is not evenly distributed. After the wealth of the Alfredian period the reigns of his successors, Edward the Elder and Athelstan, can be reconstructed only with considerable effort and not until the Benedictine Reform gets fully under way in the third quarter of the century can we feel confident in the quantity as well as the quality of the written evidence. It is probable, as I have argued later in the book, that we have consistently underestimated the importance of this movement in its impact on our secular institutions. Associated with the names of Sts Dunstan, Ethelwold and Oswald, the Benedictine Reform was from the beginning much more than an otherworldly monastic phenomenon withdrawn from society and the governance of society. Royal support in the middle years of the century was a dominant characteristic, especially under King Edgar (959–975), friend of the monks, and in return educational force became a dominant element in the monks' activities. The full might of educational achievement, in Anglo-Saxon as well as in Latin, did not make itself apparent until the end of the century and the opening decade of the eleventh century, and so coincided with the sad reign of Ethelred (978–1016) and the Danish victories of Sweyn and Cnut. We are therefore confronted with something of a paradox where a period of political misery and defeat is accompanied by signs of extraordinary vigour in government activity, learning and literature. In terms of the number of law-codes and the mass of charters, to say nothing of the quality and subtle sophistication of the currency and coinage, the reign of Ethelred in England ranks high among the reigns of early medieval kings. If by some ill chance the Anglo-Saxon Chronicle with its unhappy story of political treachery and ultimate disaster had not survived we would have had a falsely rosy picture of Ethelred *Unraed*. Legal evidence, charters, the coinage and now evidence of surviving writs enable us to trace realistically the threads of late Old-English government deep into the eleventh century to the moment of the Norman Conquest itself, though there is a falling-off in quantity of evidence, notably of original literary output.

In the three chapters of Part II we have attempted a division of theme that will give some idea of the complexities of the situation. In fact there is a great deal of intermingling of the themes covered in all three chapters at national and local levels, and no division can be perfectly satisfactory in dealing with a society that was itself changing and maturing over an exceptionally fruitful period of a century and a half. The central line of development concerns the monarchy, the shaping of a territorial kingdom, and the first chapter deals with this theme especially in relation to the need for kings to take counsel and to the growth of councils (witans) at which such counsel could be received. There follow two chapters which grapple with the working out of government in detail. The first of these treats the question of central administration operating along the main lines of activity connected with the Household, the financial attributes of government and the judicial. The second treats of local government. It is freely recognized that the divisions are arbitrary and that activities constantly overlap. Notions of sharp differentiation of office and clear separation of function are remote indeed from the period with which we are concerned.

In spite of the difficulties that arise naturally from the lack of consistency in the body of documentation the overall picture achieves a surprising coherence. Much recent work on the later Old-English period has been institutional in nature, clarifying our understanding of coinage, charters and writs, and beginning to deepen our appreciation of the nature and importance of the law codes. The imperfections in the Old-English polity are not concealed. Twice in the course of just a half a century England was conquered and passed into alien hands, Danish in 1016 and Norman in 1066. A tendency to regionalism along the lines of the ancient kingdoms of the Heptarchy is sometimes to be observed. The general line of development towards a united kingdom of England nevertheless runs straight and men as divergent as Cnut, Edward the Confessor and William the Conqueror all benefited from the resulting cohesion.

Part III consists of one concentrated chapter which attempts to sum up the immediate consequences of the Norman Conquest on the principal governmental structures in England. Recent work, notably that of Le Patourel, has emphasized accurately the element of colonization involved in the startling venture. Many Normans (and many French and Bretons, too) made a very good thing out of the Conquest. In the military field the apparatus of eleventh-century feudalism was introduced to help defend and control the ancient kingdom. We have deliberately made much of William's own insistence on the legality of his position. Conqueror he might be but that was by force of circumstance. Conquest was launched not against the legal king of England, but against Harold, son of Godwin, earl of Wessex, and usurper of the throne. The Norman case, vigorously argued and brilliantly portrayed in the Bayeux Tapestry, was that Harold was a usurper and an oath-breaker. We have tried to bring out the implications of this attitude in discussing the subtle amalgam of continuity, modification and innovation that makes up the government machine of William I, king of England, but withal throughout his life very much duke of Normandy. With the total context of the book in mind stress does perhaps fall on elements of continuity. No one would deny the concentration of vigour and wealth brought to England by the Normans: much strength persisted in the English substructure. William was well content for practical as well as abstract reasons to rule as legitimate king of England, legitimate successor to Edward the Confessor and the house of Cerdic. The contribution of the Anglo-Saxons to the strength of English medieval government was positive and permanent.

Part I
The Early Anglo-Saxon Kingdoms

1 *

The Kingdoms and their Kings to 871

The historian who approaches the question of government in the early medieval period must be constantly aware of the limitations not only of his evidence and methods but of the very nature of the question itself. Government deals essentially in its written records and theories with the rational, even though the practices of governors and governed can often lead on the part of the observer to a despairing rejection of the notion. The working-out of procedures, the framing of rules and regulations, the establishment of courts and penalties are products of human reason; and the unsettled nature of the early medieval world seemed more often than not from the plain unvarnished political record to encourage and incite the forces of violence, unreason and irrationality. The laws, customs and traditions of Rome had withered or died, and throughout the Western Empire there was no certainty about the structures of political organization and government that would take their place. This was true even among communities where Roman social and linguistic preponderance remained dominant, such as Italy, Spain and Gaul south of the Loire. It was even more true of areas where the barbarian from outside the Empire who achieved political mastery proved unreceptive to or even completely untouched by the inner motive forces of Rome and of the Christian faith which Rome had adopted late in its western imperial life. Much of Britain falls into that category, and the uncertainties and hesitations during the long period when new political units were coming into being makes the

---

* Most of the principal sources for this chapter are to be found in translation in *EHD* (vol. i) but the text of the Tribal Hidage has to be sought elsewhere, most conveniently in the work of C.R. Hart (*TRHS*, 1971) or P.H. Sawyer, with good critical comment (London, 1978). The books of W. Ullman and J.M. Wallace-Hadrill give the firmest introduction to modern thought on early medieval kingship. There has been much active work on kingship in the last generation. Of outstanding importance are the contributions of J.M. Wallace-Hadrill, especially his Ford lectures, *Early Germanic Kingship in England and on the Continent* (Oxford 1971). See also J.M. Wallace-Hadrill, *Early Medieval History* (Oxford,1975), and P.H. Sawyer and I.N. Woods, eds., *Early Medieval Kingship* (Leeds, 1977). The work of F. Kern, M. Bloch and P.E. Schramm from an earlier generation contains much of permanent value.

whole concept of rational government difficult and at times deeply suspect.

It is not only the feeling of break between ordered society and barbarian that makes for this difficulty in approaching early English society. The barbarian world had also achieved ideas of order, and the early English law-codes are among the best sources we have for studying the progress made. Laws issued by the kings of Kent and by Ine, king of Wessex, have survived from the seventh and early eighth centuries, often obscure in detail but giving an intelligible basic picture of a social order with rationally defined obligations. In three respects, in particular, they yield vital information to warn us of the inadequacies of our attempted generalizations about government. They tell us that the division between free and unfree was essential to the social structure, and that therefore full enjoyment of the law and full right to exercise government rested only with the fully free. They tell us that the kindred exercised authority in fields that later came to be taken as the province of ordered government, in matters relating to protection of its members and the duty to take vengeance, as well as in social matters relating to marriage and the transmission of land and wealth. They tell us that an elaborate scheme of compensation payments was in being, connected with the notion of the wergeld or the bloodprice that was to be paid in compensation for the death of a freeman; though the monetary payments themselves, of course, 100 Kentish shillings or 200 West-Saxon, equated with wergeld payment, were never more than approximations, setting the scale and acting as a guide to the amount of compensation that might be expected. As we shall see there are many other valuable insights, notably into the function of kingship, given to us in these early laws, but at the beginning of an investigation into government it is as well to stress these basic points and reservations. Many acts that we would term acts of government were carried out locally (and at times brutally) according to well understood principles of free kindred responsibility, and the payment of wergeld and other compensation. Such acts normally escaped the pen of the literate record maker and also of the rationalizing historian. Much government was carried out according to custom and convention transmitted orally.

There remain some further complications relating to the negative attributes of government. If payments were not made and custom denied, recourse could be made legally to personal force. The historian again is at a disadvantage. His records tell him for the most part of attempts to regularize violence and to discipline society. Even late in the Anglo-Saxon period when records are fuller and more detailed, stories of feuding violence often emerge behind the causes that are brought to local courts. Early in the period such stories must have been more plentiful and common. It is a great mistake always to equate agrarian society with peaceful society. No quarrels can run deeper or result in more bloodshed than quarrels over farm properties, succession and rights, and indeed over everyday things relating to lordship over fields, pasture, meadow and watercourses. Government itself could be brutal, all the more so in the early centuries when the Anglo-Saxons were avowedly almost aggressively slave-owners. Death, mutilation, reduction to slavery, savage corporal punishment lie behind the bland statements sometimes made about discipline and peace-giving institutions. In studying government we study the slow progress made in our western societies towards the framing of a more rational order, but we should be deceiving ourselves as well as our readers if we failed to draw attention to the substantially unrecorded acts involving the irrational exercise of physical force that continued to operate near the legal surface.

Even so, with all necessary reservations made, we can fairly state that great progress was made during the Anglo-Saxon period and that the main theme in the history of government during the early centuries may properly be isolated as a slow movement towards the creation of a territorial state. By 871 advances had been made that were to prove permanent and significant for later ages. There was by then a genuine feeling of English identity, expressed particularly in ecclesiastical, and to some extent in military matters, more so in military activities against the heathen Scandinavians than in earlier days against the British. There was also an increasing tendency for larger communities to associate themselves in sentiment and in government with their rulers and their ruling dynasties, and in consequence in elaboration of effective methods of ruling such communities. The key institution in this development of government during these centuries was kingship and most of this initial chapter will be concerned with kings and royal institutions. Anglo-Saxon settlement in the fifth and sixth centuries amounted to a migration, overwhelmingly agrarian in nature and concentrated for the most part on the abundant river valleys of south and central Britain. In the very earliest stages principles of lordship and leadership in war were clearly understood. This lordship could often be personal and local, amounting to little more than the authority of a lord over an extended kinship group, sometimes exercised from hill-forts temporarily re-occupied, as at Cissbury in Sussex or (if the place-name evidence can be given full value) at Barbury and Ebsbury in Wiltshire, Maugersbury in Gloucestershire, or Exbury in Hampshire.[1] Even so, to judge from the evidence of the Anglo-Saxon

1 Peter Fowler, 'Hillforts, AD 400–700', *The Iron Age and its Hillforts,* ed. D. Hill and M. Jesson (Southampton, 1971). K. Cameron, *English Place-Names* (London, 1961), pp.

Chronicle and from genealogical material, kingship quickly developed. The institution of kingship was known, though it was not universal, among the continental Germans, but it was not imported lock, stock and barrel into England. Only the Mercian dynasty claimed descent from kings who ruled the Angles on the Continent. English kingship and the historic dynasties were made in England.

Initially kings ruled over small areas and few people. Traces of earlier communities and political units exist in abundance in our place-name forms. In the south-east in the late fifth century enduring dynasties were established among the settlers in Kent, Sussex and Essex. One of the kings, Ælle, the South Saxon, established a temporary military hegemony over all the Germanic immigrants and settlers south of the Humber in the later part of the century. As Roman institutions crumbled and decayed the British peoples too came to recognize kingship as a proper means of political expression. Towards the end of the fifth century or early in the sixth, the Anglo-Saxons suffered repulse at the battle of mount Badon at the hands of the British who were apparently led by Arthur, their *Dux bellorum*. Later legend and the romantic imagination of the twelfth century created from him the archetype of early medieval kingship but the most the prosaic historical records tell is that 'King Arthur' represents the military leaders who, coming to the forefront at a moment of political and social disruption, sometimes emerged as kings or founders of dynasties or both. Certainly Gildas, writing in western Britain about AD 547 lived in a world where kingship was commonplace. Decisive political advance occurred in the century and a half from about 550 to 700 when the shape of the so-called British heptarchy emerged. Coincident with this period of expansion came the conversion to Christianity, initiated by the mission of St Augustine to the south-east in 597 and completed by the end of the seventh century.

The historic kingdoms of England were created in the course of this period, their shape determined by geography and pattern of settlement as well as by the need for self-defence and by the nature and extent of the resistance offered to the invaders.

There were three main points of entry for this sea-borne migration to Britain, the Humber, the Wash and the Thames estuary, and the early kingdoms radiate out from them. Geography combined with political history to ensure that effective consolidation in the period after the battle of mount Badon took place east of the highland belt which runs through modern England from the Pennines to Southampton Water. From the Thames estuary settlements sprang the historic kingdoms of

112–13, and Margaret Gelling, 'The Chronology of English Place-Names', *BAR* Brit. Ser. 6, (Oxford, 1976), pp. 93–101.

Kent, Essex (absorbing an earlier Middlesex by the end of the sixth century), and Wessex with its heartland possibly on the Middle Thames, in the modern shires of Berkshire and Oxfordshire. Sussex was intimately connected with this group though its origins owed much to political events in the north of Frankia in the last quarter of the fifth century. The settlers who used the Wash and its river systems as the chief point of entry established themselves in East Anglia, in the territory around Northampton and the Fenlands (later known as part of the sub-kingdom of the Middle Angles), and in territories occupied by a host of petty peoples whose names and obligations to their new Mercian overlords were preserved in the seventh-century tribute-taker's list that we call the Tribal Hidage.[2]

Migrants who used the Humber as their main route founded a minor kingdom in Lindsey, and laid the basis for two of the principal political units of Anglo-Saxon England, Mercia and Northumbria. Their settlements in the middle Trent, around Tamworth and Lichfield, were central to the development of Mercia, while their more northerly settlements of Deira in the fertile Vale of York and the more complex Bernicia in the harsher country of modern Northumberland and the Cheviots were eventually brought together into the kingdom of Northumbria. For a while in the course of the seventh century this composite kingdom of Northumbria became the dominant English power.

The political historian can too easily read the history of England in these centuries as an uneven but inevitable progress towards unity under the rule of one dynasty, but the creation of the kingdoms was slow and erratic. In England communities of predominantly arable farmers, facing problems of defence, mobility, maintenance of security against theft, and trading, were drawn closer together, at first into groups that recognized the leadership of one man or one kindred, the followers of *Hæsta* at Hastings or of Gilla (the Gillingas of modern Ealing), or the Gummingas whose temple and holy site lay at Harrow on the Hill in Middlesex. These developments occurred throughout early Anglo-Saxon England and can be parallelled in Germanic settlements on the continent of Europe west of the Rhine within the old imperial frontiers. Similar strivings at a slower rate and along more tortuous paths can be isolated among the Celtic communities in Wales, Scotland, and even in Ireland.

Traces, too, of settlements that were territorial and described by the common German element *gau* (or - ge in Anglo-Saxon) may be found,

---

2 C.R. Hart, 'The Tribal Hidage', *TRHS* 21 (1971), pp. 133–57; W. Davies and H. Vierck, 'The Contexts of the Tribal Hidage: Social Aggregates and Settlement Patterns', *Frühmittelalterliche Studien* 8 (1974), pp. 223–93. See below, pp. 34–7.

notably on a large scale in the familiar Surrey (*Surrige*), the south district of what was the settlement of the Middle Saxons, and in smaller units and sub-units of the south-east, at Dengie and Vange in Essex or at Penge in Buckinghamshire. Some settlements were given bluntly and directly settlement names, the dwellers in the Peak district, the dwellers in the Chilterns, the dwellers in the Wrekin.[3] Only slowly were they drawn together in the course largely of the sixth century into the historic provinces and kingdoms and tribal organizations of late pagan and early Christian England. Our first political shock comes indeed when we realize that the kingdoms described by Bede in his ecclesiastical history were themselves relatively new: Kent, Essex, East Anglia, Sussex, Wessex, Mercia, Lindsey, and even (perhaps especially) Northumbria were the creation of the first century or so of intensive Anglo-Saxon settlement.

In the early stages of the conversion of the English to Christianity much political power, in itself a symptom of success in imposing government, rested among the smaller communities of the east. When St Augustine landed in Kent in 597 he landed in a kingdom ruled by Ethelbert who enjoyed an overlordship over all the other Germanic settlers up to the Humber. The East Angles under their king, Redwald, who died about 625, also enjoyed a temporary superiority over the other kingdoms. Such superiority among the easterners was probably a product of the success of the earliest Anglo-Saxon movements as a colonizing movement, but the effects were not long-lasting. Indeed turbulence among the settled groups and rivalries between them were much more characteristic of the early centuries rather than awareness of common purpose. The turbulence and rivalry left deep scars. Common interest, possession of a common language and virtually identical social institutions, ultimately possession of a common religion, helped to counterbalance but not to eradicate the deep local hatreds which tribal warfare and later political rivalries inflicted upon the English peoples. These persisted late, sometimes surprisingly late, into the Anglo-Saxon scene. Northumbria was ravaged by local and dynastic divisions which weakened it grievously in the eighth century. The intense dislike and distrust felt by the men of Kent and East Anglia for their Mercian overlords probably owed its origin to events that long preceded the immediate causes in the late eighth and ninth centuries. One of the outstanding achievements of Alfred and his successors was to overcome the antagonism which had sprung up between the men of Wessex and the Mercians. The making of a united England was not an easy task. Yet it seems reasonable to say that there was a strong trend towards the achievement of political unity. It also seems

3 W. Davies and H. Vierck, especially pp. 236–9.

reasonable to deduce from the historical evidence that by the second half of the seventh century, with the unifying force of Christianity well established, political hopes of achieving such unity rested fair and square upon the dynasties ruling those English peoples most capable of expanding to the north or to the west against the indigenous independent British peoples, that is to say with the historic kingdoms of Northumbria, Mercia and Wessex. Such is commonplace, but it may be that we have all still to savour the full implications for the history of English government. The communities chiefly instrumental in creating permanent institutions learned their business exercising authority over alien folk.

Northumbria emerged in the second half of the seventh century as the most powerful of the early kingdoms, certainly up to the time of its severe military defeat at the hands of the Picts in 685, a defeat which put paid to its most extravagant ambitions in the north.

For a brief period under King Oswy (642–70), and especially after his defeat of Penda of Mercia in 654, Northumbria had exercised a most impressive lordship over all the English communities. It had proved unable to sustain direct political control of Mercia after 658, but its moral pre-eminence was such that, for example, the decision made at a Northumbrian council, the Synod of Whitby in 663, to favour Roman rather than Celtic customs in the practice of Christianity was enough to ensure Roman success throughout England. Northumbrian political and military authority, however, was progressively weakened by external defeat and internal dissension. The eighth century presents a dismal story of unrest and violence with many of the Northumbrian kings deposed or dying by violence. The great school at York and the northern monasteries of Jarrow, Wearmouth and Lindisfarne remained beacons of cultural light in an increasingly stormy political setting, but the sacking of Lindisfarne by the Vikings in 793 marked the beginning of the painful end of this culture.

The eighth century was dominated politically by the Middle Kingdom, Mercia. It was welded into an effective military federation by the skill of the heathen Penda (628–54), suffered temporary eclipse after Penda's death, but emerged to achieve political mastery first under Penda's sons, Wulfhere (658–675) and Ethelred (675–704) then completely and dramatically under Ethelbald(716–757) and Offa (757–796), one of the greatest of the Anglo-Saxon kings. Reasons for this are not hard to find. Success at mastery of environment in the newly-drained prosperous arable lands of the Trent valley brought comparative wealth. Dynastic acceptance by the peoples of the east Midlands, the Middle Angles of the Fens, the men of Lindsey and the settlers around the Wash, contributed a secure base. A similar acceptance of its lordship or overlordship by the hard pioneers of the west, the *Magonsætan* and the *Hwicce* of the Severn valley, and the men of the modern border shires of Cheshire, Shropshire, Herefordshire and Gloucestershire, completed the process. London became a Mercian town. Finally, although reluctantly and only after the brutal murder of their young king, Ethelbert, the East Angles were subdued. South of the Thames, after the withdrawal to Rome and subsequent death of King Ine of Wessex in 725, there was no effective resistance to Mercian overlordship. The once proud kingdom of Kent was reduced to puppet status, unable to resist Mercian pressure that threatened even the authority of the archiepiscopal see of Canterbury itself. Royal councils attended by ecclesiastics drawn from all over southern England symbolized the new far-ranging authority of the Mercian kings.

Mercian dominance did not end with the death of Offa. For the succeeding quarter of a century, briefly under his son Ecgfrith, and then under his distant kinsmen, Cenwulf (796–821) and Ceolwulf (821–823), Mercia retained its political and military control of the Midlands. The first quarter of the ninth century constitutes, however, a hinge in the political history of Anglo-Saxon England. For the first time the serious and permanent nature of the Scandinavian menace became apparent; and south of the Thames, back from a profitable exile in Frankish lands where he saw at close quarters Charlemagne's imperial might at its most effective, King Egbert (802–838) slowly consolidated his royal power, extending effective West-Saxon authority to the south-west as far as the Tamar. With the failure of the Mercian dynasty in the 820s came the West-Saxon opportunity. The Anglo-Saxon Chronicle has preserved an account of a series of campaigns between 825 and 829 which represents a move in political pre-eminence from Mercia to Wessex. This was not as dramatic nor as immediately effective as the Chronicle read in isolation would suggest. By the 830s the Mercians were again under the rule of independent kings and exercising authority over London, Essex and lands in the Upper Thames; but it was no longer the aggressive, overbearing Mercia of Offa's day. The sub-kingdom of Kent remained firmly under the control of Egbert who now ruled directly or through strong dynastic ties all the territories south of the Thames. London's situation was a shade anomalous, still Mercian but with West-Saxon access completely secure. Mercian overlordship of East Anglia was shattered, and an independent East-Anglian dynasty in control. The generation before the accession of Alfred in 871 saw a gradual (and again not fully smooth and consistent) extension of West-Saxon authority and prestige within the English kingdoms.

All is obscured and distorted by the opening stages in what were to prove the true moulding and formative campaigns of Anglo-Saxon

1 The early kingdoms

Boundaries fluctuated greatly in the seventh and eighth centuries. Mercia, for example, is shown around its early centres of Lichfield, Tamworth and Repton before its expansion under Ethelbald and Offa.

history. In 851 the Danes wintered for the first time in England, in the south-east, in the Isle of Thanet in Kent. In 866 they opened their massive onslaught that was to end with the conquest of half of England and the near achievement of a complete conquest. The effects of this new set of migrations on government and administration will be considered later, but it must be emphasized that already before the Danes attacked in strength Wessex had emerged as the hope of a united England and the West-Saxon dynasty had come to occupy a very special place in English affairs.

This brief political sketch makes clear that the ideals and wishes of the English communities found expression through the activities of their kings, and no discussion of government in these early centuries can avoid giving special prominence to the institutions of kingship. The institution itself, however, is far from simple. Monarchy was regarded universally as the most appropriate of political institutions, and where kings were not found writers tended to express surprise bordering on scandal: *Cyning sceal rice healdan* (a king must protect his kingdom) and *cyning bio onwealdes georn* (a king is eager for authority) became maxims embodied in Anglo-Saxon folk verse, and one gnomic poet refined this pride in regal authority further by stating that it was an attribute of a king to hate anyone who claimed land from him just as it was true that he would love anyone who would offer him more. There is stark realism in the juxtaposition of king, land and authority.[4] Lack of kingship was a matter for comment, and it is by no means fanciful to identify a note of disapprobation in the writings of Bede when he described the institutions of the Old Saxons in the following terms:

> These same Old Saxons, however, do not have a king, but many satraps are placed in authority over that people. When war breaks out they cast lots on a basis of equality, and all of them follow as leader, as long as the war lasts, him on whom the lot falls, and give their obedience to him; once the war is over, however, all the satraps become equal in power again.

The reasons for the pre-eminence and universality of kingship are clear enough. The Anglo-Saxon invasion of Britain represents the north-west wing of one of the great folk-migrations of recorded history, movement of a large mass of the Germanic peoples into what was to prove their permanent homes. The invasion and subsequent settlement had demanded exercise of personal leadership, and of all

4 T.A. Shippey, *Poems of Wisdom and Learning in Old English* (New Jersey and Cambridge, 1976), pp. 76–7 (Maxims II, l. 1: the Cottonian MS), and pp. 66–7 (Maxims I, ll. 59–60: the Exeter Book).
5 Bede, *HE* v. 10.

the terms employed king (*cyning* in Anglo-Saxon) in its various forms became the normally accepted word used to describe such leaders. In origin *cyning* probably carried some family or dynastic undertones, signifying membership of a specially selected kindred, divinely called to rule over a people. A member of such a kindred was expressly king-worthy. All manner of reasons contributed to this, genetic as well as economic. The hardy sons of a successful warrior-household had a better chance of careful upbringing, and so of survival. The family itself could husband resources gained from successful enterprise to the advantage of the kindred group. The process of consolidation of a people around a potential king could operate on a large scale with the Ostrogoths and Visigoths or on a small scale with the East Saxons or South Saxons or the smaller groups still of Chiltern-settlers or Wrekin-settlers or followers of individual chieftains such as the *Hæsta* who gave his name to Hastings. Religious or at the least supernatural sanction followed rather than preceded successful acquisition of power. Publicists and poets, operating according to clear-cut conventions, quickly set to work to establish or to fabricate a genealogy for the most successful of the princely houses. A genealogy, accurate if possible to living memory of four or five generations, would be attached to descent from a recognized kin of Germanic heroes. In turn this would be attached to a further set of figures, largely supernatural. The vast majority of English princely houses looked back to Woden, the war-god, as their ultimate progenitor. It is a mark of the peculiar conservatism of the East Saxons that they chose to favour the obscure local Saxon God, *Seaxneat*. As Christianity was accepted the genealogies needed fresh modification. It was an easy step to tack on the elaborate genealogies of Genesis and Exodus to the line of Germanic descent from Woden. The most elaborate of these exercises went in easy stages to the son of Noah, who was born in the Ark, and from there happily and directly to Adam himself. The genealogy of Ethelwulf, father of Alfred the Great, is given in full in the Anglo-Saxon Chronicle for the middle years of the 850s, and provides a superb example of the genre:

And Æthelwulf was the son of Egbert, the son of Ealhmund, the son of Eafa, the son of Eoppa, the son of Ingild. Ingild was the brother of Ine, king of the West Saxons, who held the kingdom for 37 years and afterwards went to St Peter's and ended his life there. And they were the sons of Cenred. Cenred was the son of Ceolwold, the son of Cutha, the son of Cuthwine, the son of Ceawlin, the son of Cynric, the son of Creoda, the son of Cerdic. Cerdic was the son of Elesa, the son of Esla, the son of Gewis, the son of Wig, the son of Freawine, the son of Freothogar, the son of Brand, the son of Bældæg, the son of Woden, the son of Frealaf, the son of Finn, the son of Godwulf, the son of Geat, the son of Tætwa, the son of Beaw, the son of Sceldwa, the son of Heremod, the son of Itermon, the son of Hathra, the son of Hwala, the son of Bedwig, the son of Sceaf, i.e. the son of Noah. He was born in Noah's ark. Lamech, Methuselah, Enoch, Jared, Mahalaleel, Cainan, Enos, Seth, Adam the first man and our father, i.e. Christ.[6]

Solid convention, adapted and elaborated in England from basic Germanic roots, already assumed the universality of kingship in pagan days. The reception of Christianity intensified the hold of the institution of kingship on Anglo-Saxon society. Those who were interested in reading and writing received an education that was religious in a sense that is hard for the modern liberal Westerner completely to envisage and understand. The written record that was most prominent in the minds of educated men was the Bible, and the reading material available was predominantly biblical or the writings of the Fathers, who were themselves steeped in biblical learning. This meant that many were made familiar at an impressionable age with the deeds of the kings of Israel. Favoured passages in manuals for the instruction of the young would be chosen with the deliberate aim of extolling the virtues of good kings or explaining the vices of bad. Puzzles relating to the tangled involvement of Church in State and State in Church could be resolved or expressed by discussion of the priest-king, Melchisedek. David was the complex example of good kingship, Saul of a kingship that had degenerated towards tyranny but still should be patiently endured. Wisdom and kingship met in the person of Solomon. Judith's slaying of Holofernes could inspire direct action against the foreign tyrant. Puzzles and problems and subtleties apart, the Bible served to impress one political fact upon all who read it or listened to it — the association of legitimate authority with kingship. A king was a fit and proper person to rule a settled Germanic people. Legitimate Christian authority over a settled people was unthinkable except in royal terms.[7]

Kingship was therefore the main instrument by which men were governed; but we must guard against making the processes too abstract. Who were these kings, how were they chosen, and above all what was their range of activities? Upon a satisfactory answer to these questions depends an understanding of nearly all questions concerning government and administration, not only in geographical range of

6 *ASCh* 855–58. Professor Whitelock translates MS C varies at one or two points from the Parker MS (Plummer I, p. 66). She comments that the Christus at the end of the genealogy must be an error for Christi (cf. Luke iii 38 'which was *the son* of Enos, which was *the son* of Seth, which was *the son* of Adam, which was *the son* of God.').

7 J.M. Wallace-Hadrill, *Early Germanic Kingship in England and on the Continent* (Oxford, 1971) gives the best single introduction to this complex topic.

kingship but also in intensity of royal control over the community in depth.

If knowledge consists merely in ability to name people we know a surprising amount about our early kings. Queen Elizabeth II can properly claim descent through named persons from Cerdic the West-Saxon king with a Celtic name who flourished in the early years of the sixth century. Unfortunately we have little but names to rely on for the sixth century. With the seventh century − thanks to Bede who completed his magnificent *Ecclesiastical History of the English People* in 731 − we are much better informed. Anecdotes, serious historical analysis, written evidence of their actions help to make understandable men such as Ethelbert of Kent, Edwin, Oswald and Oswy of Northumbria, Redwald of East Anglia, and even Penda of Mercia. One general characteristic is conspicuously clear. By the middle of the seventh century the tally of royal dynasties in England was complete. The last to emerge was the Mercian under Penda; the very anxiety of the Mercian line in later years to establish links between their dynasty and those who ruled the Angles when they were still on the continent may well indicate some basic uncertainty on their part. From the seventh century forward no ruler who could not claim membership of one of the royal dynasties governed an English folk without earning for himself the opprobrium of some of his people. It was held even by the most restrained commentators as shameful that a man not of the royal kin should be elevated to the kingship. Ælle of Northumbria was bluntly described by the Anglo-Saxon Chronicler (under 867) as an *ungecynde cining,* a king not of the proper ruling stock. Belief in the importance of the blood royal may therefore be isolated as an early and basic characteristic of English political thought. This did not carry with it other attributes that we associate with monarchy in the modern western world, attributes such as the assured succession of the eldest son, the ability to transmit rights of succession (or not to transmit them) through the female line, the right of females or minors of tender age to succeed. In all Anglo-Saxon communities − as throughout the Germanic world − the general custom was for the man from the royal kin who was fittest to rule to be selected as successor. How closely the kin was defined is not easy to estimate. In later theory a kindred to the seventh or even to the ninth degree was often assumed when it came to matters of paying compensation for injuries or for death. In practice an inner kindred of men who shared a common great-grandfather was almost certainly the effective kin, and in matters affecting inheritance (as with the supervision of the first instalments of wergeld) a still closer group of kinsmen may normally have been the people directly concerned with succession. Records are imperfect but in Wessex after Cenwalh's death in 672 there is no case known of son succeeding father until Ethelwulf succeeded Egbert in 839. We have already seen from his official genealogy that Ethelwulf traced descent beyond Egbert through many generations of princelings before reaching a ruling king of Wessex in the late sixth century; though he was, at pains to point out that his great-great-great-grandfather was King Ine's brother. The Mercian succession moved somewhat erratically between 654 and 823 though almost exclusively (the only exception is Beornred who ruled for a few months by usurpation in 757) within the descendants of Penda, Penda's brother Eowa, and Penda's father Pybba; but direct succession of father by son is rare. The great Offa himself (757 – 796) was descended through princes not kings from Pybba in the fifth generation, and the Mercians had to look remotely again to descendants of Pybba in the persons of Cenwulf (796 – 821) and Ceolwulf (821 – 23) after the brief reign (only 141 days) of Offa's son, Ecgfrith. Northumbria was tormented in the seventh century by rivalries between the two recognized dynasties of Deira and Bernicia, and in the eighth century by general uncertainties, rivalries and usurpations whether by men who claimed to be 'of the stock of King Ida' or by men not of the royal stock. The lesser dynasties of Kent, East Anglia and Lindsey tell similar stories.[8] And yet under normal circumstances close kinship to the reigning king was expected as a characteristic of royal succession. This makes sense. Control of the hearthtroop of picked warriors around the king and control of the treasure-hoard were essential if a bid for the throne was to have a good chance of success. The most natural step of all in theory was that, as the poet of Beowulf expressed it, a prince's son should prosper, succeed to his father's rank and virtue, protect and hold the people, the treasure and the stronghold, the kingdom of heroes, his native homeland.[9] Where such 'natural' succession was in doubt, either from lack of heirs or incapacity, or because the sons were too young, the result was only too often civil war and fierce disruption. The question rests uneasily with us wherever we turn in the historical record of the early Anglo-Saxon period. If succession of the eldest son or indeed of any son to his father was the 'natural' sequence, why then was it so rare? Alcuin, writing to the Mercian ealdorman, Osbert, in the year after Ecgfrith's death, associated the young king's early death with the blood shed by his father in order to secure the kingdom on the son. The implication was clear. Great and unusual and much-resisted effort was needed to ensure the direct succession of Offa's son; and the

8 The material is well assembled in an unpublished doctoral thesis by Mrs Barbara Yorke, 'Anglo-Saxon Kingship in Practice, 400–899' (Exeter University, 1978), pp. 56–98.

9 Beowulf, ll. 910–13: the son of the prince (*peoden*) was expected to flourish before he could hope to take over his father's rank and duties (*faeder-æpelum onfon*).

result was, as Alcuin put it himself, not the strengthening but the ruin of the kingdom.[10]

A son would not succeed if he was incapable of affording protection; and yet under the right circumstances his position might be safeguarded. The poet of Beowulf again gives precious insight into the attitudes of the age. After the death of Hygelac king of the Geats, Hygd the young widow entrusted the treasures, the kingdom, riches and a throne to Beowulf himself because she could not trust her young son to defend royal possessions against foes from outside. The noble Beowulf refused, in spite of the entreaties of the bereaved people, and nurtured the young prince, Heardred; it was only after Heardred's death at the hands of the Swedes that Beowulf took the throne – and ultimately exacted vengeance on them.[11] An element of choice was clearly often present, most often within the group surrounding the old king. In some measure the successor would in fact be called upon to choose himself. He would be well known to the men who held the substance of physical power, would presumably have shown promise as a warrior and as a ruler, in other words would be acceptable as a possible guardian of the folk. In another sense he was chosen to be king, and such was the terminology of the day. The Chronicle tells of men who were *gecoren to cyninge* (chosen as king). Some symbolic act of choice must indeed have been made by the people around the old king, anxious to give legal sanction to the successor. Coupled with this element of choice and selection throughout the whole Anglo-Saxon period was an element of designation by the old king though it is hard to see how effective in practice such designation could be except in cases of concealed abdication for religious or political reasons. It may be very significant that the practical examples that came to mind are to be found very late in the age. Pledges to Henry I in the more sophisticated age of the early twelfth century were not enough to ensure the succession of Matilda to the English throne. Succession was a matter of choice by the living; the wishes and words of the dead could be influential only if supported by a political party anxious to implement them. The most famous example concerns the apparent deathbed designation *in articulo mortis* by Edward the Confessor of Harold of Wessex. The contemporary English source, the *Vita Eadwardi,* tells how Edward entrusted Edith (the queen who was also Harold's sister) and the kingdom to Harold in the presence of witnesses who included the royal ladies, Archbishop Stigand, and Robert Fitz-Wimarc, a staller or court officer. The Bayeux Tapestry gives visual expression

10 *EHD* i, no. 202, p. 855.
11 Beowulf, ll. 2367–90: also ll. 2200ff. He then ruled for fifty winters, an old guardian of the people.

to the same scene though we may be sure that in Norman eyes the handing-over of the kingdom was meant to involve a temporary trust until the rightful heir, William, duke of Normandy, could enter into his inheritance. Indeed, the theoretical Norman claim to the throne of England rested essentially on a purported designation of William by Edward the Confessor, probably as early as 1051. Harold's succession could then be dismissed as unlawful, and the character of Harold blackened by describing him as an oath-breaker and usurper.[12]

By a variety of methods therefore succession to the kingship was achieved. The new king had proved himself to be fit for the task; he possessed the blood-royal; and elements of choice and of designation were involved in his elevation. It used to be customary to stress the element of choice and to see in the selection of a successor to an Ethelbert or a Cenwulf procedures reminiscent of a formal election in an assembly of magnates. This view was certainly anachronistic, though not lacking in historical perception. Consent was needed if a ruler were to be fully effective. Methods of obtaining consent were unsophisticated, but not the less important for that. At the very root of the principle of leadership among freemen lies an element of consent. The warrior leader was freely accepted by his fellow freeman, and the earliest kings, often heads of their own kindreds or extended kinship groups, must have been sensitive to the nature of the acquiescence in their rule of other free kindreds, all the more so if they wished to sustain their authority permanently.

Deposition was always a possibility in the early Anglo-Saxon period and examples can be found from most of the kingdoms. Redwald's son, Eorpwald, was killed by a heathen soon after his accession, possibly because of his conversion to Christianity, and in Essex Sigebert died at the hand of two kinsmen because they could not stomach his new morality. Sigebert took his Christianity seriously, sparing his enemies and calmly forgiving wrongs, an affront to traditional Germanic morality of revenge or composition.[13] These may be no more than examples, under stress of the conflicts of the conversion period, of that pattern of despotism tempered by assassination characteristic of the Merovingian world. Evidence of greater formality comes in the eighth century. In 757 Cynewulf and the West-Saxon *witan* deprived Sigebert of his kingdom (except for Hampshire) because of his unjust acts. Northumbrian kings were deposed at formal councils or synods, and at Easter 774 the Northumbrians drove

---

12 H.R. Loyn, *The Norman Conquest* (London, 3rd edn 1982). Ann Williams, 'Problems connected with the English Royal Succession, 860–1066', *Proceedings of the Battle Conference* 1 1978 (1979), pp. 144–67, argues neatly that designation became more important as 1000 approached.

13 Bede, *HE* ii, 15; iii, 22.

Alhred from York and took as their new lord Ethelred, son of Moll, who reigned for four years or so until he in turn was deposed in 778 or 79. Indeed Ethelred was recalled in 790 married Offa's daughter Ælfflæd, in 792 and reigned in Northumbia until his murder in April, 796.[14] Just as kingship was transformed, in Wallace-Hadrill's words, between the fifth and the ninth century into 'an office with rights and duties defined by churchmen', so did notions harden concerning the inviolability of the act of making a king. Asser's sentiments are clear even if his history is unsound when he expresses his horror at the deprivation of Ethelwulf's kingship as an act 'unheard of in previous ages'.[15]

To this point we have considered the relatively prosaic and straightforward matter of succession to an already established king. There is inadequate historical evidence for proper and complete discussion of a deeper and more interesting problem, the basis of such kingship, though genealogies and knowledge of royal actions and dynasties help to further our understanding. Fortunately more information is available on the way in which the king was identified physically and set apart as a special person. Bede in a fine description of Edwin, king of Northumbria and also overlord of the greater part of Britain, gives an indication of his royal style:

> Truly he kept such great state in his kingdom, that not only were his banners borne before him in war, but even in time of peace his standard-bearer always went before him as he rode between his cities, his residences and provinces with his thegns. Also when he walked anywhere along the roads, that sort of banner which the Romans call 'tufa' and the English 'thuuf' was usually borne before him.[16]

At Sutton Hoo, near Woodbridge in Suffolk, the most sensational find in Anglo-Saxon archaeology has much to tell us about the trappings and nature of royalty.[17] The discoveries were made in the course of excavating a great burial mound, situated as the most prominent of a group of well over a dozen mounds, on a sandy bluff overlooking the river Deben, about six miles from the sea and four from the royal vill

---

14 *ASCh* 757 and 774. Simeon of Durham, *Historia Regum,* ed. T. Arnold, *RS, s.a.* 774 adds the information that Alhred was deprived of the society of the royal Household and nobles by the counsel and consent of all the people: *EHD* i, no. 3, p. 269.

15 J.M. Wallace-Hadrill, *Early Germanic Kingship in England and on the Continent* (Oxford, 1971), p. 151. Asser, c. 12.

16 Bede, *HE* ii, 16.

17 R.L.S. Bruce-Mitford, *The Sutton Hoo Ship-Burial,* vols. i and ii (Cambridge, 1975 and 1979) provides a splendid authoritative guide. Two further volumes are planned. Bruce-Mitford's short guides to Sutton Hoo, published regularly by the British Museum since 1948, remain of great value. Also R.L.S. Bruce-Mitford, *The Sutton Hoo Ship-Burial (Reflections after 30 years),* University of York Medieval Monograph Series, 2 (York, 1979).

of Rendlesham. It seems quite certain now that the site itself was the royal burial place of the East-Anglian dynasty. Inside the flat-topped elliptical mound estimated to have been originally some 110 feet by 98 feet in maximum diameters, was a large burial ship, over 80 feet long and 14 feet in breadth at its widest point, with a maximum depth amidships of 5 feet, a ship built about AD 600 as a vessel primarily to be propelled by oars, with space for forty oarsmen though capable also of carrying sail. At the centre of the ship stood a burial chamber. It is still not certain that the burial chamber ever contained a corpse, but it was certainly arrayed with all the panoply considered proper for a royal burial, precious and beautiful goods, a riot of gold and garnet, buckles, shoulder-straps, weapons, a fine ceremonial sword, a shield, spears. There were also silver dishes, including a great platter bearing the mark of the emperor Anastasius who ruled at Constantinople in the late fifth and early sixth centuries. Humbler apparatus, pots and drinking-vessels, indicated the remains of a funeral feast. Gold coins, originally contained in a splendidly adorned purse, were assembled at a date not far from 625 AD, and it seems likely that the Sutton Hoo ship burial commemorated the death of Redwald, the East-Anglian king who briefly achieved overlordship over the Anglo-Saxons. Details of the warrior-king's battle harness, his helmet and the precious goods give proof of a contrived setting apart from ordinary folk, but two other features of the Sutton Hoo treasure are important in any discussion of the attributes of royalty. An iron standard over five feet high with an iron grille and cage has been generally interpreted, probably accurately, as a standard of the type described by Bede in his description of Edwin's royal state. Even more sensational was the discovery of a massive stone implement, nearly two feet in length and weighing over six pounds, the so-called whetstone-sceptre, in such splendid condition that it was clearly never used as a whetstone. Bearded faces were carved in relief on the tapered ends, and affixed to the one end was a ring and a bronze replica of a stag. At the other end was a saucer fitting which could be placed comfortably on the kneecap if the sceptre were held vertically by a seated figure on a ceremonial occasion after the fashion of imperial and consulate dignitaries in the late Antique period. The symbolism of this amazing piece has been variously interpreted, the whetstone with its connection with cutting edges signifying male virtues and success in war, the stag a straightforward sign of male virility. The eight bearded faces have also been taken as attempts to symbolize the ancestry of the ruling East-Anglian dynasty, the Wuffingas. There is indeed still room for much doubt and speculation in detail over the sceptre and over the other finds from Sutton Hoo, but cumulatively the evidence in favour of the close association of the find with the royal dynasty in the royal cemetery is very strong. The helmet itself, bronze-adorned and silver plated on an iron base, was constructed as much for show as for use. Sword, buckles, shoulder-straps and mountings, exquisitely ornamented in gold and garnet also signify special rank and distinction. One remembers Bede's story of Sigebert, the East-Anglian king, who was taken from his monastic retirement to lead his people in battle because he had formerly been such a resolute warrior. Because of his monastic vows he went into battle armed only with a stick, and he was cut down and killed. His presence was needed as a symbol, and we can be sure that he was dressed to look the part. The king was no modest, home-spun governor. He was the visible, easily recognizable symbol of authority over the folk.

The discovery at Sutton Hoo was extraordinary, too, in being a ship burial, a type of burial known in pre-Viking England only in East Anglia and the Thames estuary. The rowing galley appears to have been hauled up to the site and then ceremonially lowered into a pit dug on ploughed land newly excavated for the occasion. Earth was placed over it so that the new mound came to extend some 110 feet in length and to stand 10 feet above the surrounding countryside. Sutton Hoo gives an invaluable tangible picture of an elaborate heathen burial ceremony. The poet of Beowulf in the following century gave a vivid account of a comparable ceremony in a passage describing the burial of Scyld Scefing, the founder of the Danish royal dynasty:

> There stood at the sea-shore a vessel fit for a prince, a ship with prow adorned with rings, ready and eager for the journey. Then they laid the dear prince, the giver of rings, in the bosom of the ship, a mighty lord by the mast. Men brought there from far and wide a mass of treasure and ornaments. I have never heard of a more comely ship with its battle-weapons and harness, its swords and mail-shirts. On the hero's own breast many treasures were placed that were to travel further with him into the sea's possession. In no wise were they equipping him with less in the way of precious goods than had those who in the first place when he was yet a child sent him forth alone over the waves. Then further they set high over his head a golden standard, they let the sea bear him, gave him to the ocean.[18]

The poet completes his epic with an even more vivid account of the burial of Beowulf himself, and on this occasion the actual interment takes place in a great mound on a cliff top, high and broad to be seen from very far off by seafarers, an interment of the already cremated remains.

---

18 Beowulf, ll. 32–49, and ll. 3156–80 for the ceremonies following the cremation of Beowulf.

The widow sang her lament and prophesied disaster after the cremation. Further laments from chosen followers, a solemn and formal riding around the mound, and the framing of words of praise for the dead king took place after the interment. Scyld was buried in a ship and launched out to sea; Beowulf was cremated and the ashes placed within a massive and conspicuous mound. Sutton Hoo represents a combination of both, the most impressive of all such memorials to survive from the period, a fine example of pagan royal burial and yet in a sense the end of a cultural sequence since the ceremonies took place in a Christian or semi-Christian milieu. Methods varied but the principle remained the same; a king's funeral was an impressive moment in the life of a people.

Sutton Hoo is the outstanding archaeological discovery but there are also other burials where rich grave-goods, at times within a mound, suggest a special setting-apart of the man commemorated, a princely burial if not strictly and certainly royal. Modern work at Cuddesdon in Oxfordshire and at Coombe in Kent have revived interest in older discoveries, at Benty Grange in Derbyshire, at Broomfield in Essex, at Asthall in Oxfordshire, at Salisbury Racecourse in Wiltshire, at Snape in Suffolk, and especially at Taplow in Buckinghamshire. Precious goods, weapons, and preparation for feasts were not unique to Sutton Hoo. The Taplow burial with its luxurious array of gold braids, a possible symbol of royalty, was exceptionally wealthy and well endowed. The place-name, Taplow, Tæppa's mound, preserves the name of the man so honoured. The burial mound lies within the later churchyard, and Taeppa himself may well have been a ruler of a coherent group, perhaps even the dwellers within the Chilterns of later record, in the later pagan period.[19]

Possession of the trappings of royalty must from earliest times have been associated with a special investiture, a public acceptance of royal symbols and royal vestments. Christianity slowly took over responsibility for this function. Every effort was made, though not with consistent success, to provide each kingdom with a bishop; and the bishop would take care to provide proper blessings to the king and the royal court. Consecration of the monarch with full Christian ceremonial was another matter which developed only slowly. Ecgfrith, the son of Offa, appears to have been the first of the English kings to receive unction. Carolingian precedents were probably instrumental in prompting the Mercian kings to adopt this ceremony, although there were biblical precedents in plenty which must have had

---

19 The best guide remains Audrey Meaney, *A Gazetteer of Early Anglo-Saxon Burial Sites* (London, 1964), supplemented by records of individual investigation by archaeologists recorded in the periodical *Medieval Archaeology* or in *Abstracts relating to British Archaeology*, published by the Council for British Archaeology.

some force in Christian England. The papal legates to Offa in 787 could refer freely to the Lord's anointed. Later legends associated the coronation of St Oswald in the 630s with the bringing of holy oil by a sacred crow for the ceremony — an analogy with Merovingian traditions concerning the anointing of Clovis — but there is no hard evidence for anything worthy to be called a coronation ceremony in England before the end of the eighth century.

All that has been said so far about the person, kin, dress and ceremonial of the king applied to a kingship, recognized and legitimate, over a settled people. Identification of the king and dynasty brought about an attendant self-awareness among the people: the dynasties and the kingdoms of the Heptarchy developed together. The kingship about which we know most is that of the larger units of the Heptarchy, but smaller kingdoms or sub-kingdoms survived. It is more difficult to say anything of kingship over them, over the people of the *Gyrwe* or the *Magonsætan* or the *Cilternsæte* because they were absorbed into larger groupings. A genealogy reminds us however that Lindsey had a dynasty of its own well into the eighth century. Penda's son, Peada, a man fit to be king in name and in person, ruled over the Middle Angles to whose throne he had been appointed by his father. A ruling kin over the Hwicce appears in the witness lists to seventh and eighth-century charters; they subscribe firstly as *reguli* and then as *subreguli* to their Mercian overlords. They demand some special mention in any discussion of Anglo-Saxon kingship because they appear to have clung tenaciously to principles of partible inheritance over some five generations. In 690 Oshere, ruler of the Hwicce, was succeeded jointly by no fewer than four of his sons. The Hwicce were so dependent on Mercia (and may in origin have been Bernicians owing everything to the favour of Penda) that excessive weight should not be placed on their customs.[20] By and large however our basic knowledge of kingship rests on evidence relating to the larger units of the Heptarchy.

One of the principal developments of the pre-Alfredian period as has already been stated, was the extension of royal authority in the direction of an ultimate unification of the English under the rule of a single dynasty, but this does not mean that all moves in the direction of the creation of large units were permanent and unchanging. Kingdoms could be shared, and kingdoms could be divided. Such arrangements could be perilous. Division sometimes seemed the reasonable solution to succession problems when more than one kinsman was well placed to contend for the throne. Asser proves good witness not only to the fact but to the feeling of the community on one famous occasion. The

20 H.P.R. Finberg, *Early Charters of the West Midlands*, (2nd edn. Leicester, 1972), pp. 167–80.

widower Ethelwulf returned from his long visit to Rome with a young Frankish bride, the princess Judith. His eldest son Ethelbald with powerful support in the south-west had been ruling in his absence, and resented the new situation. Asser commented, as we have seen, that his attempt to deprive Ethelwulf of his kingdom was unheard of in previous ages.[21] A compromise was effected. Ethelbald kept the more prosperous west and his father retained the east. Judith was accorded royal dignities (up to this point unfamiliar in the English world) and in the event − to the scandal of all − married Ethelbald, her stepson, after his father's death in 858. Asser reflects again the anxieties of the situation when he tells how the restored Ethelwulf made his will so that after his day his two eldest sons should succeed to the kingdom. In fact the West-Saxon dynasty maintained the integrity of the kingdom, though the second son, Ethelbert, ruled as a sub-king in Kent 858 − 860, before his own accession; but Ethelwulf's difficulties are a reminder of the precariousness of a situation when a reigning monarch left a multiplicity of vigorous male heirs. There were also occasions when kingship seemed to be extending its reach beyond the bounds of the Heptarchic kingdoms. Up to the end of the seventh century this development was associated with the careers of a group of rulers later described as Bretwaldas, a title that apparently contained some element of meaning of a wider rule over at least a substantial part of Britain. In the eighth century mastery passed to the Mercian house and in the following century the West Saxons slowly showed themselves to be the heirs both of the Mercians and the Bretwaldas. Indeed the term Bretwalda or *brytenwalda* is used in the Anglo-Saxon Chronicle when it describes the climax of Egbert's career in the year 829:

> In this year there was an eclipse of the moon on Christmas Eve. And that year King Egbert conquered the kingdom of the Mercians, and everything south of the Humber; and he was the eighth king who was 'Bretwalda'.[22]

The Chronicler then named the seven earlier rulers to hold that title, taking his information from Bede who gave the identical list to name the kings who had enjoyed a wider authority in England. Bede in his comment on the death of Ethelbert, king of Kent, described Ethelbert as the third English king to exercise such an *imperium* over all the provinces south of the river Humber. The first two were Ælle, the South-Saxon king who evidently headed a confederation of Germanic peoples in the late fifth century, and Ceawlin, the ruler who set Wessex

---

21 See above p. 19
22 *ASCh* 829: the root meaning of the term may well have been 'broad ruler' but it is easy to see how a 'British' connotation could quickly have been acquired in Anglo-Saxon England.

on its way to become a powerful military unit in the late sixth century. After Ethelbert, the overlordship passed to Redwald of East Anglia who had been aiming at such leadership for his own people when Ethelbert was still alive, and then to the Northumbrian King Edwin, who ruled all the peoples of Britain, Angles and Britons, except for Kent, and extended his authority to the Menevian Islands of Anglesey and Man. The last of the seventh-century 'Bretwaldas' were the Northumbrian brothers Oswald and Oswy, and we are told that Oswy further conquered and made tributary the Picts and Scots in the northern parts of Britain. To judge from Bede's concentration on the age of Conversion with the two backward glances to Ceawlin and Ælle, the title Bretwalda (if indeed it was in general use in the seventh century) may have possessed some special significance as the kingdoms consolidated and accepted Christianity. This significance did not survive, and it seems likely that the Chronicler indulged in a piece of antiquarianism when he attached the title to Egbert and associated it with a list of those whom Bede had recognized as holding an *imperium* over other English peoples.[23] Adamnan, the biographer of St Columba, writing in the late seventh century, also referred to Oswald as *imperator,* and it does seem that some hazy imperial ideas were still present in newly converted England, possibly associated with some feeling of special privilege and influence over the Church.[24] One outstanding feature of these powerful seventh-century rulers deserves emphasis. They were leaders of military federations against the Britons, or against the heathen and the Britons, but little indication is given of their exercise of governmental authority within other kingdoms. Even Oswy, the most powerful of them, exercised no direct secular authority outside Northumbria. His attempt to do so for a brief period in Mercia after Penda's death ended in failure. For three years, 655–658, Northumbrian ealdormen ruled the Mercians; but the Mercians then revolted against *principes* who were not of their own people. It seems that seventh-century England recognized what we would call principles of nationality in the smaller units. The *imperium* signified military leadership, a pre-eminence in prestige and ability and a readiness to take tribute, but little else in the secular field.

Eighth-century Mercian overlordship was very different, and the Chronicler may have been more justified than he realized in withholding the title Bretwalda from the Mercian rulers. Even in the reign of Ethelbald this difference was apparent. Bede tells us that all the English provinces to the south of the Humber, with their kings,

---

23 Bede, *HE* ii, 5.
24 *Adomnan's Life of Columba,* ed. A.O. and M.O. Anderson (Edinburgh, 1961) p. 200: *victor post bellum reversus postea totius Brittanniae imperator a deo ordinatus est.*

were subject to him, a clear indication that Bede himself placed Ethelbald in the line of continuity from the Bretwaldas. In an important charter of 736 by which the Mercian king granted land to the ealdorman Cyneberht at Stour in Ismere, Worcestershire, Ethelbald subscribes as *rex Britanniae* and is referred to the body of the text as 'king not only of the Mercians but also of all the provinces which are called by the general name "South English".'[25] Mercian overlordship reached its peak under Ethelbald's effective successor, the great Offa, 757–96. Offa was a fine military commander and a skilful negotiator. Offa's dyke, a realistic border between the English and the Welsh, bears ample testimony to his skill in both directions. From the point of view of government his relationships with the other English communities are very revealing. Northumbria lay outside his main concern; the kingdom was disintegrating from within and punitive raids were enough to meet Offa's purpose. Wessex maintained a degree of independence under Cynewulf (757-786) but after his assassination King Beorhtric married Offa's daughter and seems to have been dependent upon him. The Franks under Charlemagne showed a spasmodic interest in affairs in both the kingdoms, but this may have been no more than a desire not to let Offa have his own way too sweepingly throughout Anglo-Saxon England.[26] In the south-east Offa was very powerful. He confirmed charters issued by the south-Saxon kings, conquered the province of Hastings in 771, and acted so arrogantly towards Kent in matters concerning the transmission of land and the Church that he provoked at least one serious revolt. Essex was completely subservient and London was a Mercian town. The final stage was reached in the 790s. East Anglia preserved its own dynasty but had caused no trouble to Offa. In 793, in the simple words of the Chronicle, Offa ordered the head of King Ethelbert to be struck off. Later legends told of this murder as an act of special treachery, perpetrated when the handsome young prince was a guest at Offa's court, negotiating a marriage settlement with one of Offa's daughters. In this instance legend may well have a strong stratum of poetic truth. Loose ties of marriage after the West-Saxon model were proving insufficient for Mercian ambition.

This bare outline of events in enough to indicate one of the principal differences between the seventh and eighth-century exercisers of *imperium*. The leadership of the former contained an element of common purpose against outside enemies, the massing of English forces

---

25 P.H. Sawyer, *Anglo-Saxon Charters* (London, 1968), p. 94, no. 89; *CS* 154.

26 J.M. Wallace-Hadrill, *Early Germanic Kingship*, p. 117, makes the shrewd comment that Ecgfrith's successor, Cenwulf of Mercia, 'may well have watched his step early in the ninth century when men with strong Carolingian connections were in power in both Wessex and Northumbria'.

against Celtic peoples. Consolidation of dynastic authority over at least the southern English was more in the Mercian minds. Royal titles in charters again reflect reality, particularly under Offa. In a charter to Rochester in 764 he describes himself as sprung from the royal stock of Mercia and made king by the dispensation of almighty God. In 774 he is king of all the *patria* of the English. Experiments in title included the straightforward 'king of the Mercians' and 'king of the English'.[27] If the latter title is taken as a statement of objective, Mercian success was indeed only partial. Nevertheless partial achievement of the basic Mercian aim did much to make possible the future unification of England, and the Mercian contribution to English institutional development was greater than used to be recognized in Church as well as in State even though the very severity of their military rule bred resistance. We are learning, however, to recognize that political circumstances were at work in late eighth-century England as strongly as in the Frankish lands, and that Alcuin, the English scholar who dominated for a while the Carolingian school at Aix-la-Chapelle, had influence on kingship that was potent on both sides of the channel. The king was to be a *doctor,* a teacher, to his people as well as a *dux,* a war-leader. In a letter to an English king, Alcuin associated a people's luck, its success in war, the wealth of harvests, its freedom from plague with the king's personal morals and behaviour. In a fine rhetorical passage he asserted that the goodness of the king represented the prosperity of all the people because the justice (*æquitas*) of princes is the exaltation of the people (*populi*).[28] The summons of papal legates, the holding of great Church councils under royal patronage, the creation of a new archbishopric at Lichfield and the unction given to his son Ecgfrith all indicate Offa's anxiety to benefit from and to work with the Church. The theory of the monarchy benefited greatly from the period of Mercian dominance.

In practice, too, the Mercians clarified the situation, though not without harshness that brought its own reactions. Control of the Severn Valley became complete. The dynasty of the Hwicce depreciated visibly in the charters as their rulers became *subreguli* (ealdormen) in place of their earlier and prouder titles as *reguli*. Unpopularity followed, probably because the Mercians were driven to more ruthless discipline in their attempts to build up an effective defensive system within southern England. The construction of Offa's dyke threw great burdens particularly on the border folk and it may be

---

27 F.M. Stenton, *Anglo-Saxon England,* (3rd edn Oxford, 1971), pp. 211–12.
28 *MGH,* Ep. IV, ii: *legimus quoque quod regis bonitas totius est gentis prosperitas, victoria exercitus, æris temperies, terrae habundantia, filiorum benedictio, sanitas plebis.......quia æquitas principum populi est exaltatio.* J.M. Wallace-Hadrill, *Early Germanic Kingship*, p. 105ff makes important comment on this passage.

that later attachment to the cult of St Ethelbert (of East Anglia) among the *Magonsætan* of Hereford indicates folk memory of Mercian unpopularity. Kent, which felt the full force of Mercian energy, became bitterly hostile. Active and successful kingship bred reaction among people who had to pay for the action and the success, and it is probable that both Kent and East Anglia were more aware of their identity in the 820s than they were on Offa's accession seventy years before. They played a prominent part in the overthrow of the Mercian hegemony. The beneficiary proved to be the West-Saxon king. Egbert succeeded to his kingdom of Wessex in 802, and slowly consolidated his authority. In 825 he defeated Beornwulf, king of Mercia, at Wroughton. Another force under his son Ethelwulf, drove the Kentish king north over the Thames, and the people of Kent and of Surrey and of the South Saxons and the East Saxons submitted to him because they had previously been wrongfully forced away from his kinsmen.[29] In the same year the king of the East Angles and the people appealed to King Egbert for peace because of their fear of the Mercians; and the East Angles killed Beornwulf, king of the Mercians.

It is likely that Wessex, even under the strong rule of Egbert, represented something of a reaction from Mercian austerity and harshness. Egbert holds a special position in West-Saxon history because he restored the fortunes of his dynasty and people. The Chronicler had this in mind when he called him Bretwalda, and linked him directly with Bede's emperors to the exclusion of the powerful Mercian dynasty. More than West-Saxon rivalry with Mercia may be involved in this omission and (as has already been suggested) some awareness of the difference in the nature of the overlordship may well have been involved. Egbert, like the *imperatores* of Bede before him, did not deprive other English kings of their kingdoms nor kingdoms of their kings. His sweeping military successes left him for a while in virtual command of England south of the Humber but only south of the Thames did he set out to build an organized kingdom. Kent acquiesced in West-Saxon overlordship, probably because of Egbert's own direct family connections with princes who ruled in Kent. Sussex became a dependent sub-kingdom, and pressure, already strong in 815 when Cornwall was ravaged from east to west, was maintained further in the south-west. Egbert's last campaign in 838 culminated in a victory against both Danes and Cornishmen. North of the Thames a very different picture emerged. In Mercia the old dynasty had died out in the early 820s, but new lines appear: Wiglaf obtained the kingdom in 830.

---

29 *ASCh* 825: *from his mægum ær mid unryhte.*

The East Angles also continued to enjoy the rule of their own indigenous princes.

Egbert died in 839 after a long and successful reign of more than thirty-seven years. He was succeeded by his son, Ethelwulf, who established his own son Athelstan as sub-king in the south-east over 'the kingdom of the people of Kent and of the kingdom of the East Saxons and of the people of Surrey and of the South Saxons'.[30] Athelstan died before his father and the succession passed to the younger brothers, Ethelbald and Ethelbert (again in the south-east). On Ethelbald's death in 860, Ethelbert succeeded to the whole of greater Wessex, to be succeeded in turn by the fourth of Ethelwulf's sons to reign, Ethelred, in 865. None of these young rulers, all powerful men in their way, showed signs of usurping authority north of the Thames. At all events politics were now dominated by the presence of the Danes; it was this Danish presence that finally prompted the creation of a united England.

30 *ASCh* 839.

2*

Kingship and the Ranks of Men

The conspicuous developments of these early centuries, the conversion of the English to Christianity, the Mercian hegemony, the slow assertion of West-Saxon leadership, must not conceal from us the intensity of the less conspicuous but equally important developments in the field of government. A healthy reticence on the part of Christian thinkers towards the exercise of secular lordship, even of legitimate royal lordship, began slowly to give way to more positive attitudes. The themes that were discussed were understandably the person of the king and the attributes of royalty in military and financial and legal matters more than any other single feature; but the nobility also went through something of an institutional crisis of identity during these centuries as emphasis appeared to shift from blood to service as a determinant of noble status. We can also see definite progress made in what is sometimes termed the process of territorialization of political power. Certainly the territorial divisions within the familiar kingdoms of England became neater and more precise in their physical definitions.

It is difficult to consider the exercise of authority of man over man because of the spasmodic and fitful nature of our sources. No Mercian law-codes have survived, and the distribution of surviving charters has been largely determined by the presence of great churches with continuous life in the favoured areas. Kent is disproportionately well represented; Mercia (except for Worcester and the Severn Valley), East Anglia, and Northumbria are under-represented. We suspect that many of the things that we are going to say about royal government apply to all the English kingdoms though evidence in support of this conjecture is scanty. On the other hand institutional differences which tend to be ascribed to Danish influence may, for example, owe

---

* This chapter draws heavily on the evidence provided by the laws and by Bede, but for the eighth century other sources come to assume great significance, notably evidence from ecclesiastical councils (Haddan and Stubbs), from charters mostly available in the collection of de Gray Birch, *Cartularium Saxonicum* (*CS*), and from the coinage.

something to pre-Danish variations within an English pattern, between Northumbrian and West-Saxon or between Kentish and Mercian or East-Anglian. In the event Wessex became the nucleus of a united England, and West-Saxon peculiarities in nomenclature and nature of the territorial subdivisions of the kingdom and in the nature of the royal officers became models and types for extension throughout England. This very fact alone provides some justification for emphasis on developments south of the Thames throughout these centuries.

The positive attributes of kingship make up the most prominent feature of administrative history to emerge from the surviving records, and are perhaps best considered under the two interlocking attributes of leadership in war and control of wealth.

Leadership in War

A king was expected to lead his people in war, a prime duty that lay as heavy on kingship in the more settled days of the ninth century as in the more mobile and uncertain fifth and sixth. Egbert of Wessex (802–839) was a formidable war-leader up to the last years of his reign. His grandson, Alfred, succeeded more or less on the field of battle after the death, on campaign, of his brother, Ethelred: the year of Alfred's accession (871) was known as the year of battles. Poetry supports the prosaic record. A king was expected to be active in defence of his people, to be victorious in battle against encroaching neighbours, to extend the living-space of his community. In old age he might sit back and trust the younger men (whom he had rewarded well) to bear the brunt of the active fighting. Involvement in war and control of warriors was a basic and formative element in royal authority.

From the earliest days two institutions were closely connected with these military responsibilities. The heart of a fighting force consisted of a hearthtroop gathered together at a king's court, but at no stage except possibly in the period of migration itself, was this of exclusive importance. As communities coalesced and settled so did the importance of the epic fighting-troop, operating around a personal lord, inevitably diminish. Kings extended their range. Retainers grew old and were rewarded with farms and lordship under the king over men and possessions. The active, warlike force at the king's court became more complex, and widespread recruitment became necessary as the kingdoms were consolidated. It remained the essential privilege of the freeman, the mark of his status, to bear arms, and his essential duty to fight in defence of the king and the community. The laws are unambiguous on this point, but as the agrarian element in the settlement came to predominate it was inevitable that differentiation sprang up in the nature of this duty. For a noblemen, an old retainer who had served his thegnly apprenticeship in the king's court, constant readiness to fight was a condition of his rank and of the holding of his estates. Equipment was always ready at hand, and royal summons or circumstances or both would be enough to prompt active military service. The condition of the ordinary freeman was somewhat different. In Wessex, at least from the time of Ine (688–725) and probably earlier, a fine *(fyrdwite)* was exacted from an ordinary freeman or from a man of higher rank who neglected his duty to serve in the army. An ordinary freeman was to pay 30 shillings, a nobleman who did not own land was to pay 60 shillings, and a nobleman owning land was to pay 120 shillings and to forfeit his estate.[1] Military duty rapidly became a charge on land as well as on persons. The device favoured in Carolingian Europe in the late eighth and ninth centuries was to group freemen into companies of four or five and to place responsibility for the actual physical performance of military service on one of the group. Evidence of similar moves in the direction of a select fyrd and the evolution of a five-hide unit may be found in Anglo-Saxon England.

As early as the ninth century it is certain that the service of one warrior from five or six hides of land was regarded as reasonable, but it is highly unlikely that universal rules applied. In 801 when Pilheard, a *comes* of King Cenwulf of Mercia, explained how a large estate of 30 hides, probably Wycombe in the Chilterns, had come to him in return for a down-payment of 200 shillings and an annual render of 30 shillings to the king, he was at pains to stress the freedom of his land apart from the three public causes, that is the construction of bridges and fortresses and also, in time of need, service of five men only for the army. Such a privilege, for privilege it clearly was at this stage, the exaction of five men's service from 30 hides, needed emphasis in the solemn charter. The hearthtroop and the general obligation of all freemen to serve in the *fyrd* remained the dominant element in Anglo-Saxon military service. Charges on land and the creation of a select *fyrd* were complementary institutional growths attendant on the administrative processes needed to keep the army royal and efficient.[2]

Control of the hearthtroop and *fyrd,* of the active fighting men, important though it was, represented only one element in this military aspect of royal authority. It is too easily forgotten how much the community depended on material methods of defence against in-

1 *EHD* i, no. 32, p. 404; Ine 51 – *gesithcund* men owning land, *gesithcund* men not owning land and *cierlisc* men are the three grades considered.
2 *EHD* i, no. 73, pp. 500–1: an endorsement by Cenwulf, king of Mercia, to an exchange of 30 hide estates. The service of five men to fulfil the military obligation of the estate (probably in the Chilterns) was regarded as adequate. Also below pp. 163–5

vaders, whether the invaders were fellow-Englishmen, Britons or Irish or Scandinavian invaders from across the sea. To provide some measure of security formal fortifications in the shape of earthworks and timbered stockades were essential. There gradually emerged in the written records of the eighth century references to a combination of charges upon estates that were later known as the *trimoda* or *trinoda necessitas,* the three necessities. Provision of men to fight in the *fyrd* and provision for the maintenance and repair of the fortifications, the *burhs,* were two of these necessities. The third, equally essential for military purposes, concerned the repair of bridges, and on many sites bridges and fortifications coincided. Control of bridges also meant effective control of communications, particularly significant in relation to a valley-settling people. The association of bridges with fortifications and the army reminds us how closely general administration comes to be linked with military affairs. The idea that the highway was the king's is as old as the highway itself, and the law-codes give plentiful evidence of the basic function of the king to maintain full royal control of communications within his kingdom.[3]

Recent subtle and convincing work has enabled us to see how the concept of the *trimoda necessitas* grew in the course of the eighth century, notably under the dynamic direction of the Mercian kings and their advisers.[4] It is probable that the growth in the custom of granting immunities from the ordinary processes of government to great churchmen and more slowly to laymen may have occasioned the formulation of such a concept. By 796 at the latest the three burdens were obligatory on all estates granted by the king in the Mercian kingdom. Reservations had appeared in Mercia at an early date, when possibly in reaction to criticisms made by English missionaries in Germany, special privileges were granted to the churches at the council of Gumley in 749; but even there repair of bridges and the maintenance of fortresses were mentioned specifically as matters outside the other public burdens from which the Mercian churches were to be freed. No self-respecting Mercian king was to be deprived of his right over the army, fortifications, and bridges. It may well be that the question of compulsory army service rendered to the king ante-dated the other two; men on Church lands as well as men with secular lands were not to be exempted from military service; and the Gumley charter with its emphasis on financial burdens appears to have taken simple military service for granted.[5] Evidence is strong enough to suggest that Mercia

3 H.R. Loyn, *Anglo-Saxon England and the Norman Conquest,* (London, 1962), pp. 98–100.
4 Nicholas Brooks, 'The Development of Military Obligations in Eighth and Ninth-Century England', *England before the Conquest,* ed. P. Clemoes and K. Hughes (Cambridge, 1971), pp. 69–84.
5 Wilkins, *Concilia,* i, pp. 100–1. Haddan and Stubbs, iii, *AD* 749, pp. 386–7. W.H. Stevenson, 'Trinoda Necessitas', *EHR* 29 (1914), pp. 699–702.

was the centre for the formulation of the *trimoda,* though army service alone was an undoubted basic obligation in every kingdom. Late in Offa's reign bridge and fortress service seems to have been introduced into Kent, presumably in reaction to Viking threats. In similar fashion Sussex seems to have been subject to similar burdens. Offa was clearly reacting with accustomed vigour *contra paginos marinos,* and it is one of the ironies of early Anglo-Saxon history that his methods in turn bred some active dislike of Mercian overlordship among the men of the south-east. Wessex seems to have lagged behind the Mercian kingdom in this respect and it may be significant that pre-Alfredian work has been discovered by archaeologists at the Mercian *burhs* of Hereford and Tamworth while West-Saxon *burhs* such as Wareham, Cricklade or Lydford, though carefully excavated, have yielded none. The Mercian kings have not been given enough credit for their creative work in organizing a realistic form of local defence based on service due from persons and from land on the inhabitants of Greater Mercia and of the kingdoms directly under their influence.[6]

Control of Wealth

Many of the positive manifestations of royal authority in the military sphere involved control of wealth both in cash and in kind. An army could not be sustained without considerable call on manpower and resources. An ability to call on manpower was indeed a basic right of kingship. The poem 'Beowulf' is illuminating on this point. We are told that when the Danish king, Hrothgar, built his great palace of Heorot he summoned men from far and wide to help with the task. In the same passage, almost as a justification of this royal right to exact service, we are told that a king had power over men, except for the 'folk-share' (presumably the ownership of allodial lands) and the lives of men.[7] One of our earliest surviving English administrative documents, the Tribal Hidage, which may well be roughly contemporary with the poem of Beowulf, gives some insight into how resources were collected. This was a tribute list, probably, drawn up in the later seventh century and brought up to date by one of the Mercian war-lords of the eighth century and catalogues the obligations of the primitive folk that went to make up the greater Mercia of the eighth century. Some of the topographical problems involved in an interpretation of the names are still uncertain, but the main outlines are clear. The document gives first the names of territories or peoples in

---

6 H.R. Loyn, 'Towns in Late Anglo-Saxon England', *England before the Conquest,* pp. 115–28, especially pp. 126–7, and Martin Biddle, 'Archaeology and the beginnings of English Society', *ibid.* pp. 391–408, especially pp. 392–8.

7 Beowulf, l. 73, *buton folc-scare ond feorum gumena.*

Anglo-Saxon, usually in the genitive plural form, followed by an assessment of hidage. After twenty entries it offers an accurate running total of 66,100 hides. It then gives a further fifteen names, finishing with an assessment for five large kingdoms obviously reckoned as dependent on Mercia, and a final total of 242,700 hides which is incorrect (the correct figure is 244,100). The complete list is:[8]

Name	Hidage	Location
1 Myrcna landes	30,000	The Trent valley stretching to the south-west
2 Wocen sætna	7,000	The Wrekin settlers, presumably well into modern Cheshire.
3 Westerna	7,000	The land between the Severn and Offa's dyke.
4 Pecsætna	1,200	The Peak District.
5 Elmedsætna	600	Leeds and 'Elmet.'
6/7 Lindesfarona..... mid Hæpfeldlande	7,000	Lindsey with Hatfield Chase.
8 Suþgyrwa	600	Small peoples in the Fenlands
9 Norþgyrwa	600	
10 Eastwixna	300	
11 Westwixna	600	
12 Spalda	600	Spalding in Lincolnshire?
13 Wigesta	900	Norfolk Fenlands around the Wash.
14 Herefinna	1,200	Wooded territory in Huntingdonshire and Northamptonshire.
15 Sweordora	300	Whitlesey Mere, Huntingdonshire.
16 Gifla	300	Land in Bedfordshire.
17 Hicca	300	Hitchin, Hertfordshire.
18 Wihtgara	600	Isle of Wight.
19 Noxgaga	5,000	Possibly land to the south of the Thames, substantially modern Surrey.
20 Ohtgaga	2,000	
	66,100	

At this point the original list probably came to the end of one folio, though in surviving form its information is compressed and runs straight on to the remainder of the list :

21 Hwinca	7,000	The land of the *Hwicce* in the Severn valley
22 Ciltern sætna	4,000	The Chilterns
23 Hendrica	3,500	Oxfordshire stretching west to the Cotswolds and south to the Middle Thames and Dorchester provides a possible home for these two obscure
24 Unecungga	1,200	but substantial peoples

8 C.R. Hart, 'The Tribal Hidage', *TRHS* 21 (1971), pp. 133–57; Wendy Davies and H. Vierck, 'The contexts of the Tribal Hidage: social aggregates and settlement patterns', *Frühmittelalterliche Studien,* 8, (1974), pp. 223–93.

25 Arosætna	600	The river Arrow in Warwickshire
26 Færpinga	300	Charlbury in Oxfordshire
27 Bilmiga	600	Small Fenland peoples, possibly in Rutland around Wittering and Warrington, and in Cambridgeshire
28 Widerigga	600	
29 East Willa	600	
30 West Willa	600	
31 East Engle	30,000	East Anglia
32 East Sexena	7,000	Essex with parts of Hertfordshire and of Middlesex
33 Cantwarena	15,000	Kent
34 Suþ Sexena	7,000	Sussex
35 West Sexena	100,000	Wessex

242,700

(correctly 244,100)

There are great difficulties in interpreting this document. The raw assessment of Wessex at 100,000 seems penal, and may possibly have been so. All the smaller peoples are assessed in units of or multiples of 300 hides (five at 300, no fewer than eleven at 600, one at 900 and three at 1,200). 7,000 hides was regarded as a proper figure for a larger compact grouping, and seven peoples appear with that assessment (taking Noxgaga and Ohtgaga as one joint unit), indeed possibly eight if one could link the Chiltern-settlers with the *Hendrica* and discount the extra 500 hides that combination would involve. For the larger peoples an assessment based on a 300 hide unit would again apply : 15,000 for Kent, 30,000 (surely heavy to the point again of the penal for East Anglia) and 30,000 for the central heart of Mercia itself. Only the 100,000 hides for Wessex stands out as the complete oddity, and short of postulating a small hide for all of the West-Saxon lands (a rash postulation on the evidence available) there seems no logical mathematical reason for this oddity.[9]

The importance of the Tribal Hidage is obviously great. Whatever the difficulties of exact topographical identification and whatever the complexities of the sums involved in calculating the hidage one thing is sure : a method of assessment had developed which was capable of wide application throughout the English communities, and it was based on a unit known as the hide, the division described by Bede as the *terra unius familiae,* the land sufficient to support one family. There must have been a time when hide held this meaning, though the size and extent of the primitive *familia* is a matter for legitimate debate. It is probable that the hide consisted of several farms held by a

---

9 Davies and Vierck argue strongly for the penal nature of the West-Saxon assessment.

2 The England of the Tribal Hidage

Identifications are based largely on the work of David Hill. Tribal names have normally been used in the nominative but oblique cases have been retained (as in Hendrica and Willa) where there is still doubt over site.

group of kinsmen, an extended family.[10] Convention established over a large part of the country that a long-hundred of acres (120 acres) was a seemly holding of arable to be described as a hide, though it would be utterly wrong to envisage exact mensuration at this stage in social development : indeed a small hide of 30 or 40 acres became customary in some prosperous parts of the country.[11] Quickly, if not indeed from the very beginning, notional ideas entered the fiscal scene, and a consequent flexibility in the relationship of real acres to notional assessment was inevitable. There was no easier and more reasonable way of rewarding faithful service than by granting an estate at a reduced or even nominal assessment to public burdens. Beneficial hidation, that is to say the granting of land at a reduced assessment, is likely to have been as old as hidation itself. The evidence becomes clearer as charters begin to survive, that is to say from the last thirty years or so of the seventh century. It is generally accepted that the charters were not themselves dispositive, that is they did not constitute the act of donation but rather recorded such an act which would be made orally by a solemn declaration before witnesses or symbolically by the handing over of a turf or a knife or a sod of earth. Early missionaries may indeed have drawn up such record in the form of a private Roman charter though the charters attributed to the first Christian king, Ethelbert of Kent, are all forgeries. It is not however until the time of the great archbishop of Canterbury, Theodore of Tarsus (668−690) that authentic documents survive from most of the southern kingdoms. Northumbrian evidence from the writings of Eddius Stephanus and Bede confirm that the practice of issuing charters in favour of churches was widespread. Taken together with a recognized system of measuring and assessing lands in hides, charters provided greater flexibility at the administrative level. Composite estates could be described more neatly. For example a very early Sussex charter (688−705) testifies to the grant of 38 hides in five named places, made up of parcels of 12, 10, 11, 2 and 3 hides, for the foundation of a monastery.[12]

Bede again provides an essential source-book for the early period. There are many passages in the Ecclesiastical History where Bede refers to the hidage of different areas. These can range from substantial sub-kingdoms such as Sussex with its 7,000 hides, a figure cor-

10 T. Charles Edwards, 'Kinship, status, and the origins of the hide', *Past and Present* 56 (1972), pp. 3−33.
11 The fundamental study is that of J. Tait, 'Large Hides and Small Hides', *EHR* 17 (1902), pp. 280−2: in parts of Wessex, notably Wiltshire, a small hide of 40 acres of arable was customary, in Cambridgeshire the normal hide was 120 acres.
12 *EHD* i, no. 59, pp. 485−6. Also pp. 375−82 for a compressed and valuable account of the origin and development of the Anglo-Saxon Charter.

roborated by the Tribal Hidage, to Iona with only five hides. Mercia in the mid-seventh century after the death of Penda is described as consisting of two territories divided by the river Trent: to the north was the land of the northern Mercians with 7,000 hides : Peada, Penda's son, succeeded to the land of the South Mercians, assessed at 5,000 hides. Iona itself was described as not big but about the size of five such units, according to the system of reckoning of the English. The Isle of Man at about 300 households and more fertile and prosperous Anglesey at 960 could also be fitted by Bede into this convenient assessment pattern.[13]

Bede's information is confirmed by our earliest land-charters. The object of most of our surviving charters was to testify to a grant of land by the king to a religious house, or to a layman with prospects of reversion to a religious house. Chance survival brings about this impression of ecclesiastical dominance, and it is probable that a much higher proportion of grants went to the laity than used to be recognized. Land grants, virtually without exception, measure the estates in terms of hidage, that is to say the degree of assessment to public burdens. Terminology was still indeterminate and the main components of the whole estate could be described as *mansiones, cassati, mansae, tributarii* or *manentes,* terms reminiscent of the contemporary Frankish world. The implications of this simple concentration on hidage, or its Latin equivalent, are immense for any study of government. Assessment of estates involves some central directing institution, the king himself, the king's court or the collective wisdom of the folk, again presumably under the guidance of the king or royal officers. It also involved some apparatus, no matter how rudimentary, for the conversion of the assessment into manageable renders or even hard cash. In its earliest forms an equation in kind would suffice for conversion into payment. A fully armed soldier, a stated number of oxen or sheep or measures of corn would be exacted from each hide of land. Hidage was used as a convenient means of measuring a variety of burdens imposed upon the land. On royal estates food-rents and levies would be exacted in this way. A charter of Offa in the last years of his reign (793–796), for example, granted 60 hides at Westbury and 20 hides at Henbury to the church at Worcester free from all renders except for a food-rent from the estate at Westbury which was described in the vernacular as 'two tuns full of pure ale and a coomb full of mild ale and a coomb full of Welsh ale, and seven oxen and six wethers and 40 cheeses and six long "peru" and 30 ambers of unground corn

---

13 There is a good discussion of Bede's use of *terra unius familiae* and its relation to the hide in P. Hunter Blair, *An Introduction to Anglo-Saxon England* (2nd edn Cambridge, 1978), pp. 267–70.

and four ambers of meal.'[14] From 60 hides this was a modest imposition, and represents a reasonable render to the king from a subject's estate. The unspecialized nature of so many of these burdens led to complications which persisted in some measure throughout the Middle Ages. Customary obligations refuse to fit into the lawyer's neat categories.

The available evidence points to one important general truth about the attitude of eighth-century kings towards the transmission of land. The most efficient kings were careful about their donations to churches. Service could be exacted but virtual permanence in tenure inevitably detracted to some extent from the authority of the donor. In this respect there is something of a contrast between Northumbria and Mercia in the eighth century. Bede tells of the abuses that had sprung up in Northumbria from the establishment of false monasteries, endowed with land that should properly have gone to provide homes and sustenance for young noblemen and sons of veteran thegns who could lead the defence of the country against barbarian attack.[15] The scandal seems to have been widespread, royal servants, thegns and reeves taking the opportunity of enrichment by setting themselves or their wives or their kinsfolk in charge of such so-called monasteries, or using the pretext of intention to found monasteries to have lands ascribed to them by hereditary right in royal edicts and confirmed to them by the subscriptions of bishops, abbots and secular persons. Break-up and neglect of royal demesne contributed to the weakening of the Northumbrian kingdom. The Mercians were more careful. Offa made it transparently clear that he alone could authorize the granting of land in perpetuity to churches, even revoking what seems to have been a perfectly proper grant by the Kentish king, Egbert, to Christ Church Canterbury.[16] It may well be that a greater concern for the integrity of royal demesne, coinciding with a period of expansion over lesser surrounding folk, played a greater part than has always been realized in the rise to prominence of the Mercian kingdom.

Concern with royal demesne should be coupled with a positive attitude towards the medium of exchange, towards the coinage. At some stage, probably again during the years of Mercian ascendancy and most probably during the reign of Offa, cash substitution for other types of render in the payment of hidage became more common. Currency reforms in the late eighth century may well have been connected

---

14 *EHD* i, no. 78, pp. 507–8. Sir Frank Stenton commented, *Anglo-Saxon England,* p. 288, that 'these details can hardly be regarded as a heavy charge on the men of 60 hides'.

15 *EHD* i, no. 170, pp. 799–810; Letter of Bede to Egbert, archbishop of York (5 Nov., 734).

16 *EHD* i, no. 80, pp. 510–1: Offa's objection rested on the grounds that it was improper for a thegn to give land allotted to him by his lord without the lord's witness. In the body of the charter Egbert is referred to as Offa's *minister,* i.e. his thegn.

with attempts to create a system of regular cash payments based on hidage, in short a geld-system (see pp. 34–8) that would apply to all territories under Mercian control. Some such efficiency lay behind local and regional reactions against the Mercian ruling house. By the end of the eighth century we can talk of a royal treasury in terms very different from those used of the treasure-hoards in jewels, gold and precious personal adornment of the earliest Anglo-Saxon kings.

The currency reforms of Offa's reign have received much attention in recent years.[17] Discussion has tended to focus on two problems of considerable interest and importance, on the analogies with secular developments in the realms of Charlemagne on the continent and on the general significance of the reform to the economic and above-all the trading life of the English communities. In essence the reforms led to the creation of the true silver penny, larger and thinner than the earlier pence (often known for convenience in differentiation as *sceattas*), a coin that was to remain virtually the sole current native type of coin to be minted in England during the succeeding 500 years. The first examples known were struck by two minor Kentish kings, Heabert and Egbert, but the impetus for wide-spread adoption of the coin came from the court of the Mercian overlord and seems firmly to be connected with increased sophistication in the practice and symbolic strength of kingship both in England and on the continent. At their best the coins of Offa achieve a rare beauty of design which makes them much coveted collectors' pieces. The obverse comes to bear the king's bust (coins were issued, too, in the name of the queen, Cynethryth, and of Archbishop Jænberht) and in time the regular pattern in inscription is achieved of royal name on the obverse with the moneyer's name on the reverse. Evidence of find-spots suggests that the striking of coins tended to be confined to the south and the east, roughly in an arc from East Anglia to Southampton Water, with Canterbury and London the principal mints. A gold dinar struck in Offa's name but with blundered Arabic inscription found in Italy indicates the wider ranges of Offa's extraordinary currency, but it is more important to note the administrative implications.[18] The provision of a respectible standard silver penny must have facilitated greatly the collection of royal taxes and revenues.

The King and Law

The king possessed a Court at which judgements were made, and all

---

17 The following paragraph is based on the important article by C.E. Blunt, 'The Coinage of Offa', *Anglo-Saxon Coins,* ed. R.H.M. Dolley (London, 1961), pp. 39–62.
18 C.S.S. Lyon, 'Some problems in interpreting Anglo-Saxon Coinage', *Anglo-Saxon England*

discussion of abstract rights, of the relationship of the king to law, is meaningless unless that one basic fact is taken into account. Literature, poetry and the charters, as well as the more clear-cut legal records, testify to this and suggest a jurisdiction that was exceedingly powerful. A royal court, presided over by a king, could send a freeman to the gallows, sell him into a slavery or inflict ruinous financial penalties. The jurisdiction was not however limitless. Custom, precedent and the status of the offender provided some curbs and restraints. A freeman was not to be subject to mutilation or the lash. The king should seek the counsel of the wise men of the realm. But it would be wrong to assume a passive presidency of the court on the part of the king. Biblical example, poetic tradition and the necessities of everyday life demanded that positive judicial action of substance be given to the notion of a king as a defender of right or suppressor of wrong and of evil-doers.

The law that was administered is not easy to define in modern terms. Its origins were complex and further complicated by the distortion inevitable when custom that is normally expressed orally is put into writing by men whose principal interests were ecclesiastical rather than secular. Two elements predominate, the existence of a body of customary law common to the community (which we term folkright) and royal initiative. Folkright applied to all the fields of law that came later to have exact and carefully drawn borders, personal law, the law of tenure. Folkland is essentially land held according to folkright. The prologues to the earliest law codes, insofar as they preserve the spirit of the age from which they purport to come, are revealing. The Kentish laws stress royal initiative. We hear of the decrees (dooms) which Ethelbert established in St Augustine's day, of the decrees which the kings Hlothhere and Eadric established (adding them to the law which their forefathers had previously ordained) and of the decrees laid down by Wihtred at an advisory assembly attended by the great men of the kingdom.[19] The West-Saxon evidence hints at a more subtle situation. King Ine (688–725) in the prologue to his laws explained that he, together with a great assembly of the chief men in his kingdom, had taken anxious thought over the salvation of their souls and the state of the kingdom, that true law *(ryht æw)* and true statutes *(ryhte cynedomas)* might be established.[20] The special object of the exercise was stated to be in order to prevent later perversion of the royal decrees by ealdormen and other subjects. The assumption lurking

5, (Cambridge, 1976), pp. 173–226. Also B.H.I.S. Stewart, 'The Coinage of Southern England, 796–840', *BNJ*, 1963, pp. 1–74.

19 Lieb. i, pp. 3, 9 and 12.

20 Lieb. i, p. 88.

behind all these statements is that there existed for every ordered community a body of law to which the name folkright may properly be given and which from time to time was clarified by royal decree. Reference to old law (eald riht) even in trivial matters such as procedures to be followed when violence breaks out in a drunken brawl, highlights the existence of folkright.[21] Indeed to draw a sharp antithesis between folkright and royal decree is to intrude fake modern concepts into what is of necessity an amorphous situation incapable of sharp differentiations. Royal decrees clarified and added authority to existing received law; and additional new decrees drawn up in solemn assemblies had the force of closer definition of existing folkright.

As kings became rulers over settled peoples it became necessary for some records of royal administration to be kept. In England it is possible that the reintroduction of writing came about in Kent even before the coming of Augustine. Contact with the Frankish courts in the late sixth century, the marriage of Ethelbert to Bertha, a Frankish princess who came to Kent accompanied by her bishop, Liudhard, and general intensification of both economic and political ties with the Frankish and Romanic world may have been enough to ensure such a development. With Augustine's arrival and the conversion of Kent to Christianity further development became essential in literacy and royal administration. The conversion was no small-scale venture. Augustine was accompanied by some forty well-trained, zealous and disciplined men and their impact was considerable. Record of this on royal administration came especially from the legal field, though it may well be also, as some of our leading diplomatic historians have argued, that in matters of land-tenure the Augustine mission was responsible for the introduction of the solemn land charter into England.[22] In matters affecting law Bede is our prime but not our only authority. The 'Laws of Ethelbert' have survived, in later recensions, it is true, but still bearing firm signs in language and contents of early seventh-century origins. Bede notes in his summary of Ethelbert's achievements how, among other benefits, the Kentish people enjoyed as a result of the conversion the writing down in their own native tongue of judicial decrees according to Roman patterns or examples *(iuxta Romanorum exempla)*. It has been shown in recent years that this phrase *iuxta Romanorum exempla* was likely to be, not as many of us had been inclined to take it, a general reference to the Romans as

---

21 Lieb. i, p. 11, Hl and Ead. 12; *EHD* i; p. 395.
22 P. Chaplais, 'Who introduced Charters into England? The case for Augustine', *J. Soc. Archivists,* 1969, pp. 526–42. Nicholas Brooks, 'Anglo-Saxon Charters', *Anglo-Saxon England* 3, (Cambridge, 1974), pp. 211–31 gives full reference to work of the preceding twenty years.

men of written law, accustomed to the framing in writing of elaborate codes and law-books, but a specific reference to sixth-century continental practice where ecclesiastically trained administrators committed the barbarian Germanic laws to writing in their predominantly Romance-speaking communities. Affinities exist, as Sir Frank Stenton long ago suggested, between the laws of Ethelbert and the *Lex Salica;* they also existed in other statements of laws, Burgundian, Alemannic, Gothic, not all of which have now survived.[23] The commitment of the legal customs and practices of a people to writing in the royal name was an important stage in the stabilization of a dynasty and also, in a more subtle sense, in the infusion into Germanic kingship of the Christian notion of the kingly office, a *ministerium,* exalted but not different in kind necessarily from other secular office. A king who issued judicial decrees with advice from his secular and ecclesiastical wise men was *ipso facto* in the long traditions of lawgivers of Israel and the biblical past; and the suggestion of a just king with responsibility for the proper government and administration of the people committed to his care was implicit if not fully formulated or always understood.

In practice the law expected the king to be energetically active in the suppression of theft and violence, especially where other redress was lacking or doubtful. Insistence in the early law-codes on the royal responsibility in protecting widows, orphans and traders emphasize these elements. The Church was in a special position. Conversion to Christianity and the adoption of written law brought a new situation into being. The king needed literate servants and only the Church could provide them. In return the Church expected legal protection. Ecclesiastical property was to be safeguarded and so too were payments made to the Church by the faithful. The Church came increasingly to rely on the king and in so doing built up a series of precedents in the field of the upholding of the law that were to have deep effects also on secular society. A fuller and more active equitable content was given to the king's rights to supervise legal processes under the new dispensation. The Church had immediately to be fitted into the social structure and already in the earliest days of the Conversion it was laid down by King Ethelbert of Kent, that formidable compensation had to be paid for any attacks on ecclesiastical property, a twelve-fold compensation for the property of God and the Church, eleven-fold for the property of a bishop, nine-fold of a priest, six-fold of a deacon, and three-fold of a cleric. Infringement of the peace of the Church was equated with infringement of the peace of a meeting; and both were to be remedied with a double compensation

23 J.M. Wallace-Hadrill, *Early Germanic Kingship*, pp. 37–8.

payment.[24] Royal authority alone was powerful enough to make such legal statements at all significant. In late seventh-century Wessex, as in Kent, the kings supported the Church in its basic observances, enjoining baptism on pain of financial penalty, favouring communicants in the assessment of oaths, exalting the status and monetary protection given to the clerical order, especially the bishops, and supporting the keeping of the Sabbath, the payment of church-scot, and ecclesiastical rights of sanctuary. If a man liable to be flogged reached a church, presumably for formal sanctuary, the flogging was to be remitted. Concern with trade was also regarded as a matter substantially within the province of a king. Anything that was outside the ordinary agrarian routine and demanded mobility was a matter for direct royal cognizance. The laws of the Kentish kings Hlothhere and Eadric (673 – 685?) are particularly enlightening in this respect.[25] A man of Kent buying property in London had to have two or three honest *ceorls* or the king's town-reeve as witness. If his title were questioned he was to vouch to warranty at the king's hall in London the man who sold it to him, that is to say produce witnesses who would testify to the identity of the seller. If he could not do that he was to declare at the altar with one of his witnesses or the king's town-reeve that he had bought it honestly. Concern over foreigners, over men wandering away from the main roads, over the province of good witness, suggests royal anxiety to supervise honest trading and to avoid theft.

To this point we have dealt with the positive side of the royal position. There was also a strong negative advantage which came to him because of his royal rank. All society was graded according to blood-price, that is to say according to the *wergeld* or the sum of money reckoned as proper compensation in case of homicide. This is a characteristic common to many human societies and is especially typical of the peoples we know as Indo-Europeans. Among all Germanic societies with minor variations the same basic principles of bloodprice and compensation apply. The ordinary freeman in late seventh-century Wessex had a wergeld of 200 shillings which, reckoned at the standard West-Saxon equation of five pence to the shilling, amounted to 1,000 pence. Earlier in the century the Kentish freeman enjoyed a wergeld of 100 gold shillings which was equivalent to 2,000 silver pence. In both societies noblemen had equal wergelds equivalent to 6,000 silver pence, 1,200 shillings in Wessex and 300 gold shillings in Kent. An intermediate 600 shilling class in Wessex probably represented a British nobility absorbed into the social structure as the

---

24 *EHD* i, no. 29, p. 391, Eth. 1: *ciricfrip and mæthlfrip.*
25 *EDD* i, no. 30, pp. 394–5, cl. 16–16.3.

kingdom extended deeper into the south-west.[26] But a king was rated well above these groups again, and attempts were made to bring the royal kin also into a special category. Of course we must never forget that legal statements are often no more than attempts to establish reasonable standards and that the arbitrary element of sheer force could often enter the picture when it was a matter of exacting compensation in the place of vengeance. Ine, the powerful king of Wessex, exacted what appears to be a thirty-fold compensation from the men of Kent in compensation for the murder of the West-Saxon prince Mul, brother of the previous king Cædwalla. In Mercia after the eighth century the king enjoyed a wergeld twelve times that of a nobleman, half of which belonged to the king's person and half to the kingdom. A similar attempt to set a special and ruinous protective price on the king appears in Northumbria.[27] No great store should be set by the details of such attempts. It is much more important to recognize the principle that in all the Anglo-Saxon kingdoms prohibitive protection prices were established as a safeguard to the king and to the coincident peace of the kingdom. Other devices, some probably of primitive origin, served the same ends. The royal throne, his high-seat, was specially hallowed. Protection of the royal person within his own court was often in the lawyers' minds: and reports of assassinations and attempted assassinations indicate the reality underlying the concern. His *borh,* or special hand-giving power of protection, was considerable. Forcible entry into his residence and also, incidentally into the residence of a bishop within his diocese was punishable by the heavy compensation of 120 shillings. His thegns and other servants, including Welsh horsemen who acted as messengers for him, had special protection. A king's godson had a double *wergeld,* one to be paid to the kindred and the other to the king. Anyone fighting in the king's house was to forfeit all his possessions and it was to stand in the royal judgement whether or not he was to forfeit his life.[28] In a multitude of other ways a mystique was built up around the person and the office of the king with all the religious and legal authority society could bring to bear. Similar developments on the continent reached their culminating point in the late eighth century with the elaborate consecration ceremonies afforded the new Carolingian

26 H.M. Chadwick, *Studies on Anglo-Saxon Institutions* (Cambridge, 1905), provides a guide of permanent value to the topic. *EHD* i, no. 32, p. 401, Ine 24.2: a Welshman with five hides was reckoned as a 600 wergeld man.

27 *ASCh*, 694 (30,000 'pence'); Lieb. i, p. 462 (30,000 *sceattas*); *Be Mircna Laga*, Lieb. i, p. 458, *Norðleoda Laga* (30,000 prymsa).

28 *EHD* i, no. 32, p. 399, Ine 6 and *passim* throughout the laws, especially Ine 33 and 76.1 which offered special protection to the king's Welsh horseman who could carry his messages and to the king's godson.

dynasty first as Christian kings over the Franks and then as emperors. It was no accident that Offa spent much time, patience and energy arranging that his own son Ecgfrith should be consecrated king in his father's lifetime. The experiment did not prove a political success. It nevertheless points clearly to future developments and represents in many ways a culminating point in this early period in the trends that go to provide maximum prestige and safety to the now Christian kings.

Fragmented though the evidence may be the picture given is in the last resort clear enough. The finest of the ecclesiastical thinkers, Bede, Boniface, Alcuin, retained their sceptical reserves about the kings as people. Honest Augustinian doubt about the virtue of princes remained in men's minds. Humility was the characteristic that received the highest praise from Bede when he considered the kings and princes of the age of the Conversion. The most powerful rulers, Ethelbert, Edwin, Oswy, were all flawed in one respect or another, Oswald, the saint, was a special case, and Oswin, humble and thoughtful, was seen by the devout Aidan to be not too long for this wicked world.[29] The poet of Beowulf was in many respects more positive. He consciously sets out his models of good kings and bad kings, Hrothgar and Heremod; and Beowulf, protector of heroes, emerges as the supreme example of great kingship, the wise king, the old guardian of the homeland who held his dominion in justice for fifty years. In the magnificent last scenes of the poem when the hearth-companions lament the passing of the king they extol his qualities of gentleness, mercy, and kindness, as well as his love of glory and renown.[30] Our more prosaic records show with increasing accuracy the areas of social life where such virtues could best be exhibited, in council, in court, and in the increasing complexity associated with the governance of men.

Ealdormen, Gesiths and Thegns

Principles of government of permanent importance developed from the exercise of royal authority, but this was not the only significant type of authority known to the Anglo-Saxon world. The king was in a special position elevated over lesser mortals; his authority possessed a capacity for residual growth denied to that of other men. He could not however act alone. As the kingdoms grew in size his advisers were drawn increasingly from a noble class, the 'twelve-hundred' men of the laws who were protected by a the high wergeld or blood-price of 1200 shillings, six times that of the ordinary freeman in

29 Bede, *HE*, ii, 14.
30 Beowulf, ll. 3180–2, the last lines of the poem: cwædon þæt he wære wyruld-cyning, manna mildust ond mon-ðwærust, leodum liðast, ond lof-geornost.

Wessex. Some of these men were themselves royal princes, kinsfolk of the king with possible rights in the succession. Others were representatives of former ruling dynasties which had lost royal title and independence as they were absorbed into the larger heptarchic kingdoms. Others again owed their status to service which they or their ancestors had performed to kings. Their privileges mirrored the privileges of the crown. Protected by their high blood-price they also enjoyed their own *borh,* their rights to compensation if their own peace were disturbed. Anyone fighting in the home of an ealdorman or other important councillor was to pay 60s. compensation and to give another 60s. as a fine. There are superficial peculiarities about the penalties. The fine was only half that exacted for fighting in a peasant's house or indeed in open country but the inference is clear. No compensation was to go to the peasant. The ealdorman was expected to be able to look after himself, presumably to provide the physical force needed to exact the fine, and to receive compensation in return for his trouble.[31] Terminology to describe the nobility is naturally still fluid in the early Anglo-Saxon period. The three vernacular terms in most frequent use were *ealdorman, gesith* and *thegn*; and it is probable that *gerefa,* particularly in the northern kingdom, signified a high officer (*prefectus* appears occasionally as the Latin equivalent) more exalted in status than the later reeves. The ealdorman already had closer links with the kings and possessed more of an official status. He could lose his office (unless the king wished to pardon him) if he failed in his duty, particularly in his duty against thieving. Forcible entry into an ealdorman's dwelling made an offender liable to the heavy penalty of 80s. An ealdorman was expected to be prominent in the army and in the courts, leading contingents of the *fyrd* in the field, acting as the royal deputy in active military service and in the more prosaic business of delivering judicial judgements. Privileges, an extra weight to the value of his oath in the courts, brought correspondingly heavy penalties if privileges were abused.[32] This applied to the ordinary nobleman as well as to the man who held an ealdorman's office. *Gesithcund* (gesithborn) was the common term in use in late seventh-century law tracts to describe such men. The laws of Ine were particularly explicit on the matter of military service. Neglect of such service was to be punished by forfeiture of land and a fine of 120 shillings from a nobleman who owned land, by a fine of 60 shillings from a nobleman who did not own land, and by a fine of 30 shillings from an ordinary freeman.[33] In time the term *gesith* became

31 *EHD* i, no. 32, p. 399, Ine 6.2.
32 *ibid.,* p. 401, Ine 19: a king's *geneat* who was a communicant could give an oath to the value of 60 hides.
33 *ibid.,* p. 404, Ine 51. Above p. 32.

somewhat antiquated, chiefly used in poetry, but it served a useful purpose in early Anglo-Saxon society to describe noblemen possessing estates of their own, with some considerable measure of authority independent of that of the king. The *thegn* on the other hand, and even more so the king's thegn, though a 'twelve-hundred' man, was normally more of an exalted servant, one who performed an office about his lord. *Thegn* indeed covered a wide range of service from men with great privileges and status to humble retainers: in law an element of nobility was to be expected in a thegn, but the term still lived in the language of the seventh or eighth century in its root sense of 'one who served'.[34]

We know much about the nobility of early Anglo-Saxon England but some matters, vitally important to an effective study of government, escape us completely. We can assume that a nobleman's undoubted military obligations had corresponding fiscal obligations. There is no direct statement on the nature or limitation of his powers of jurisdiction, but the value of his oath, and the fact that the presence of a man of his rank was essential among oath-helpers in certain cases if exculpation was to be effective made him an important figure in all early judicial processes. A key text occurs in the laws of Ine. If a gesith-born man interceded with the king or the king's ealdorman or with his lord for members of his household, slaves or freemen, he, the gesith, had no right to any fines because he would not previously at home restrain the offenders from wrong-doing.[35] There are possible ambiguities and proper hesitations over the interpretation, but it seems reasonable to infer that a nobleman had a prime duty to keep order in his own household even if matters leading to formal fines *(witeræddende)* were the concern of public courts in the presence of royal officers. The extent of such dominical jurisdiction is hard to establish. There were certainly stringent restrictions on the exercise of authority over free dependents. The whole complicated system of wergelds and kin-protection stood as a permanent safeguard against a tyrannous lord. An unjust striking down of a free dependant would invite retribution from the freeman's kindred. No such sanction was offered the unfree. The safeguards of a slave were tenuous, or so they appear in retrospect, and were of a social and religious order rather than a legal.

It seems evident, too, that a nobleman's authority over a village community rested on his social rather than his legal dominance, and

---

34 H.R. Loyn, 'Gesiths and Thegns', *EHR* 70 (1955), pp. 529–49. The association of thegns with the Anglo-Saxon verb 'to serve', *thegnian,* was direct and continuous; *ealdorman's* sense of seniority in age and *gesith's* sense of companion on a journey were a shade more oblique.
35 *EHD* i, no. 32, p. 404, Ine 50.

would be determined in part by sheer physical and material factors, now outside the historian's knowledge. Wealth, size of hall, nearness in kinship to the king or the ealdorman, past prestige as a warrior, judge or royal servant, could determine the degree of authority exercised more so than mere physical force or apparent status. The idea of a 'twelve-hundred' man having automatic rights of a legal nature over other freemen should be summarily dismissed. The nobility of early Anglo-Saxon England operated as far back as the written record goes in a framework of law that was both royal and communal. When the Anglo-Saxon poet discussed the special 'gifts of men' he placed high on the list those who knew the law 'where men deliberate' and also those who 'in the assembly of wise men determine the custom of the people'; such gifts were not exclusive to one class.[36] This is not to deny variation in authority. The nobleman, already distinguished by speech, dress and appearance from the ordinary freeman, could, particularly in a military context, act in an apparently arbitrary fashion. Bede tells how in a war between Mercia and Northumbria a young Northumbrian king's thegn, Imma by name, was taken captive. The nobleman *(gesith)* who held him captive noticed from his face, bearing and speech that he was not of the meaner sort, as he had said, but of the nobler class. He persuaded him to tell him the truth and when he did so, confessing that he had been a king's thegn, the *gesith* replied:

> 'I realized by all your replies that you were not a peasant, and now indeed you deserve death, for all my brothers and kinsmen were killed in that battle; yet I will not kill you, that I may not break my promise.'[37]

In the event the young thegn was sold into slavery to a Frisian in London. The passage is of considerable importance in illustrating the authority of a military commander over his captives and in reminding us of the active world of warfare and kindred vengeance that flourished in the seventh and eighth centuries. Such arbitrary action should not however be taken as typical of noblemen in their dealings with civil dependants.

Freemen and the Unfree

To judge from the law-codes an ordinary freeman, a *ceorl*, the basic unit in organized society, was a man who paid or was paid for. This was only part of the story. A freeman in one of our early ter-

---

36 D. Whitelock, *The Beginnings of English Society* (London, 1952), p.135. *EHD* i,no.213, pp. 874–5. *Exeter Book,* ed. G.P. Krapp and E. van K. Dobbie (London and NY, 1936), p. 138: sum in mæðle mæg modsnottera folcrædenne forð gehycgan, þær witena bið worn ætsomne.
37 Bede, *HE,* iv, 22.

ritorial kingdoms still bore the characteristics of a free member of a tribe. He was oath-worthy and weapon-worthy, a person of repute, possessed of a free kindred and capable of playing a full part in the army and the courts. Such a part involved much more active self-help than would have been considered proper or seemly in a later age. Provided that he paid the recognized dues, a *ceorl,* a 200-shilling man, with or without a recognized link of lordship between himself and the king, would rarely need the services of anything resembling public authority. His personal safety was recognized by his own arms and his free kindred. Similar sanctions ensured his safe possession of a share in the village arable, his homestead and his flocks. Marriage and the rearing of his children were matters for arrangement among free kindreds and personal control. Public duties at the army and in the courts, it is true, had to be performed on pain of fines and intervention by royal officers. Restraints of an ordered society lay heavy on him in that sense, but these restraints were as much internal as external. As a free member of the people of Deira or East Anglia or Kent or Wessex he fulfilled his duties without an elaborate hierarchy of officialdom to sustain him.

Discussion of courts, of simple freemen and of kindred obligations and sanctions can be helpful. It can also mislead. Anglo-Saxon England was a slave-owning society, and in no period is this more true than during the early centuries, even after the conversion to Christianity. The laws of Ethelbert show a considerable sophistication in the gradations of slavery and anyone lying with a ceorl's woman-slave had to pay compensation to the ceorl according to the category of the slave, six shillings for one of the first class, 2½ shillings for one of the second class, and 1½ shillings for one of the third. It seems certain that these classes were determined roughly according to function and training, and in connection with royal women-slaves we are told that the penalties were 50 shillings for anyone lying with a maiden belonging to the king, 25 shillings for a grinding slave. and 12 shillings for a slave of the third class.[38] Legal concern was naturally concentrated on compensation to the slave-owner. Distinctions of dress, mien, appearance and sometimes language, thickened the social lines and barriers between the free and the unfree. The West-Saxon lawyers of the late seventh century were particularly anxious to incorporate whole classes of Welshmen, free and unfree, into their social structure as the kingdom extended to the south-west.

38 *EHD* i, no. 29, pp. 391–2, Eth. 10, 11 and 16.

A slave would have no legal redress against the will of a powerful master. Public courts could not interfere, and he could be punished corporally or even killed without penalty. A master could offer protection against others, though such protection had its clear legal limits. For example if a Welsh slave killed an Englishman his master was to surrender him to the lord and kinsmen of the slain man or to pay 60 shillings in compensation. If he did not wish to pay compensation (and the element of decision-taking involved must have prompted the creation of at least an *ad hoc* private court) the master was to set his slave free. The slave's free kindred was then to settle for him, if he was fortunate enough to possess one: if not, the avengers were to have their will.[39] Manumission under less dramatic circumstances was always a possibility and reduction to slavery, too, was less rare a happening than we are sometimes led to believe. The laws of Ine make provision for the punishment of offences by newly enslaved penal slaves.[40] Conflict between slaves, of which we hear little directly, would have been a matter for settlement by the free slave-owners. The public courts could take no cognizance, but loss of a slave, or of a slave's work, harmed a freeman, and so indirectly brought even the most vulnerable and miserable of slaves into some sort of communal protection. The very processes of manumission and of reduction to slavery demanded some degree of recognition at public courts.

From the point of view of the growth of institutions of government the treatment meted out to slaves has a special importance. More than the arbitrary commands of a master were at stake. At the lord's central household, or at the ceorl's farmstead, some disciplinary court, no matter how informal, must have been in existence. Bede on occasion mentions the reeves, the *vilici* or *tungerefan,* who hold positions of authority within an estate. When Caedmon (the first English poet according to the delightful story told by Bede) discovered that he had the gift of song he reported to the reeve who was in authority over him.[41] There were none of the agencies of a full-fledged territorial state such as there had been in Imperial Rome to safeguard slave-owners against their own slaves. The balance of social forces was more delicate in the Anglo-Saxon world. The Church played what to modern eyes so often appears an ambiguous role in relation to slavery. Archbishop Theodore legislated widely but with only a flicker of humanitarian thought towards the slave.[42] Lawyers at witans and at Church synods concerned themselves with proper observance of ec-

---

39 *EHD* i, no. 32, p. 407, Ine 74, 74.1.
40 *ibid.*, p. 404, Ine 48.
41 Bede, *HE*, iv. 24.
42 H.P.R. Finberg, *The Formation of England* (London, 1974), pp. 59–60.

clesiastical routine and ceremonial, and accepted slavery as part of the human condition. If a slave worked on Sunday at his master's command he was to be freed and his master to pay a fine of 30 shillings. If he worked on Sunday without his master's knowledge he was to be flogged; and a freeman working on that day without his lord's command was to forfeit his *healsfang,* that is to say a proportion of his *wergeld* or bloodprice, half of which was to go to the man who discovered the infringement together with half the proceeds of the guilty man's *borh.*[43] Some safeguard to person was recognized implicitly. The most hopeful text for the early Christian centuries as for the later was that he. whom Christ had redeemed with his precious blood was indeed worthy of a shepherd's care. David was more pleasing in God's eyes when he was a *servus* than when he was *rex et dominus.*

Territorial Divisions

By the end of the seventh century, as we have seen, England had come to be divided into a few large kingdoms, and during the period of Mercian hegemony the movement towards consolidation in one kingdom had been greatly advanced. The growth of large units increased the need for systematic and relatively standardized subdivisions of territories. Traces of units smaller than the historic kingdoms have already been discussed in relation to the Tribal Hidage. Placenames provide further evidence. The archaic element -ge (corresponding to modern German *gau*) appears occasionally in the sense of province, as in Surrey, Ely, Chertsey, and the Kentish names, Lyminge and Sturry. It is probable that these were all tribal or sub-tribal divisions which were only with difficulty turned to territorial administrative use. The conversion to Christianity, accompanied as it was by the growth of literacy and by the incorporation of new Romanic administrative techniques into the structure of the community, accelerated developments in local government. Church buildings became more permanent and so did delineation of the areas they served. In some parts of the country the evolution of more or less permanent administrative territorial units was more advanced than in others. Recent careful investigation of medieval shires in southern Scotland and northern England in the light of similar complexes of lordship elsewhere in England has established the probable proposition that many of the medieval 'shires' characteristic of areas around Hexham, Bamburgh, Coldingham, and such centres, ecclesiastical or lay, owed their origins to seventh-century Northumbrian practice.

43 *EHD* i, no. 31, p. 397, Wihtræd 9–11.

Durham was an important administrative centre in the 650s and Hexham was described as a *regio* by Eddius Stephanus.[44] The word 'shire' (*scir*) was still unspecialized, and continued to be used well into the tenth century to describe a sphere of office, but already in Wessex it could carry the significance of a territorial division, though not necessarily with the same precision as later usage. According to the laws of Ine, a man leaving his lord without permission and making his way into 'another shire' was to return to his former home and to pay his lord 60 shillings in compensation if he was discovered there.[45] There was a confused and blurred line between personal lordship and territorial jurisdiction. Extensive lordship as opposed to intensive control of a single estate or village was a feature of early settlement. When a prince or great lord was granted rights over territory these rights could often amount to full customs, fiscal and judicial. Differences of terminology have concealed similarities in structure not only from part to part of England but throughout much of Britain. Sokelands or manors with appendages were later legal expressions calculated to describe similar situations. Extensive lordship was not the only feature of settlement, early or late. The range of lordship was wide from great thegns governing lands equivalent to a shire to owners of no more than a few parcels of sokeland; and terminological usage was fluid.

By the side of the later and relatively clear-cut pattern of territorial shires, lathes, hundreds and wapentakes the administrative patterns, as well as the terminology, of the seventh and eighth centuries appear intolerably vague. Records leave clear traces of larger *regiones* and *provinciae,* and it is reasonable to assume that smaller divisions existed in more or less permanent form. If group discipline of any consequence was to be imposed popular courts had to be held within tolerable riding distance of all farms and townships in the area. Natural features and topography accounted for the location of the meeting places of such courts, and it is likely that these meeting places were quickly hallowed by what came to be regarded as immemorial custom. Some of the later English hundredal centres were located at what must have been in later centuries highly inconvenient but traditional sites in open country, great mounds, conspicuous trees or stones, that may well have been used as administrative and legal meeting places in the earlier centuries.

Occasionally of course the administrative task was easier and its record less intangible. Royal estates served as useful and convenient

---

44 G.W.S. Barrow, *The Kingdom of the Scots* (London, 1973), ch.1 'Pre-feudal Scotland: shires and thanes', pp. 7–68. The following paragraph draws heavily on this perceptive analysis.
45 *EHD* i, no. 32, p. 403, Ine 39.

points and later boundaries or patterns of landholding preserved strong hints of their former role. Historic Wessex, where the pattern was unobscured by successful Danish occupation, provides the most clear-cut examples. The royal manors at Somerton and Wilton gave their names ultimately to the great shires of Somerset and Wiltshire. Within Wiltshire itself Domesday evidence discloses a network of manorial rights and attachments and of petty jurisdictions in the shire that suggests that Cricklade, for example, with a multiplicity of contributory burgesses drawn from hamlets and villages between the Thames and the Kennet, was an administrative centre at a very early stage.[46] In Somerset very acute work by archæologists in a hitherto somewhat neglected part of the shire has disclosed an even more remarkable phenomenon. In the Vale of Wrington, in the delectable stretch of country that leads from Chew to the south-west of Bristol through Batscombe, Wrington, Banwell and Congresbury to the sea, early medieval estate divisions and topography suggest some possibility of continuity (not necessarily without a temporary break) between Roman land use and Anglo-Saxon.[47] The coincidence of villa site with Saxon estate may be fortuitous but it is worth recording. In Kent indeed it has long been recognized that the territorial divisions, the lathes, were modelled strikingly on Roman precedent. Common needs of territorial government in the same territory may be enough to account for the phenomenon, but the inference, especially in Kent, that there is some continuity in tradition and practice, dating back to sub-Roman days, is not to be dismissed out of hand. Evidence is strong for *villae regales* such as Lyminge, Wye, Faversham and Milton, as well as the larger and more famous towns of Canterbury and Rochester.[48] Further north the search for primitive administrative units has been more difficult because of the double impact of Danish successes and West-Saxon simplification after reconquest, but the rough outline of an Anglian administrative system based on royal and ecclesiastical divisions is beginning to emerge. In some areas the pre-Anglian Celtic *clas* church arrangements appear to have been significant; and in Scotland a resurgence of interest in the Pictish people has led to some suggestion that the institutional heritage of the Picts may be more important than previous generations thought. The disruptions of civil strife and of Viking attacks, however, overwhelmed what elements there were of a working and effective system in the Northumbria of the eighth and early ninth centuries.

46 H.R. Loyn, 'The origin and early development of the Saxon Borough with special reference to Cricklade', *WAM* 58 (1961), pp. 7–15.
47 P.J. Fowler, 'Vale of Wrington', *Recent Work in Rural Archaeology,* 1975.
48 J.E.A. Jolliffe, *Pre-feudal England: the Jutes* (Oxford, 1933), provided the pioneer study.

Vital developments appear to have taken place in the kingdom of Wessex at the time when Northumbria suffered its first taste of Viking attack. It may be that Egbert's period of exile at the Carolingian court now began to bear fruit. In the very first year of his reign we hear of the success of ealdorman Weohstan with people of Wiltshire in battle against the Mercians; by the middle of the century the Chronicle recounts as a commonplace that the ealdormen fought in command of the people of Dorset, or Somerset or Devon.[49] As far as military affairs were concerned the ealdormen and the territorial shire were closely linked before the beginning of the Alfredian period. The true creative work at this particular level of administrative life seems very much to have been a West-Saxon achievement.

The Church

A word should now be said of the Church, and its contribution to the growing orderliness of life. In the earliest days of the conversion the chief concern was clearly to safeguard the new Church of the missionary phase within the existing structure of society. Much depended on the cooperation of the kings with the Church, and Church organization itself came to rely in a very direct and personal sense on the bishops. It was not always easy in the initial stages for continuity to be achieved, but it became customary for each kingdom to have its own bishop. At various points within the kingdoms missionary centres were established, early minsters reminiscent of Celtic *clas* churches, side by side with other more formal monastic institutions. These were the power-houses for local effort, preaching, teaching, educating, building up the reputation of the new religion and the new Church. It was Theodore of Tarsus, archbishop of Canterbury (668–90) who proved, however, to be the first great organizer on a large scale of the Christian Church in England. His work had such importance both in itself and by example for the development of secular government in England that it is useful to consider it in some detail. When Theodore arrived in England the episcopate as such was in considerable disarray. South of the Humber the only bishop in office, Wine, former bishop to the West Saxons, appeared more or less to have bought his new office of bishop of London from the Mercian king. North of the Humber things were a little better. Ceadda was bishop of York, though of doubtful title, and Wilfrid, chief apologist for the Roman party at the Synod of Whitby (663), was bishop of Ripon in western Deira. Theodore quickly appointed bishops to Rochester, Dunwich and Winchester, and in September 672 held a great Council for the

---

49 *ASCh* 802, also 840, 845, 851.

whole Church in England at Hertford which did much to secure the legal authority and integrity of each bishop within his own diocese. The Council was important for itself as well as for what it did. Example was given of a body of literate, influential men laying down rules on moral, social and organizational matters for implementation throughout England, irrespective of existing political divisions. Arrangements were even made for annual synods to be held in August at *Clofeshoh,* a place still unidentified but possibly an alternative name for Brixworth in Northamptonshire where there is a church which by its size and geographical position would certainly have provided a suitable location for such synods, given the known ecclesiastical shape of the English Church in the second half of the seventh century. Proposals were also made at the Council for an increase in the number of dioceses as the number of converts grew, but these proposals were deferred. Aleady vested interests were at work to resist radical change, and Wilfrid of Ripon and York, who ruled the whole vast Northumbrian diocese from 669 to 677, even proceeded to an appeal to Rome against Theodore's attempts to divide his see. Although unsuccessful in his main aim Wilfrid won much support at Rome, and persuaded a council held at the Lateran in Rome in the autumn of 679 to issue a decree that the number of dioceses in England should be limited to twelve. The decree was contrary to the known plans of Gregory the Great for England and seems essentially to have been no more than an uneasy statement that the *status quo* in the late 670s should be maintained. It is a striking indication nevertheless of the difficulties Theodore had to face in the ecclesiastical as well as in the secular world. Even so, acting cautiously and slowly as political opportunity offered, Theodore brought the political organization of his English Church into more realistic and practical form. He was particularly successful in East Anglia where, initially by the use of coadjutor bishops, he set the shape for the establishment of sees for the two principal constituents of the East-Anglian folk, at Dunwich for Suffolk, and at Elmham for Norfolk. In western Mercia he won his most enduring monument in the creation of sees for the Hwicce and the *Magonsætan* at Worcester and at Hereford respectively. As part of the elaborate, complicated, and in part indecisive dispute with Wilfrid Theodore also took his opportunity to establish a see for Lindsey at *Syddensis civitas* (still unidentified) and to regularize the creation of sees at Hexham and Lindisfarne. For the secular historian Theodore's work is a powerful reminder of the force of feeling of integrity among the smaller groups that lived within the greater kingdoms of the seventh-century world. His successors carried on the good work. The great sprawling bishopric for the West Saxons was subdivided. In 735 a second archbishopric was created at York. By the middle of the eighth century England was divided into manageable territorial dioceses, many of them in familiar and very long-lasting historical form. South of the Thames there were the five sees of Canterbury, Rochester, Selsey, Winchester and Sherborne. In the great Midland belt, apart from London and the East-Anglian sees of Dunwich and Elmham, there were the chief Mercian sees at Lichfield, Lindsey, Hereford, Worcester and Leicester (stabilized as a see in 737 though the continuous series of bishops among the Middle Angles originates in Theodore's days). To the north of the Humber the situation clarified into the archbishopric of York with bishops at Hexham, Lindisfarne, and (after the early 730s) Whithorn.

Theodore of Tarsus with his concentration on diocesan organization and holding of English synods may therefore be truly said to have left a permanent imprint at the top level on an important aspect of English life. It is more difficult to assess his further undoubted achievements at the local level. With his background firm in the world of Roman and Mediterranean civilization he knew all about parochial organization, particularly urban parochial organization. England with its overwhelmingly agrarian nature and few towns needed a different type of ecclesiastical polity. There were only the slow glimmerings of the beginning of a parish system in the seventh century, and even then with a different emphasis from the image of the central Middle Ages with its village church as an essential attribute of nearly every village. Much depended on the endowment available, and the kings, great nobles and bishops tended still to support the larger churches, the minsters or *monasteria,* served by a community of priests who would look after substantial areas from their common centre. Brixworth in Northamptonshire, although its building pattern is exceedingly complex, still gives an impression of such a substantial minster from the early period. East Kent, deep into the Middle Ages, still preserved indications of the time when ecclesiastical organization of the whole area depended under the bishop on the twelve principal churches or minsters. The best example of a lesser church to survive physically is probably to be found at Escomb in County Durham, but many districts still relied on no more than high crosses to signal the place where mass would be said or even the former site of an altar that had moved elsewhere. The magnificent sculptured crosses of Bewcastle in Cumbria or Ruthwell in Dumfriesshire hint at the range of 'church' organization to be found in communities emerging from the missionary stage.

Brisker development took place in the eighth century. Bishop Egbert received the pallium from the pope in 735 and so marked the permanent establishment of an archbishopric at York. Attempts in the latter years of the century to establish a third archbishopric at Lichfield met with only temporary success, but diocesan arrangements and divisions were rationalized. Great schools for clergy flourished, notably at Canterbury and at York. Better provision of better clergy led to a positive increase in the number of lesser churches within England. Some of these were typical Germanic territorial churches. As the nobility became more a landed nobility it was regarded as more and more natural that a church should be provided with the primary duty of serving the estate. In England (in contrast to the continent) the bishop retained his authority and the worst abuses were avoided. An unfree priest, for example, was exceedingly rare in Anglo-Saxon England.

As for the parish system itself, steady progress was made. Much of the evidence is negative, coming from complaints by Bede, Egbert of York, or Alcuin of abuse or inactivity, or from the enactments of Church Councils. Great stress was placed on the health of the monasteries and on the need for the bishop to make more frequent progresses through his diocese: and Bede complained specifically that the dioceses were too large.[50] Payments to churches such as soul-scot, plough-alms and free offerings, were systematically enjoined upon the population. Tithes were still a matter of voluntary payment, though in 787 the papal legates in council at *Clofeshoh* laid it down that tithes were to be paid by all men.[51] The general elaboration of financial payments involved also an elaboration of physical building and development. Some well-established minsters proliferated subordinate churches and chapels. There were still large tracts of England with nothing approaching the familiar parish system of later centuries, but in Wiltshire, Hampshire, Devon, and parts of Somerset, parish priests were familiar figures even in pre-Danish days. Egbert of Wessex and his son Ethelwulf (Alfred's father) encouraged the process. Ethelwulf's work was of particular importance since he proved himself an active and energetic patron of the Church. There has been much discussion of the importance of his grants of royal land, sometimes referred to as his 'decimation', to the Church.[52] The Anglo-Saxon chronicle reports that he conveyed the tenth part of his land throughout all his kingdom 'to the praise of God and his own eternal salvation'. He appears in fact to have granted land to his thegns, giving them the power to leave it after their days to religious houses if they so chose. Whatever the exact sequence of

---

50 *EHD* i, no. 170, pp. 803–4. Letter of Bede to Egbert, archbishop of York.

51 Wilkins, *Concilia*, iii, p.203. Haddan and Stubbs, iii, pp.456—7: *ut omnes studeant de omnibus quae possident decimas dare.*

52 H.P.R. Finberg, 'King Æthelwulf's Decimations', *The Early Charters of Wessex*, (Leicester, 1964), pp. 187-213. *EHD* i, no. 89, p. 525 – comment by D. Whitelock on Æthelwulf's grant of land near Rochester to his thegn, Dunn.

events, one result is clear. On the eve of the massive Danish invasion the Church was strengthened institutionally and financially; and the release of substantial endowments aided greatly the development of the parish system.

Enough has been said to indicate the massive changes that had come over the British scene in the period from c.AD 450 to 871. At the earlier date we deal with a world that was primarily Roman and Celtic. The Roman armies had departed and the frontiers of Roman Britain had been overrun but the social mix was still Romano-British, the vernacular tongues Celtic, and the Latin element not negligible. The immigration of Germanic peoples and the imposition of their institutions, language and culture over the greater part of the lowlands of Britain brought about a permanent alteration in the nature of the islands. Acceptance of Christianity in the seventh century and renewed intense contact with the continent, with Frankia, Italy, Rome and also with the continental Germans, modified dramatically the social and cultural patterns. Political fragmentation persisted but gradually in State as well as in Church the idea of a unified England began to take active shape. The skill of powerful rulers, notably in Mercia, and the awareness that came from corporate support in a joint and perilous enterprise – the conversion of the continental Germans – sharpened the feeling of community. The Scandinavian raids of the late eighth century heralded a period of political and religious uncertainty lightened only by the rise of Wessex under King Egbert. Even so England in the middle of the ninth century exhibited some of the signs of a community that had fallen away from her best days culturally and spiritually. In the field of government there was still evidence of great potential. No Mercian law code has survived but there is no reason to think that the Middle Kingdom was inferior to Wessex. The shires of Wessex were taking their historic shape. Administrative apparatus for the collection of money and the hearing of judgements was well developed. From the middle years of the reign of Offa a good silver currency had been introduced. The dynastic situation was slowly clarifying and the ancient House of Wessex emerging as the hope of a united English kingship. The potential was to be realized, but in an unexpected form in the face of intensified savage attack from Scandinavian pirates and settlers who were initially both barbaric and pagan.

3*

The Reign of Alfred, 871–899

Special attention has always properly been given to the reign of Alfred in all general histories of England. He succeeded, during a year of battles, 870–71, to a West-Saxon kingdom that was fighting for its very existence against heathen Danish armies, exultant with success. They had already taken control of the most fertile parts of the north and east of England. Northumbria and East Anglia had been overcome, and Mercia brought to terms that placed its continued political existence in doubt. Resistance was proving resolute in the south, but it seemed only a matter of time before final opposition was crushed and Scandinavian warlords were in triumphal command throughout the British Isles. The Scandinavians controlled communications by sea. From their secure permanent bases in the Scottish Isles, Ireland, and now after 869 from the estuarine strongpoints of Northumbria and East Anglia, they could ravage and recruit more powerful armies at will. Their English adventures were part of a general European move: effective command of much of the Frisian, Flemish and north French coast intensified the danger to Wessex. Sustained, persistent, at times heroic leadership saved the day for the Christian English. King Alfred died in 899 the acknowledged king of Wessex and lord of all the English not subject to the Dane.

The main crisis point in his reign came between the years 878 and 886. The Danes ravaged and settled, sharing out the land of the Northumbrians in 876, partitioning the Mercian territories with an English leader, Ceolwulf, in 877. An unexpected onslaught at Chip-

---

* The *Anglo-Saxon Chronicle,* the biography of Alfred by Bishop Asser and the laws are the essential sources for Alfred's reign. The only manuscript of Asser's *Life* (in itself incomplete) to survive the Middle Ages was destroyed in the Cottonian fire of 1731 but there is no doubt about its substantial authenticity. It was written in 893, contains a Latin translation of a version of the *Anglo-Saxon Chronicle* and much personal material, some hagiographical in nature. Asser was from Dyfed in South Wales and became one of the principal advisers to King Alfred in his programme of translation. *The Laws of Alfred* survive in full in two manuscripts, one written in the mid-tenth century (CCCC 173) (printed Lieb. i, pp. 16ff, MS E) and the other in the early twelfth-century Textus Roffensis (*ibid.,* pp. 17ff, MS H).

penham over midwinter in early 878 almost brought Wessex to disaster. Alfred retired to Athelney and, helped by a victory won by the men of Devon under their ealdorman, Odda, at Countisbury, he rallied the Christian forces, defeated the Danish leader, Guthrum, at Edington, bringing him to terms and to conversion. Guthrum and his army departed from Wessex, settling first for a year at Cirencester, and then in 880 in East Anglia. At some stage in the succeeding years, possibly soon after 886, Alfred established a treaty with Guthrum that laid down what was to prove the main boundary of social division in the following centuries between English England and Anglo-Danish England. King Alfred and King Guthrum and the councillors of the English race and all the people in East Anglia agreed and confirmed on oath that the boundaries should lie up the Thames to the Lea (that is east of London), and then along the Lea to its source, thence on a straight line to Bedford and up the Ouse to Watling Street. With a further natural extension along the line of Watling Street towards Wroxeter and ultimately to Chester this was to mark the bounds of the Danelaw. According to twelfth-century sources Mercian law applied as far north as the administrative shires of Oxford, Warwick, Stafford and Cheshire. The shape of virtual future permanence in the English social scene of the Middle Ages emerges from the settlement between the West-Saxon king and the converted Danish ruler of East Anglia.

In 886 Alfred achieved a political success of the first importance when he occupied London after fighting that involved (according to Asser) the burning of cities and the massacre of people, and received the submission of all the English people not under Danish domination. He entrusted London to the charge of his son-in-law, Ethelred, a Mercian, married to Alfred's daughter Æthelflæd. Ethelred and Æthelflæd became effective rulers of western Mercia until the time of their death (Ethelred in 912 and Æthelflæd in 918), so preserving a measure of autonomy for the province.[1] Our sources for the heroic story are exclusively West-Saxon and we sometimes wonder how the Northumbrians, the East Mercians and the East Angles regarded this realistic southern English king as they repaired their farms and paid tribute to their Danish lords. The outstanding value and merit of Alfred's achievement remain incontestable. He preserved a nucleus of traditional English kingship and government. The two centuries which followed his death elaborate and complicate the structure, but the basic lines of development were firmly drawn in their distinctive paths during the reign of King Alfred.

1 *ASCh*, 886. Asser, *Life of Alfred,* ch.83, p.69 and p.324. Florence of Worcester associates the recovery of London with the acquisitoin of that part of Mercia which Ceolwulf had held: *Chronicon ex Chronicis,* ed. B. Thorpe (London, 1848–9) vol. i, p. 267.

This is a large claim to make and it demands a little explanation. At the most general level justification is simple. Alfred emerged from the period of Danish invasion as the only representative of an English royal dynasty still to occupy a throne. Even at the end of the reign he was not effectively king of English England, though some contemporaries were seeking after the title for him. He was nevertheless the only native Christian king in England. This very fact gave special force to his governmental activities, and here we come to the deeper justification for our proposition. Alfred and his close advisers were unusually thoughtful men, self-conscious in their acts, critical of the means of government, ultimately proud of their achievements. It is often said that there are direct analogies, with things altered which have to be altered, between the reign of Charles the Great (Charlemagne) and that of King Alfred. This is very true. The Church was actively involved in the business of government. The king actively promoted and supported an elaborate programme of Christian education. He himself took part in a thoughtful and constructive project of translation, intelligently calculated to bring to the people of England in their own tongue those works most needful for them to know. In face of the direct heathen menace every attempt was made to foster and to encourage awareness among the English of their Christian heritage. Scholars were brought in from the continent and from west Mercia and from Wales to help in the general educational effort. Emphasis, unusual and almost unique at the time, on the vernacular helped to focus all thoughtful English eyes on the West-Saxon court. Resistance to the Dane and resistance to heathenism became associated with the royal dynasty of Wessex, an association not completely broken even as late as the grim and inept days of Ethelred the Unready. Theocratic ideas began to germinate. The Christian nature of kingship and of government was recognized and strengthened.

From the point of view of government and administration, the law code of Alfred the Great is the fundamental document that demands close analysis, and, properly supplemented by the Chronicle and Asser's biography of the king, provides a reasonably coherent picture of an ordered society in creation. In addition to the two full texts of the laws there are several other manuscripts which give some of the laws.[2] Extensive use of the code by later Anglo-Saxon kings and translators shows how widely it was known. Its issue was a calculated political move of the first importance, and was also in a sense an act of faith. It is unlikely that the laws were declared before London passed into Alfred's hands in 886, but many leading scholars are now inclined to place their issue in the 880s rather than in the traditional and long-

2 *EHD* i, no. 33, pp. 407–8: there is a further useful note on the manuscripts *EHD* i, p. 358ff.

accepted early 890s. They demand attention not only for the substance, the importance of which is self-evident, but for the manner in which they were promulgated. It has not been recognized sufficiently that they differ from the voluminous output of law in tenth and early eleventh-century England in the emphasis placed on the official nature of the promulgation and in the clear statement of government purpose embodied in the text. With the possible exception of the Laws of Cnut, which were held as the basic model of Anglo-Saxon law well into the Norman period, no law-code of late Anglo-Saxon England provides a comparable insight into the mechanics of government and indeed into the thought that went into law-making activities.

There is, to begin with, a long and somewhat neglected introduction to the laws, consisting of extensive quotations (in Anglo-Saxon) from biblical passages that have a bearing on principles of law-making.[3] A full text is given of the Decalogue and many passages from Exodus xx–xxiii are provided in translation. The transition is then made, dramatically and effectively, to the New Testament. Christ's words are quoted, 'think not that I am come to destroy the law,' and the biblical section concludes with the statement:

> A man can think on this one sentence alone, that he judges each one rightly: he has need of no other law-books. Let him consider that he judge to no man what he would not that he judged to him, if he were giving the judgement on him.

In typical fashion (one suspects) Alfred then turned from biblical inspiration to the immediate situation. His sense of history demanded a direct link. He referred to the many synods held throughout England after the reception of Christianity at which were established, for the mercy which Christ taught, prices of compensation in money for almost every misdeed at the first offence. Only treachery to a lord was excluded from these merciful decrees: Almighty God adjudged none for those who scorned him, nor did Christ for those who gave him over to death. As a vital introduction to the substantive passages of the code a basic principle was enunciated of immense moment in later Anglo-Saxon history. Everyone was charged to love his lord as himself.[4]

The king then proceeded to give an important explanation of the methods he used to compile his lawbook. He collected laws together which had previously been observed, selecting those which he liked and rejecting with the advice of his councillors those which he did not like. Some legislative power is implied in this process of selection. He

---

3 Lieb. i, pp. 26–46, especially cl. 49. 6, p. 44.
4 *ibid.* cl. 49. 7, p. 46. Christ himself is said to have laid this charge on men.

denied however the ability to make new law on the grounds that he could not legislate in that way for the future. There was no knowing what would be pleasing to men in time to come. In diffident and rather charming manner he confined his own activity to discovering what seemed him most just 'either of the time of my kinsman, King Ine, or of Offa, king of the Mercians, or of Ethelbert, who first among the English received baptism'. The collection was finally shown to all the councillors who declared that they were all pleased to observe it. Alfred, as king, took a firm initiative in selecting the laws for his kingdom. He relied on the advice and cooperation of his chief men in formal council to make his selection effective and practicable.

Alfred's introduction to his laws gives one further practical insight into the very nature of law in early medieval Western society. Eternal law was not of this world but the law of God, reflected in the human condition in the Old and New Testaments. Precise laws as such, even a relatively elaborate and thoughtful code such as Alfred's, were subject to the changeability of time, to be accepted or rejected by the properly constituted authority, according to circumstances. They were indeed no more than comments in particular instances of a general supernatural law that governed an ordered Christian universe. The proper authority was the Christian king and his council. The laws of Alfred, king of the West Saxons, could therefore be published as a standard rightly to be followed by all Christian people capable of understanding the English tongue. They were not exclusive to the West Saxons, and Alfred himself made a special point of saying that he had drawn from the legal experience of the Mercians and the men of Kent as well as from his native West-Saxon antecedents. Nor was obedience to the laws in any sense limited to groups, noble or simple, free or unfree: the king himself, though specially protected, was below and subject to law.

When we turn to the substance of the laws we find plentiful evidence of the king's special position.[5] He was not above the law, but he was elevated above all other men below the law. His person was privileged. Anyone plotting against the king's life, directly or by harbouring exiles or traitors, was liable to forfeit his life and all he owned. Violation of the king's *borh* or surety was to be penalized by the heavy fine of five pounds of pure pennies. Fighting or even drawing a weapon in the king's hall could be punished by death if the king so wished it. Forcible entry into the king's residence rendered the offender liable to a fine of 120 shillings. Similar legal protection in matters affecting surety, breach of peace and forcible entry (though on a lesser scale) was allotted to archbishops, bishops, ealdormen, secular lords and ordinary

5 *EHD* i, no. 33, pp. 409ff. Alf. 3 (*borh*), 4, 7, and 40.

freemen. The king was at the summit of lordship in his kingdom, and in all manner of ways the law strengthened his position. The king also possessed residual authority which other lords did not.[6] He had special duties when dealing with men who did not fit into the normal patterns of society. If a man with no kindred was slain half the compensation due was to pass to the king and a half to the dead man's associates. Traders, men outside the settled community, lacking the immediate protection of a kindred, were to be brought before the king's reeve at a public meeting, to declare how many of them were going on their trading expedition up country, so that they could be brought to justice at a public meeting if the need arose. The king and the bishop were to act as special witnesses in case of dispute over the disposal of bookland outside the kin. Treason was the most serious of offences, and the law of the Church encouraged loyalty to the king, and incidentally to all secular lords by every method at their disposal.

Theoretical authority and prestige is one thing, effective exercise of government quite another. To help him King Alfred had to depend on the royal court, the mainspring of his actions. To it there came the great men of the realm, the bishops, the ealdormen, the king's reeves and the most important among the thegns. It is customary to call such councils or assemblies *witenagemots,* or meetings of wise men. The king was responsible for government but it was convenient for him to make decisions known in such assemblies. The ordering of armies, preparation for naval defence, building of fortresses and general matters concerning the physical or spiritual well-being of the country would be discussed there. Asser has described Alfred's methods of handling his royal court and Household.[7] Those who held office about the king were divided into three sections, the one to serve day and night at court for one month in three while the other two groups were about their duties at home. Alfred could therefore rely on service from able followers all the year around.

The court was by its nature firmly committed to action on financial affairs. It is again Asser who tells us that Alfred divided his revenue into two equal parts, the first to be put to secular use, as reward to warriors and thegns, as payment to craftsmen, and as gift to strangers. The second half went to spiritual purposes, to support churches, and particularly the monasteries Alfred had built, to sustain schools and other institutions of learning, and to feed the poor.[8] We know that Alfred sent regularly, probably annually, alms to Rome, both his own

6 *ibid.* Alf. 30–1 (kindred), 34 (traders), and 41 (bookland). He also shared with the bishop and the lord of the church the 120s fine laid on a person bringing a nun out of a nunnery without the permission of the king or the bishop, the king taking half the fine.

7 Asser, *Life of Alfred,* ch. 100, pp. 86–7.

8 *ibid.* ch. 101 and 102, pp. 87–9.

personal alms and those of the West-Saxon people, and further that he was exceedingly grateful to Pope Marinus (d. 884) who had, at the king's request, freed the English quarter at Rome from papal taxation.[9] We are not so well informed on the receipt of finance. References to the hidage of estates suggest that land taxes were indeed levied, presumably mostly in kind. A substantial part of the royal revenue came in kind, in traditional customary dues from the king's own estates. He also possessed rights over judicial processes which could bring in much wealth. The care taken over the currency suggests that there was a surprising amount of minted silver in use even in the darkest days of Danish advance. The Danes were quick to adopt a silver currency, and indeed relied on English moneyers to strike their coinage in East Anglia and in Northumbria.[10]

Administration of justice was profitable and occupied much of the king's attention. Alfred had a direct and personal interest in the business. A famous charter issued in the reign of his son, Edward the Elder, referred back to a judgement made by Alfred, as he was washing his hands in his room at the royal manor of Wardour in Wiltshire. The charter provides splendid evidence for the general reputation of Alfred when, in the course of affirming that the particular judgement in question should stand, it asks rhetorically 'when would any claim be decided if every judgement which Alfred made were in dispute'.[11] Alfred made many judicial decisions, but they were not made merely in the light of pure reason or vague equitable notions. Judgement underlined knowledge of the law. It is significant that when Alfred drew up his will sometime between the years 873 and 888 the king asked his councillors not to hesitate to declare the folkright, the customary law.[12] The royal court, king and councillors alike, constituted an active positive body in matters concerning the declaration of law and the administration of justice.

Inevitably there were occasions when important judicial business had to be transacted away from the king's immediate court and presence. Increasingly the assemblies of responsible men joined together for military and peace-keeping purposes at the convenient level of the shire came to offer the proper occasion for such transaction. Within Wessex it is clear that Alfred as a good and active king paid frequent visits to the shire courts, but even within the cir-

---

9 ASCh, 883–90. Pope Marinus is said to have sent relics of the Cross to Alfred (s.a. 883) and to have freed the English quarter from taxation (s.a. 885).

10 R.H.M. Dolley and C.E. Blunt, 'The Chronology of the Coins of Alfred the Great', Anglo-Saxon Coins, ed. R.H.M. Dolley (London, 1961). Also Dolley, Viking Coins of the Danelaw and of Dublin (London, 1965).

11 F.E. Harmer, Select English Historical Documents of the Ninth and Tenth Centuries (Cambridge, 1914), no. 18. EHD i, no. 102, pp. 544–6.

12 Harmer, no. 11. EHD i, no. 96, pp. 534–6, especially p. 535.

cumscribed bounds of his kingdom, it was not always possible for him to be present in person. At times it must have been enough for a trusted servant to report the king's will to the shire assembly, and this could not again always have been possible or desirable. There are hints that some administrative device, involving written instructions, was already in use or evolved during the reign of Alfred.[13] When the king himself in his preface to the translation of Pope Gregory's *Cura Pastoralis* greeted Bishop Wærferth of Worcester to whom he sent a copy of his work he used a formula strongly reminiscent of the later writ form. The preface in this particular copy opens with the words 'King Alfred bids greet Bishop Wærferth in loving and friendly fashion (*hateð gretan .... luflice ond freondlice*)'. The best evidence comes from the translation of St Augustine's *Soliloquies*. In a fine passage Reason asks 'Consider now if your lord's letter and his seal comes to you, whether you can say that you cannot understand him thereby or recognize his will therein?' The presence of the phrase 'Lord's letter and seal' (*hlafordes ærendgewrit and hys insegel*) does not of course imply the existence of a sealed writ. Seal and written document were presumably still separate physical entities. But it does imply forcibly, and all the more forcibly since the passage is an interpolation in Augustine's text, that methods of authenticating the king's orders in writing to the localities were already well known and indeed commonplace in the reign of King Alfred. Given the royal reserve of legal and judicial authority such devices were indeed essential.

It is Asser again who makes it transparently clear how the ultimate reserve in the handling of judicial business rested with the king. In a fine passage towards the end of his biography he shows how Alfred personally gave judgements both for the benefit of the nobles and of the common people. There had been difficulty in establishing judgement in the shire and other local courts, and the direct intervention of the king had been needful. In his rather elaborate prose Asser portrays Alfred as a most skilled investigator into the exercise of justice and also as a shrewd legal reformer, checking on his judges, asking them awkward questions either personally or by some of his faithful followers. It would take an honest and able judge to stand up to the sort of so-called 'mild' inquiry mentioned by Asser. The judges were to be asked 'why they had given so wrong a judgement, whether from ignorance or out of any kind of ill-will, that is for love or fear of one party of hatred of the other, or even for greed of anyone's money'.[14]

13 The evidence is carefully assessed by F.E. Harmer, *Anglo-Saxon Writs* (Manchester, 1952), pp. 10–12. The passage from the *Cura Pastoralis* is given in *EHD* i, no. 226, pp. 887–8 and that from the Soliloquies (in slightly different form from Harmer's version) in no. 237 (a), p. 918.

14 Asser, *Life of Alfred*, ch. 106, pp. 92–5.

Asser, of course, was an artist and a Welsh educationalist, and was not without ulterior purpose in setting out his account. If the judges confessed their fault Alfred is said to have reproved their inexperience and folly wisely and moderately, ordering them to resign on the spot or to apply themselves to the study of wisdom. The ealdormen, reeves and thegns, given the choice of their jobs or their ignorance, did not hesitate, preferring toilsomely to pursue unaccustomed study rather than resign authority. The old ones grumbled. Some had left it too late and had to employ others, kinsmen, free dependents or slaves, to read Saxon books to them, expressing the age-old cry against the younger generation who now had educational opportunities denied to the older folk. What books we wonder: scripture, law-codes or those that we know Alfred considered most needful for men to know – Gregory, Bede, Orosius, Augustine and Boethius? Attempts to recapture the learning of the Christian classical past had legal as well as cultural and religious implications.

We are right to stress this reserve of royal judicial authority but to strike the balance we must remember, too, that much activity that a later age would expect to be in royal hands, remained outside or only indirectly encompassed within his legal orbit. The reserve nevertheless was undoubtedly there. In an important section of his laws Alfred set out the circumstances in which it was legal to take to arms against an enemy. If he were powerful enough the correct procedure was for the offended man to surround his opponent's homestead, and to besiege him until he surrendered to the formal procedures that should eventually involve proper compensation and settlement. If the offended man were not powerful enough he was to ride to the ealdorman to ask for support: if the ealdorman could not help he was to ride to the king before having recourse to fighting.[15] The king and the royal officers had a legal obligation to bring about settlements without fighting if they possibly could. This was common sense: violence begat violence, feuding could spread, and general weakness to the kingdom would inevitably result. Royal officers were also prominent in another matter initially affecting the stability of the kingdom. It was important that secular lordship should be formalized as far as was possible, so that a lord could be answerable for his men at the king's tribunal as at all popular courts. Alfred laid down that if anyone moved from a district to seek a lord elsewhere he was to do so with the witness of the ealdorman in whose shire he had previously served. Failure to do so meant that his new lord became liable to pay 120 shillings compensation, half to the king in the shire in which the man had served

15 *EHD* i, no. 33, p. 415. Alf. 42. 3.

previously, half in that into which he had come.[16] Control of movement was important in such growing communities. It was assumed that the royal officer, the ealdorman, would have the legal apparatus of supporting courts at which witness could be given in all the shires into which the kingdom was divided. Royal legal authority did not stop at the confines of the royal Household and court. The ealdorman was protected by special fine exacted from men who fought in his presence or who disturbed public meetings by drawing a weapon, and these special sanctions were further extended downwards to the ealdorman's deputy and the king's priests.[17]

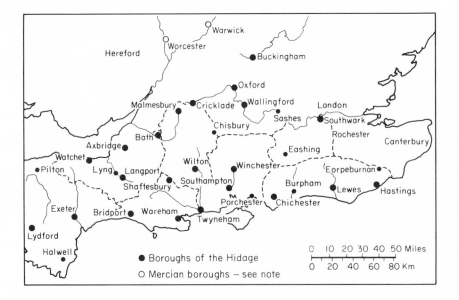

3   The Burghal Hidage

The appearance of the two Mercian boroughs, Warwick and Worcester, in an appendix to one group of manuscripts of the Burghal Hidage may be associated with the shiring of Mercia in the reign of Edward the Elder (D. Hill, 'The Burghal Hidage: the establishment of a text', *Medieval Archaeology* XIII (1969), pp. 84–92).

Enough has been said to suggest that the apparatus of royal government in ninth-century Wessex was already passing out of the rudimentary stage. The pressure of the Danish wars helped further to systematize the process. Defensive campaigning was notoriously dif-

16 *ibid*. p. 414. Alf. 37, 37.1.
17 *ibid*. Alf. 38–38.2.

ficult in the early Middle Ages. The Danes owed much of their success to their mobility and the unexpectedness of their attacks. Considerable administrative skill was needed to meet the onslaughts of these quick-moving invaders. Alfred found the answer by consistent and ultimately successful organization. All freemen were liable for army service. It was for that reason primarily that they bore arms, the mark of distinction that set off free from unfree. In his last campaigns, in the early 890s, Alfred had so perfected his techniques that his army was divided into two, half at home and half on service, apart from those men who guarded the fortifications, the *burhs*.[18] The *burhs* themselves seem essentially to have been a product of Alfred's imaginative campaigning. By the time of Alfred's death Wessex was defended by a ring of more than thirty *burhs* (boroughs in a more specialized modern sense), most of which can still be identified: *Eorpeburnan* (possibly on the edge of Romney Marsh), Hastings, Lewes, Burpham, Chichester, Porchester, Southampton, Winchester, Wilton, Chisbury, Shaftesbury, Twyneham, Wareham, Bridport, Exeter, Halwell, Lydford, Pilton, Watchet, Axbridge, Lyng, Langport, Bath, Malmesbury, Cricklade, Oxford, Wallingford, Buckingham, Sashes (an island in the Thames at Cookham), Eashing, Southwark.

Some of these were based on Roman defences, as at Chichester, Porchester, Winchester, Bath and Exeter, while others were no more than emergency forts set up on the sites of iron-age hill-forts. Some developed into important permanent urban settlements, while others faded away into complete obscurity. Walls or earthworks were common to all, generally enclosing a large area. At Cricklade, for example, where excavations revealed a long stretch of the Saxon wall, the total circuit was over 2,000 yards: at Wallingford it was over 3,000 yards. The special importance of the boroughs (as we may call them) to the history of government and administration is the way in which responsibility for their defence and maintenance was imposed on the whole community. An assessment was laid on surrounding villages or estates and measured in terms of hides of land. From each sixteen hides sixteen soldiers were to be sent to defend twenty-two yards of the wall, each pole, or 5½ yards, of the wall to be manned by four men. The system worked, and the success of Alfred's later campaigns can in large part be attributed to its efficacy. It says much for Alfred's skill

---

18 *ASCh* 893. The text of the Burghal Hidage, the key document in relation to the *burhs*, is conveniently studied in A.J. Robertson, *Anglo-Saxon Charters* (Cambridge, 1939), p. 246, supplemented by D. Hill, 'The Burghal Hidage, the establishment of a text', *Medieval Archaeology* 13 (1969), pp. 84–92. Also N.P. Brooks, 'The unidentified forts of the Burghal Hidage', *Medieval Archaeology* xiii (1964), pp. 74–90, and 'England in the Ninth Century: the Crucible of Defeat', *TRHS* 29 (1979), pp. 1–20.

that such general obligations could be imposed so thoroughly. Evidence, though patchy, leads finally to the conclusion that by the end of Alfred's reign royal government played an ever-increasing part in the lives of the Christian English community. Support given by the Church was direct and unqualified. Bishops attended Alfred's councils, and even fought actively in the royal host. At least one bishop (Heahmund of Sherborne in 871) was killed in battle. The Church trained the men who provided continuity to government in the shape of written records. The Church played a prominent part in the folk-courts, the bishop often presiding jointly with the ealdormen at the shire courts. The taking of oaths and the giving of pledges were basic instruments in the business of government, and the Church was vitally involved in both: a man who defaulted on his pledge was to endure the penance a bishop prescribed for him – and to suffer forty days imprisonment on a royal estate.[19] Excommunication from all the churches of Christ was imposed on an escaped prisoner as well as the secular penalty of outlawry. In return for its active and positive support the Church received much benefit from the germination of royal government and royal peace. Its rights of sanctuary were respected. Its holy days and holidays received official royal sanction: double compensation, for example, was to be paid for offences committed on special holy days. A fine of 120 shillings was to be exacted, presumably by royal officers, for neglect of the chief festivals and fasts. Nuns were placed under special protection. King, witan and Church cooperated closely in their attempts to create, in a time of great political upheaval, an ordered Christian society.

As so often, Asser in his special highly personal fashion reveals much of the reality that made up the business of royal government[20] His view of royal activities made good sense. He tells us how Alfred in spite of wars and pagan raids, in spite too of daily infirmity of body, practised assiduously, eagerly, and with single-minded purpose, the art of governing his kingdom. To Asser this involved what to modern eyes appears a curious combination of tasks. Alfred practised, so we are told, every branch of hunting. He gave instruction to his goldsmiths, his craftsmen, his falconers, hawkers, and dog-keepers. He erected buildings to his own new design more stately and magnificent than had been the custom of his ancestors. He observed prayers in the due season closely and excelled in generosity both to his own people and to foreigners. He brought up his children well and extended care in training to the children of the Household. Generosity, activity, care for good learning and instruction were the features specially

19 *EHD* i, no. 33, p. 409. Alf. 1.2–1.8.
20 Asser, *Life of Alfred*, ch. 91–92, and also ch. 100, pp. 76–80, and p. 86ff.

singled out; and when in a later rhetorical passage Asser came to reflect again on the incessant cares of government that faced the king the same basic features are in evidence, though with subtle twists that we may have failed in the past to appreciate properly, certainly from the administrative point of view. For Asser throws great weight on his picture of Alfred the builder, the physical builder. He tells of the cities and towns he restored and the others which he built where none had stood before, a fair comment on his burghal policy, fortified townships for effective defence against the pagans. Asser tells also of buildings made on the king's instructions with gold and silver, beyond compare, of royal halls and chambers admirably constructed in stone and timber, of royal residences in stone, moved at the royal command from their ancient sites and beautifully erected in more suitable places. The reference to gold and silver (*de aedificis aureis et argenteis ... fabricatis*) has brought some discredit to the passage but even if taken as a rhetorical flourish or exaggeration the main theme of the passage is clear and bears the mark of the eye-witness. When Asser speaks of the bridge at Athelney, made with laborious skill between two fortresses, the western front of most beautiful workmanship, defending the king's new monastery, we may be sure that Asser spoke from personal experience. Equally compelling and equally proof of the author's inside knowledge is Asser's comment on the frustrations which the king had to face in order to achieve his ideal. Men would not voluntarily undertake the labours that he imposed on them until it was too late and loss had been suffered to the pagan of kinsfolk, slaves, handmaids, goods: repentance would also then come too late and they would then set about with great energy, promising to perform *what they had before refused* with regard to the building of fortresses and the other things for the common profit of the whole kingdom. When the Danes rowed up the Lympne into the Weald in 892 they stormed a fortress four miles from the estuary that was only half made, and manned by only a few peasants. Asser knew at first hand what he was talking about.[21]

He also knew at first hand much about the administration of the court and the royal Household.[22] In the same chapter where he talks of the king's difficulties he gives also deep insight into the realities of medieval kingship. Alfred like a skilful pilot guided his ship of state through raging and manifold whirlpools! His instruments, wisely brought over and bound to his own will and the common profit of the kingdom, were his bishops and ealdormen and nobles and the thegns who were dearest to him. Asser also emphasized the role of the royal

---

21 *ibid*. ch. 91, pp. 78–9. *ASCh* 892 (*sæton feawa cirlisce men on ond wæs sam worht*).
22 *ibid*. ch. 100, pp. 86–7ff.

reeves (the *praepositi* as he calls them) to whom after God and the king the control of the kingdom rightly belonged. To get things done reliance had to be placed directly on these royal servants, men in charge of royal estates now with extended public powers. It is these men who seem very much to be in Asser's mind as he talks of Alfred's skill in handling them by gently instructing, urging, commanding and after long patience punishing sharply. Obstinacy and vulgar folly are the faults especially isolated. Men accustomed to the honour and profits of office responded slowly to the demands of an active creative ruler. As we have already seen Asser also gives us a valuable and indeed for its age unique glimpse of the organization of the court. The qualities consistently emphasized are those of the care and concern of a society consciously Christian.

Control of reeves, men who looked after estates, renders, finances, and manpower provides one important clue to Alfred's success. The infrastructure, so to speak, was well organized, and the Church played an invaluable part in keeping the royal presence known and respected at this level. Within the political structure at the higher level, at what a later age would have termed the magnate level, we also have occasional glimpses, mostly from a West-Saxon point of view, of the reasons for Alfred's success in establishing the basis for a permanent kingdom of England. In a passage at the end of the grim record of the great Danish onslaught in the 890s the Anglo-Saxon Chronicle reported under the year 896:

> By the grace of God, the army had not on the whole afflicted the English people very greatly: but they were much more seriously afflicted in those three years by the mortality of cattle and men, and most of all in that many of the best king's thegns who were in the land died in those three years.
>
> Of those, one was Swithwulf, bishop of Rochester, and Ceolmund, ealdorman of Kent, and Brihtwulf, ealdorman of Essex, and Wulfred, ealdorman of Hampshire, and Ealhheard, bishop of Dorchester, and Eadwulf, a king's thegn in Sussex, and Beornwulf, the town-reeve of Winchester, and Ecgwulf, the king's marshal, and many besides them, though I have named the most distinguished.[23]

An impression is given by this entry of an organized administrative hierarchy, including both ecclesiasiastical and secular officers, and charter and chronicle evidence enables us to fill out the record a shade further. Much of the weight of political leadership fell on the ealdormen, great men sometimes of ancient lineage, sometimes close in blood and person to the king, consistently in fact as well as in terminological usage royal representatives or distinguished servants in

23 *EHD* i, no. 1, p. 205.

their shires. It was customary under Alfred for each territorial shire in Wessex to have its own ealdorman which means that at any one time one would expect to find nine or ten men holding that exalted office, enjoying special privilege and prestige, status, estates and dues, and probably bearing some distinguishing mark of rank in clothes, insignia or arms. Kent was something of a special case, and was normally led by two ealdorman, probably corresponding in sphere of office to the ancient divisions into East and West Kent represented at ecclesiastical level by the two sees of Canterbury and Rochester. The Ceolmund of the annal mentioned above does not appear in surviving charters as *dux* but a Ceolmund *minister* subscribes to Kentish charters from as early as 855.[24] Brihtwulf of Essex is a mysterious figure, possibly to be associated with a Beorhtulf *dux* who subscribes to Kentish and West-Saxon charters in the 860s.[25] It may be that the vigorous campaigning in the Thames estuary in the 890s brought about a revival in an office one would have expected to fall into disuse after the agreement between King Alfred and Guthrum. Wulfred of Hampshire appears in charters from 879 to 892 and was clearly an important person in the stabilizing of the kingdom after the peace of Wedmore.[26] Some became very great men indeed. In 897 the Chronicle specifically mentions the death of Ethelhelm, ealdorman of Wiltshire, and we know a little more about him. In 887 he took the alms of the West Saxons to the pope at Rome, and was granted estates in Wiltshire. According to William of Malmesbury his daughter became Edward the Elder's second wife.[27] Further west Odda, ealdorman of Devon, played a critical part in the campaigns of 878 while Somerset was in the charge of the ealdorman Æthelnoth. He was a close companion of the king, had accompanied him on his flight to Athelney and was one of those present at the christening of Guthrum. He subscribed to charters in the years following Wedmore, attended what might have been a decisive meeting of the Mercian council at Droitwich in the late 880s, led the West-Saxon armies at Buttington in 893, and led a mission to Northumbria in 894 (the probable year of his death) after a Viking at-

---

24 *EHD* i, no. 89, p. 525 (*AD* 855), also Sawyer, 327, 344, 1196, and 1202–3. If these are indeed the same man an intelligible picture is offered of a young Kentish thegn (*miles* or *minister*) still a *minister* in the 870s rising to ealdorman's office later in life.

25 Sawyer 327,337. Essex passed into Danish hands in the 870s, but the recovery of London must have had effect on part at least of the old province of Essex.

26 Sawyer 345 (*AD* 882). N. Banton *Ealdormen and Earls in England from the reign of King Alfred to the Reign of King Æthelred II* unpublished D. Phil. thesis (Oxford, 1981), p. 40.

27 D. Whitelock comments on the unlikelihood that Æthelhelm is the king's nephew of that name in 'Some Charters in the Name of King Alfred', *Saints, Scholars, and Heroes*, ed. M.H. King and W.M. Stevens (Minnesota, 1979), p. 92. William of Malmesbury, *De Gestis Regum*, i, p. 136 ff.

tack on the south coast of England.[28] It is notable that several of the king's companions who had weathered the storms of the most anxious period of his reign in the late 870s lived on to prosper as the kingdom stabilized.

Evidence tends to be even more scanty and scattered for other areas of Wessex, but enough survives to suggest that Sussex, Surrey and Dorset, for example, conformed to the general pattern with one ealdorman in charge.[29] Two areas deserve special mention. Berkshire had long been disputed territory between Mercia and Wessex. In 871 it was governed by an ealdorman named Æthelwulf of Mercian extraction. Over his long period of office he subscribed initially to Mercian charters and then from the 850s to West-Saxon. After his death during the year of battles in 871 his body was taken for burial to Derby.[30] Asser reminds us at the beginning of his Life of Alfred that the king had been born, of a Mercian mother, at Wantage in Berkshire, and there can be no doubt that the passing of Berkshire under West-Saxon control foreshadowed the slow but ultimate absolute merging of West-Saxon and Mercian administrative interests in the tenth century.[31] The placing of London and unconquered Mercia under the charge of the Mercian ealdorman, Ethelred, must be read as a pointer in the same direction. Ethelred, as we have already seen, was married to Alfred's daughter, Æthelflæd, who was herself of the Mercian blood royal. Sources other than the West-Saxon occasionally refer to them in royal terms, and it is clear that particularly after Alfred's death they exercised an authority greater than that of the normal ealdorman, issuing charters, taking the initiative in campaigning and building permanent fortifications. Her brother, Edward the Elder, had to act decisively to assert his authority after their death and even at the end of his substantially successful reign he had to face dissidence that led even to cooperation of the Mercians in the north-west around Chester with the Welsh. But by and large the Mercian situation was altogether exceptional and the system of ealdormanries encouraged by Alfred in Greater Wessex seemed set fair to become the model for extension to the rest of Christian England. In the event under pressure of political events the model was not followed exactly. The number of

---

28 *EHD* i, no. 1, pp. 195–6. Ethelweard, whose information about these events was good, mentions Æthelnoth *ibid.* pp. 203–4 and Ethelweard, *Chronicle*, ed. A. Campbell (London, 1962) p. 51. F.M. Stenton, *Preparatory to Anglo-Saxon England* ed. D.M. Stenton (Oxford, 1970), pp. 8–13.

29 N. Banton, op. cit., chapters 2 and 3, including very valuable comments on the position of Ethelred and Æthelflæd, pp. 63–79, where full attention is drawn to the sub-regal status (to say the least) of the two rulers, clearly more exalted than the ordinary ealdormannic role.

30 *EHD* i, no. 1, p. 192. Ethelweard adds that the body was taken to *Northworpige*, later known as Derby (ed. A. Campbell, p. 37).

31 Asser, *Life of Alfred*, ch. 1, *in illa paga, quae nominatur Berrocscire.*

ealdormen diminished, and it became rare in the tenth century for there to be more than four or five ealdormen at any one time in Mercia and as few as two or three in Wessex.[32] After 965 it was customary for there to be only one in the whole of Northumbria. Nevertheless the office of administrator over a territorial complex known as a shire became the standard way of exercising royal control in Alfredian Wessex. Ultimate responsibility under the king for the army, the building of fortifications, the levying of taxes and their collection, the collection of dues, rested in the hands of the ealdormen or their representatives. The 'earl's third penny', a third of the judicial renders and proceeds of the shire court, was the ealdorman's proper reward. Increasingly and early in the tenth century more and more of the routine business passed into the hands of the ealdorman's representatives, often a royal officer or reeve. The ealdormen themselves tended to take on great magnate status, exercising office over several shires and acting indeed as powerful provincial governors. The complexity of their office grew as society itself became more complex.

This chapter has emphasized royal authority and royal officers and in succeeding sections of this book heavy emphasis will be placed on the growth, at some stages spectacular, of royal authority. Kings, even when weak or unreliable, were at the centre of governmental activity, and progress in written records and in practical affairs was associated with their name. Yet it is wise to remember that great tracts of activity that we now associate with government were still in Alfred's time and in the tenth and eleventh century matter for the individual freeman and his kindred. Only slowly did the functions that we now attribute to the State pass from the ordinary freeman. He was still expected to protect himself, his family and his property: there was no police-force to do the work for him. If he was imprisoned his kindred had the duty of feeding him. Under specified formal conditions it was his duty to take vengeance. A man could fight on behalf of his lord if the lord were being attacked without incurring a feud, and a lord could do the same for his man. A man could also fight on behalf of his kinsman if wrongly attacked, though not against his lord: that the king did not allow.[33] The special care and concern of the king that the bond of loyalty between lord and man should not be broken, even if kinsfolk were involved on the other side, is the best single indication we have of the way in which society was settling into a stabler territorial mould.

---

32 N. Banton, *Ealdormen and Earls,* p. 95, makes the interesting suggestion that the reduction in the number of ealdormen in Wessex to two or three may have been conducted in stages and may have been something of a response to the conquest of Mercia.

33 *EHD* i, no. 33, p. 415. Alf. 42.6.

Alfred's contribution to the development of Anglo-Saxon government needs therefore to be read in terms that take full account of the severely practical as well as the idealistic. He undoubtedly left behind him a formidable example of Christian kingship in action, but the action involved minute exercise of care and attention to judicial matters, financial matters, and also to mundane matters connected with the organization of shires, appointment to the offices of ealdorman and reeve and above all to the building of fortifications and the establishment of means of ensuring their permanent manning. As an intelligent innovator Alfred deserves full praise but credit must also be given to him for the creation out of ancient moulds of forms of practical government that could be used and extended by his son and by future generations. He left a reputation for mildness and mercy though he could act decisively and even brutally when occasion demanded it. Too successful perhaps to be regarded as a saint, Alfred achieved much in the fields of law, education and administration that goes far to justify the high reputation he was accorded by later generations.

Part II

The Later Anglo-Saxon Kingdoms 899–1066

4*

Kingship and the Kings

The period from the death of Alfred to the Norman Conquest is not at first sight an obvious political unit. It is true that for the first few days of 1066 a direct descendant of Alfred was king of England, for Edward the Confessor was Alfred's great-grandson's grandson in the male line of descent. But for more than a quarter of a century, from 1016 to 1042, an alien dynasty of the Danish line of Gorm the Old had sat on the English throne, and the succession was to pass out of the West-Saxon line again in 1066 to Harold Godwinson and William of Normandy. Nevertheless from 899 to 1016 the throne was occupied by men in legitimate male descent from King Alfred, and in 1041–42 it was thought right and proper that Edward, son of Ethelred, brought back from his forced exile in Normandy, should be regarded first as heir and then as successor to the Danish Hardicnut.   There is also good justification for treating the period as a unit in the field of government and administration. Change of dynasty there was, but no corresponding change in monarchy. Cnut, as has so often been said, proved more English than the English after his succession to the throne. He advanced the cause of monarchy, fitting in easily to a process which culminated in the creation of a relatively powerful and united kingdom. The successors of Alfred, English or Danish, gradually brought the whole of England under their control and political unity coincided with a development of royal authority. Government became overtly territorial, a kingdom of England rather than a kingdom of the English, or of tribal units among the English. A high point in development of the monarchy was reached under Edgar (959–975). His spectacular coronation at Bath in 973 and subsequent ceremonies on the Dee near Chester symbolized the range and vigour

---

* There is a vast literature on Germanic kiingship (see also Chapter 1). The work of Dr J.L. Nelson provides a useful insight into modern ideas on the late period. Sources are best explored through an examination of the laws, the charters, and the work of Wulfstan, especially valuable since Wulfstan, archbishop of York 1002–23, was a practical statesman and adviser both to Ethelred and Cnut. Wulfstan's key text *The Institutes of Polity* has been brilliantly edited by K. Jost (see footnote 9 below).

of the Christian monarchy. The ineptitude and distrust of Ethelred's reign was to some extent made good under the Danish Cnut (1016–35). Edward the Confessor (1042–66) governed a realm whose institutions were advanced and successful for their mid-eleventh-century date, and William of Normandy was well aware of the strength and potentiality of the prize he gained by his victory at Hastings.

The Theory of Kingship

Throughout Western Europe great changes came over the nature of kingship in the course of the tenth and eleventh centuries. The basic pattern had already been etched in by Peppin and Charles the Great in the Frankish realms. Close cooperation between Church and State with the king as the dominant partner, active involvement of the Church in the business of government, sturdy protection of the Church and its missionaries by the king and intensification of proper spiritual sanctions for the kingship, were the predominant features. The ninth century was too torn by barbarian invasion and civil wars for much active progress to be made, except in the field of theory by a few ecclesiastical thinkers, but revival, recovery and undoubted economic progress from the beginning of the tenth century made positive advance possible. This advance manifested itself at its most spectacular level in the German lands. Under Otto the Great (936–73), Edgar's elder contemporary, Germany was welded into an effective monarchy, the first Reich, and indeed after 962 into an empire, consciously modelled on the empire of Charles the Great. Monarchical institutions in the shape of an elaborate Household administration, a formalization of councils of magnates and a chancery were fully in operation there by the end of the tenth century. Many limitations can be identified in the German situation, partly because of the newness of the dynasty, the extent of the lands concerned and the strength of localism and particularistic feeling. Written law was not as sophisticated as in England, the coinage was inferior and instruments for articulating government so that royal orders could be effective were inadequate. French development was quite different, more backward in some respects, and yet carrying a greater potential for the future. Carolingians and Capetians shared the royal honours until, after the coronation of Hugh Capet in 987, the Capetian family emerged as the royal dynasty of France. Of the early Capetians the great French historian Marc Bloch said accurately that they possessed little more then their name and crown, neither attribute, it must be confessed, without weight and significance. Another distinguished French historian, Robert Fawtier, commended them for one achievement above all else – their power of survival.[1] Constitutional interest in France is to be found rather in the development of the great fiefs than in the monarchy itself. Normandy, Anjou and to some extent Flanders provide more evidence of solid institutional growth than the Capetian heartlands around Paris and Orleans. France in the tenth and for the greater part of the eleventh century was the land of great fiefs. The immense potentiality of French monarchy, in direct descent from Carolingian traditions, was not realized until the twelfth century: concentric centralization is the key to French medieval constitutional growth.

England was nearer the German model, creating her unity and developing central processes of government as she did so. There was one outstanding advantage in the English situation, and that was the size of the community and the extent of the kingdom. At a time when communications were poor Germany proved too extensive to be patient of strong, consistent royal government. Some of the emperors, vigorous and powerful though they were, wore themselves out with constant travel. The itineraries of the early Ottonian and Salian kings and emperors illuminate the difficulties facing them; effective royal authority demanded the regular presence of the royal Court.[2] England is and was manageable in this respect; its geographical extent did not exceed the economic and physical resources of the monarchy.

It was understandable that with the mould of Western Europe falling into the familiar shape of the three principal monarchies, England, France and Germany, much active thought should be given to the theory of monarchy. On the continent the line of distinguished writers and commentators was virtually unbroken from Carolingian times through collectors of royal capitularies, makers of episcopal handbooks to the massive achievements of Burchard of Worms in the early eleventh century or the royal apologists at the time of the Investiture Contest. The mirror of monarchy was in people's minds, and biblical examples were freely used to exhort, admonish or warn contemporary rulers. England produced its quota of political thought on the monarchy, but because much that has survived was written in the vernacular it has not been as well studied as much of the continental material. In the proems and introductions to the codes of laws, in occasional reflections in charters and wills, and in homiletic writings, comments

---

1 M. Bloch, *Feudal Society* (Eng. trs., London, 1961), pp. 422ff. : R. Fawtier, *The Capetian Kings of France* (Eng. trs., London, 1960), p. 16.

2 Acute insight into the German problem is provided by K.J. Leyser, *Rule and Conflict in an Early Medieval Society: Ottonian Saxony* (London, 1979) and in earlier articles in *EHR* (1968) and *Past and Present* (1968). J. Gillingham, *The Kingdom of Germany in the High Middle Ages* (Hist. Ass., London, 1971) gives a good general survey.

were made on the principles and practice of monarchy and of all Christian authority. Alfred himself had Gregory's *Cura Pastoralis* translated, a treatise on government, not merely on episcopal government, a work of massive influence in literate circles.[3] Under King Edgar there took place a great revival in Benedictine monasticism under the inspiration of Archbishop Dunstan, of Ethelwold, bishop of Winchester, and of Oswald, bishop of Worcester. In the early years of the 970s, before the coronation at Bath, a special version of the Benedictine Rule, the *Regularis Concordia,* was prepared for English use.[4] An outstanding and unusual characteristic of the version was the prominence given to the royal family. Prayers were to be said not only for the king but also for the queen as part of the ordinary ritual of the new Benedictine houses. In spite of some hostility and occasional setbacks no fewer than seventeen of these houses were established by the 990s. It is not too fanciful to see them, and especially the powerful and wealthy and influential houses of Peterborough, Ely and Ramsey in the Fenlands and East Anglia, as among the strongest forces in support of the united monarchy of England.

The influence of reformed Benedictine observance had its effects too on the development of English scholarship. The end of the tenth and beginning of the eleventh centuries is often referred to as the 'Golden Age' of Anglo-Saxon prose. The great scholar and homilist, Ælfric of Eynsham and of Cerne Abbas, in a famous homily for Palm Sunday provided a key text for any discussion of kingship and the abstractions of monarchy in late Anglo-Saxon England. He wrote:

> We will give you an illustration. No man can make himself king, but the people has the choice to select as king whom they please; but after he is consecrated as king, he then has dominion over the people, and they cannot shake his yoke from their necks.[5]

This is a fine clerical exposition of pre-Investiture Contest doctrine. It is as interesting in what it omits as in what it expresses. We know in fact that the process of selection was from a much more limited field than Ælfric allows. It was expected that a king should be from a royal kin. Literary sources from gnomic poems to heroic verse insist that possession of the blood royal is essential to legitimate kingship. The Anglo-Saxon Chronicle reinforces this by its constant references to the descent of the kings from the sixth-century Cerdic, and genealogical

3 H.R. Loyn, *Alfred the Great* (Oxford, 1967), pp. 52–7.
4 *Regularis Concordia,* ed. Dom T. Symons (London, 1953). There is an important article by Dom Thomas 'Regularis Concordia: History and Derivation' in *Tenth-Century Studies,* ed. D. Parsons (London and Chichester, 1975), pp. 37–59.
5 Ælfric, '*Catholic Homilies*', ed. B. Thorpe, vol. i, p. 212: *EHD* i, no. 239 (b), pp. 925–6.

lore takes the descent further back through Germanic heroes to Old Testament kings. Only in exceptional circumstances will selection not be made from the kin of Cerdic.[6] Ælfric is more in line with Carolingian ecclesiastical thought when he stresses the special sanctions given by consecration. It is clear that great care was taken over the preparation of Edgar's coronation *Ordo* at Bath, based as it was on similar ceremonies earlier in the century and ultimately on Frankish precedent. It is possible that Edgar had already been consecrated, presumably at Kingston-upon-Thames early in his reign as king of the West Saxons. As Janet Nelson has reminded us, 'to consecrate a king was to assert a society's identity'; and the ceremony at Bath should then be interpreted in an imperial dimension, a British dimension.[7] After the coronation at Bath Edgar went by sea to Chester where eight kings submitted to him and Florence of Worcester in giving the most circumstantial account (Edgar at the helm, the other kings rowing on the Dee from the royal palace to St John's church) reported that Edgar himself reflected that any of his successors could be proud to be the king of the English with so many kings subordinate to him,[8] These other kings were Cumbrians, Scots, Viking Lords of the Isles and Welsh. Unction to kingship was preparatory to this demonstration of authority. Modern British coronations preserve the shape of a very ancient ceremony in the order of proceedings: recognition, oath-taking, anointing, throning and homage. Apart from the feudal accretions the shape seems much in line with what had become accredited practice in the tenth-century West: ritual acts of election and elevation preceded anointing and crown-wearing. Acknowledgement of formal submission, an element in feudal homage, came after it.

Custom by the tenth century had enabled regular practices and procedures to be formulated. Legally and constitutionally the tripartite promise to protect the Church, to punish malefactors and to do justice to all Christian people is impressive. Later coronation charters, some would say even Magna Carta itself, seem to develop from this simple promise. Contemporaries were more concerned with the public manifestation of a special setting apart from all other lordship. No other lord received unction. In a corresponding situation in France the great nobility, even at its most independent, made special effort to attend this occasion, the coronation of a king, with all its mystical overtones. Ælfric states sound Church doctrine when he argues that this

---

6 *ASCh passim,* notably the preface to MS A, and entries under 552, 597, 674, 685, 688, 757, 786, 855–8.

7 J.L. Nelson, 'Inauguration Rituals', *Early Medieval Kingship,* eds. P.H. Sawyer and I.N. Wood (Leeds, 1977), p. 68.

8 *Chronicon ex chronicis, s.a.* 973, quoted in *EHD* i, no. 1, p. 228 (fn. 1).

consecration – not unlike the setting apart of a priest – had immediate consequences on the authority of the new king. Henceforth he could not be deposed. A bad lord was, in the central Augustinian tradition, to be suffered as a penalty for sin.

Ælfric's contemporary and friend Wulfstan, archbishop of York and bishop of Worcester, was also deeply interested in monarchy and the workings of royal government. This is no surprise for he was a prominent adviser, especially in legal matters, first to Ethelred and then to Cnut. The characteristic rhythms of his prose have been surely identified in the statements of law issued during the reign of Ethelred and it is quite certain that his was the shaping mind behind the laws of Cnut. In his voluminous homiletic work he turned from time to time to themes of lordship and of kingship, and in the course of his long career he attempted drafts of what was intended to be a thorough analysis of the rights and duties of the different grades of society, a massive work of political thought to which modern scholars have given the name the *Institutes of Polity*.[9] In what was probably intended as one of his first drafts, an initial section on the heavenly king was followed by chapters on the earthly king. A Christian king was to be a comfort to his people and a just shepherd to his Christian flock. He was to protect Christendom and God's Church with all his might, to help the righteous and to afflict the evil-doers, especially thieves, robbers and bandits. Christ and a Christian king were the means by which God's servants could hope for peace and comfort. By a king's wisdom a people became happy, healthy and victorious. A king should act resolutely against heathenism, and encourage booklearning. He should often consult with wise men if he wished to pay proper obedience to God. He should curb the overbearing who act against the law of God and the law of the people and exact compensation energetically – against their will if need be. His true function was to purify his people before God and the world. He was to take special care for his own spiritual strength. Just as the body grew weak for lack of proper nourishment, so did the soul without proper spiritual food.

Wulfstan gives much valuable insight into the function of a king by these exhortations. The idea of kingship as a spiritual office is implicit in his analysis. The object of its proper exercise was the achievement of spiritual welfare in the community. The means of achievement involved consultation with the wise, listening to the good, and the exercise of force in the basic matter of exacting compensation. Royal authority in itself should be enough to ensure that the evil-doer paid up, but if not, royal power should be so strong that justice could be done against the will (*huru unþances*) of the evil-doer.

9 *Die 'Institutes of Polity, Civil and Ecclesiastical'*, ed. K. Jost (Berne, 1959): *Be heofonlicum cyninge and Be eorðlicum cyninge*, pp. 39–51.

Wulfstan's evidence is especially valuable because he was himself long at the centre of affairs for most of the turbulent second half of Ethelred's reign and during the early years of the reign of Cnut. He had a systematic mind and attempted in much smaller compass a literary analysis of political thought after the style of the work of his contemporary Burchard of Worms. Apart from his chapter on the king he attempted also short analyses of the kingdom itself and of the royal throne. The homilist in him predominated in his analysis of the kingdom.[10] He took straight from Sedulius the eight virtues expected in a kingdom ruled strongly by a just king: truth, patience, generosity, good counsel, correction of evil-doers, fostering of the good, light taxation (*levitas tributi: lihtenges*), and equity in judgement. The seven qualities which the king himself was expected to possess were that he should fear God, love the truth, be humble to good men and resolute (*stiðmod*) against evil-doers, that he should comfort and feed the poor (one text says God's poor), protect and foster God's Church, and judge equitably according to just laws between kinsfolk and strangers. On the throne itself, the symbol of just, mystical lordship from which judgements would be determined, Wulfstan gave a condensed chapter, drawing from the scriptures and from English work (including the Alfredian translation of Boethius and his own friend Ælfric) in which he sums up his own view of the framework of a Christian society. Each just throne depended, as he saw it, on three pillars: *oratores, laboratores* and *bellatores*. The *oratores* were the men of prayer whose duty it was, day and night, to make intercession for the people. The *laboratores* were the workmen by whose labours all were fed. The *bellatores* were the fighting men whose duty it was to protect the kingdom in war. These were the three pillars on which rested all thrones – and Wulfstan added in one of his recensions 'among a Christian people'. The strict division of function between *weorcmen* and *wigmen,* workmen and warriors, is at variance with much that we know from the practice of Anglo-Saxon England, but there can be no doubt that Wulfstan was expressing current generalized thought in his own highly personal way. If any of these pillars were to weaken the throne itself would totter (*sona se stol scilfð*). If any were to break, the throne would fall and the people would be reduced to misery. Good Christian doctrine and 'just secular law' were the strengthening elements that made for an enduring kingdom. Wulfstan finished the chapter on an homiletic note which is the key to his political thought. If Christianity weakens (*awacige se cristendom*) the kingdom itself totters, and the result is universal lawlessness and evil-doing.

10 *ibid. Be cinedome* and *Be cynestole*, pp. 52–8.

Much of Wulfstan's long tract was in the nature of a commentary on this basic premise. Set side by side with the lawlessness, bad faith and treachery of much of Ethelred's reign, it serves as a reminder of the enduring forces for stability and ordered government that persisted through the most perilous times. Wulfstan was very concerned, here in the *Institutes* as elsewhere, with the role of the bishop, and spent much time and energy on the functions that a bishop should be called on to perform in this tightly structured Christian social order. He attempted an analysis of a bishop's 'daywork' which included not only the spiritual offices proper to his order, a measure of manual labour and supervision of his household, but also a direct exhortation that he should often and frequently give godly instruction to the folk *on gemote,* in the folk-courts.[11] Earls and reeves and secular judges were exhorted to give just judgements and not to favour their kinsmen against other folk. Reeves were brought under special admonition to work zealously and justly in their lord's interests. We are told that there had been a sad falling off since Edgar's day, and that reeves who should be protectors had turned into oppressors. In Edgar's time they had been chosen warily and acted well but now they afflicted wretched people without redress, grievously offended God himself, and massed up earthly treasures for themselves – for which in time, added Wulfstan, they would have to pay both to God and the world. The same strains of moral exhortation to do good and not to look for treasure in this world ran through long chapters on abbots, monks, priests, nuns, widows, God's servants, and all Christian men. The tract in the form in which it has survived was often well-shaped in detail. Individual chapters strike home with great force by skilful use of the poetic rhythms and balances of which Wulfstan was master. The work however was not subject to final review and shaping, and represents rather an enduring literary interest, written or dictated by the archbishop from time to time in his sees, at Court, or on his journeyings. The constant general theme was the unity of Christian society. The tract ended with the open analogy of the unity of the heavenly kingdom and the earthly kingdom here below:

> We should all love and honour one God and earnestly hold to one Christian faith (*cristendom*) and eschew completely all heathen belief. And let us be faithful to our one king and lord (*cynehlaford*) and protect life and land together as best we may, and ask in our inmost heart the help of God Almighty. *Sit nomen domini benedictum.*[12]

Similar emphasis on the unity of the heavenly kingdom as a mirror to the unity of the earthly kingdom is to be found in the proems to the law codes and in the charters. Wulfstan was expressing ideas common to his generation. This is to some measure unexpected, and demands comment. Wulfstan was, as well as bishop of Worcester,

11 *ibid. De episcopis* and *Item de episcopis,* especially ch. 81, p. 76.
12 *ibid.* chs. 235–6, p. 165.

archbishop of York. Loyalty to the West-Saxon dynasty was not a quality that always came automatically and naturally in Northumbria. After the Norman Conquest Lanfranc, the new archbishop of Canterbury, with the full support of King William, asserted his supremacy over the archbishopric of York in part at least to prevent any separatist movement developing there, and as a safeguard against a foreign invader attempting to have himself crowned at York. We can find plentiful evidence of regional feeling and awareness of different ancient political traditions in late Anglo-Saxon England. Special legal attention was given to the needs of the men of the Five Boroughs or to the Northumbrian priests.[13] A charter of King Edgar in 969 by means of which land at Kineton, Warwickshire, was granted to his thegn Ælfwald refers in its description of the bounds to a border that lay from the springs to the boundary of the Mercians and from the boundary of the Mercians to *Succan-pit*; and the boundary in question was the age-old line of demarcation between the Mercians and the *Hwicce*, the settlers in the Severn valley.[14] It may well be that we have underestimated the part played by the Church in bringing about the unity of England and have correspondingly underestimated the persistent fissiparous tendencies of a predominantly agrarian community, conscious of its local and regional loyalties. When the epic poet described the last fight of Byrhtnoth, the ealdorman of Essex, in 991, he talked of Byrhtnoth as one who defended the whole realm, the home of King Ethelred, protecting his lord, his people, his land. After Byrhtnoth's death the faithful survivors fought on to avenge their lord. Three of them made known their origins. Ælfwine declared that he was of a great kin among the Mercians, the grandson of ealdorman Ealhelm. Leofsunu stated that the men about Sturmere would have no need to reproach him and Ælscferth, son of Ecglaf, was of a resolute Northumbrian kin. Ælscferth, we are told, was present in the host as a hostage, a curious comment on the unity of the realm.[15] Yet the similarities between Christian men speaking substantially the same tongue were enough to outweigh the differences when the Christians were confronted directly with heathen Scandinavians. The Church was clearly taking the rising political flood when it argued firmly in favour of Christian unity, one belief, one *cristendom*, one king. On the sole occasion when there was a division of the realm among princes from the ancient dynasty, probable civil war between Eadwig and Edgar was averted only by Eadwig's timely death in 959; and the attempted compromise division between Edmund Ironside in Wessex

---

13 *EHD* i, no. 43, pp. 439–42, Ethelred III − the code was issued at Wantage. It refers to the peace that the ealdorman and the king's reeve gave in the meeting (geþincða) of the Five Boroughs. *EHD* i, no. 52, pp. 471–6, the 'Law of the Northumbrian Priests'.

14 *EHD* i, no. 113, pp. 563–4.

15 *Battle of Maldon*, ll. 216–18, 249ff;. and 265–7. The best edition is by E.V. Gordon (with supplement by J.G. Scragg) (Manchester, 1976).

and Cnut in 1016 was never put to the political test. On Edmund's death Cnut succeeded to all the kingdom of England.

The Succession

The kin of Cerdic (in practice the descendants of King Alfred or at the most remote those of his paternal grandfather, Egbert) provided the blood royal, but there was no hard and fast rule of succession to the throne within the kin in the tenth and eleventh centuries. This was a problem general to the age, solved in France where by an extraordinary combination of biological good fortune and political sagacity the Capetians were able to keep the throne in direct patrilinear descent from Hugh Capet in 987 to Philip VI in 1328. The French kings provided male heirs, and the principle of association in the kingship of the eldest son in his father's lifetime, coupled with acceptance of primogeniture in the male line and feudal investiture, ensured an easy transition from reign to reign. The English situation proved more complicated personally and in principle. Alfred's son, Edward, later known as 'the Elder', had been a prominent leader in the military campaigns of the 890s, and succeeded his father in 899. He was crowned at Kingston-upon-Thames on 8 June 900, but met with a serious rebellion from his cousin Æthelwold, son of Ethelred I, and representative therefore of the elder male line. The rebellion was suppressed and Æthelwold was killed in battle in 903. Edward was succeeded in 924 by his eldest son, Athelstan, who died unmarried in 939, and then by Edmund, born in 921 (Edward's son by his third marriage, and the much younger half-brother of Athelstan), who was murdered by a private enemy at Pucklechurch in Gloucestershire on 26 May, 946. Edmund left two small sons but the crown went to his brother, Eadred, who died unmarried in November 955. Eadred appears to have been deliberately celibate, and brought his young nephews up as his heirs. Eadwig, the elder of the two, succeeded and was crowned at Kingston by Oda, archbishop of Canterbury, in January 956. He rapidly alienated responsible ecclesiastical opinion with the consequence that his younger brother, Edgar, was declared king in Mercia and the Danelaw in 957. Eadwig died on 1 October 959, and Edgar was then recognized as king of all England. It is hard to know how much weight to give to these events of 955–959. At first sight they seem to suggest a distinct check to progress towards a united England. Yet Edgar's reign, 959–975, represents a dramatic stage in the achievement of unity within England. It may well be − as later chroniclers and writers of lives of saints tended to assume when they wrote of Eadwig and Edgar − that the troubles were limited to the palace and to the close group of higher ecclesiastics interested in power as well as monastic reform. Certainly we can see that it was precisely during these years that the principal officers who were to dominate English politics in Church and State for the succeeding generation received their appointments or promotions.[16] The existence of two royal courts was dangerous and potentially disruptive. Civil war was probably not far away when Eadwig died in 959. How serious and how deep the civil war would have been is hard to estimate. In all probability the strong forces for stability and unity in Church and State would have been enough to compel dynastic settlement just as they proved enough to bring Dunstan back from exile, to place Edgar in power north of the Thames, and to force the annulment of Eadwig's marriage with Ælfgifu on grounds of consanguinity. Edgar may have been crowned early in his reign but no records has survived of the ceremony. His formal coronation at Bath (which may have had imperial overtones) was delayed until 11 May 973, possibly until he had reached the canonical age of 30, and two years later he died, leaving two sons, the thirteen-year old Edward and his half-brother Ethelred who was born about 968. Edward reigned for only three years or so and was murdered at Corfe Castle on 18 March 978, apparently at the instigation of his step-mother. Ethelred was immediately acclaimed and crowned and so began a long, unhappy reign which lasted, apart from a winter in exile 1013–14, until his death in 1016. He was succeeded briefly by his eldest son Edmund Ironside (April to November, 1016). The attempted compromise divison of the kingdom with Cnut was given no time to succeed, and the representative of the West-Saxon dynasty were forced into exile in Normandy during the reign of Cnut and his sons. Ethelred's youngest son, Alfred, made a further attempt at a restoration after the death of Cnut but was captured, blinded and died of his injuries at Ely in 1037. Ethelred's sole surviving son, Edward the Confessor, was summoned back to England in 1041 and succeeded his half-brother Hardicnut, the son of Cnut and Emma of Normandy, in 1042. Edward seems to have made some attempt to continue the dynastic succession when he brought back Edmund Ironside's son, Edward Atheling, and his children from their long exile in Hungary, but Edward Atheling died mysteriously before he could meet his uncle in 1057. His young son Edgar was temporarily chosen king by the citizens of London after the chaos of the battle of Hastings, but submitted to William, went with his mother and sisters to Scotland in 1067, and lived on for a long and undistinguished career, dying unmarried at some unrecorded time and place after 1126. Edgar's sister, Margaret, married Malcolm Canmore, king of Scots, at Dunfermline

16 F.M. Stenton, *Anglo-Saxon England,* pp. 366–67: Ælfhere to Mercia, Byrhtnoth to Essex, Æthelwold to East Anglia, and Ælfheah shortly afterwards to Hampshire.

in 1069. Three of her sons in turn became kings of the Scots and one of her daughters, Edith, married Henry I of England, so bringing back the blood of the ancient royal kin into the ruling Norman dynasty. In the event Edward the Confessor was succeeded by his brother-in-law, Harold Godwinson, the strongest man in the kingdom in troubled times. After Hastings William attempted to emphasize his kinship with Edward, but this kinship lay of course with Edward's maternal kin not his paternal. The Confessor's mother, Emma of Normandy, was indeed William's great-aunt, but this brought no drop of Cerdic's blood into his veins.

The main rules of succession are clear enough. The king's son was the natural person to succeed. Division of the kingdom was to be avoided if possible. Politics and the inadequacy (in the eyes of some very influential magnates) of Eadwig brought Edgar to partial power in 957. Politics and possibly a scheming step-mother brought about the murder of King Edward the Martyr in 978. Emphasis on the importance of the coronation undoubtedly increased during these centuries, and helped to contribute to the maintenance of the integrity of the kingdom. Edgar's success in Mercia was possible only with the active cooperation of an influential body of the clergy, notably Dunstan; and it seems increasingly likely that some ceremony was held at a relatively early stage in his reign. Efforts to create a successful *Ordo* at the coronation reached their triumphal climax in England with Edgar's crowning at Bath on 11 May 973, though it is certain that *Ordines* based on Carolingian precedent were in use earlier in the century.[17] There are indications of attempts to formalize proceedings relating both to the coronation and to the burial of kings at this time. All the tenth-century kings except Edgar and Edmund are known to have been crowned at Kingston-upon-Thames. Edmund's place of coronation is unknown and it is possible that Edgar's first coronation may have been held there. Edmund Ironside was chosen king by 'all the councillors who were in London and the citizens' after the death of his father, Ethelred, in April 1016, but we are not told specifically where he was crowned. Nor are we told where Cnut and his two sons were crowned, but their fondness for Winchester – all three were buried there – may point to a conscious effort to build up prestige at the heart of the old West-Saxon kingdom. Edward the Confessor was certainly crowned at Winchester though buried at his newly consecrated abbey of Westminster in the early days of 1066. Harold Godwinson was crowned at Westminster, thereafter recognized as the proper place for the coronation of the English kings. As for the tenth-

17 J.L. Nelson, 'Kingship, Law and Liturgy in the Political Thought of Hincmar of Rheims', *EHR* 92, (1977), pp. 241–79.

century choice of burial places there was undoubtedly some variety. Alfred and his father and grandfather had been buried at Winchester — though two of his brothers had been buried at Sherborne, and one at Wimborne Minster. Edward the Elder and Eadred were also buried at Winchester, but the tenth-century revival in monasticism came strongly to have its effects on royal custom. Athelstan was buried at Malmesbury in 939. The great revival of Glastonbury made it a natural centre for ceremonies connected with the obsequies of a monarch and possibly the selection of his successor. Edmund, Edgar and Edmund Ironside were buried there, Eadwig was probably buried, presumably without great ceremony, at Gloucester where he died on 1 October 959, and Ethelred, a shade incongruously, was buried at St Paul's Cathedral in London in April 1016. The overwhelming preponderance of coronations and burials in the south is impressive. It is sometimes hard to realize that we are dealing with kings of all England. Their social life appears to be so heavily concentrated south of Watling Street, and for the most part south of the Thames.

5 *

Government at the Centre

The reputation of Anglo-Saxon royal administration has suffered in the past from faulty comparisons with institutions not proper to its own time. Many scholars have approached it with questions of the Norman Conquest and settlement in mind and undue emphasis has been placed on its inadequacies and failures. It is well to remember that the Norman Duke William in 1066 succeeded to a kingship whose range and strength in law and administration exceeded that of any contemporary European monarch with the possible exception of Germany where the Salian kings and emperors were poised to endure a most disruptive half a century in the course of the Investiture disputes. To recognize that many aspects of Old-English administration were frankly primitive by the side of the Norman Exchequer or the Angevin courts of justice is not to criticize it, but rather to point to the value of its potential. Even some of the detailed legitimate criticisms levelled in the past prove to be only partially justified. There was, for example, no capital in the full modern sense, but Winchester and London were both highly favoured centres in the eleventh century, and the more or less permanent homes of men and women who played prominent continuous roles in the business of royal government and administration, princes, princesses, exalted treasurers and other officers as well as humble cooks and servants at royal palaces.[1] Emma, queen first of

---

* Original material on the workings of central government is plentiful but diffuse. There is no stable body of contemporary descriptive material. Much valuable evidence is preserved in the numerous royal charters of the period, and Nicholas Brooks and S.D. Keynes give good modern and up-to-date guides to this difficult material. For coinage and currency the work of Michael Dolley and his fellow workers is invaluable. Pierre Chaplais, N.R. Ker, M.B. Parkes and P.H. Sawyer also provide very helpful guides to the basic diplomatic material. There is much of value still in Liebermann's work on what he calls the 'national council', but an up-to-date study of the witan is much to be desired.

1 *Winchester in the Early Middle Ages*, ed, Martin Biddle, vol.i (Oxford, 1976), especially the essay by Martin Biddle and D.J.Keene 'The Late-Saxon burh', pp. 449-69. Biddle refers ac-

Ethelred and then of Cnut, was so closely associated with one of these centres that she was known as the 'Lady of Winchester'. She was indeed, as one might expect from a Norman of her generation, so interested and active in affairs of state that her son, Edward the Confessor, shortly after his accession made it his business to see that his mother was rendered harmless politically, yielding up the royal treasure to him and keeping to her residences in Winchester. The treasure was tangible physical wealth in the shape of gold, silver, precious jewels as well as current silver coins. The need to safeguard it in fortified buildings within fortified towns was closely associated with moves, already well in evidence before 1066 and brought to a further fine point by the Normans, to centralize government and administration in the south.

The Household

Palaces, repositories for treasure, residences of officers were important, but the principal active mainspring of government remained the king, his Household and his Court in the full domestic sense of the term. The Court itself was peripatetic, almost certainly following a set rhythm of movement which depended on both natural and liturgical motives. We must not paint too naive a picture of constant forced movement simply because many estates or complexes of estates were charged with the provision of one night's farm for the king and his elaborate Household and entourage. There may have been a time when the king wandered from manor to manor eating up his renders as he passed but that time was well past by the eleventh century. In some parts of England such as Wiltshire with its high proportion of royal estates, the farms of one night were often expressed in standard money terms. Chippenham, Tilshead, Calne, Bedwyn, Amesbury and Warminster were all known as royal estates responsible for the collection and payment of such farms at the time of Domesday Book.[2] Even if direct commutation into money was not universal the provision of food renders did not imply that the food was eaten on the spot. Moving the Court could be a slow and painful business and the king and those who looked after the logistics of the moves would aim at a succession of quite lengthy stays at favoured centres. The high festivals of Christmas, Easter and Whitsun might well entail a stay of three weeks to a month respectively in the west country, London, and the

curately to Winchester in terms of the development of an early capital (see below p. 152). C.N.L. Brooke assisted by Gillian Kerr, *London 800-1216: The Shaping of a City* (London, 1975), provides the essential guide to London developments.

2 J.H. Round, *Feudal England* (London, 1895, reissued 1964), pp. 109-14.

Winchester-Oxford area. Other fixed points are more obscure to us. There was a season for all things, Lent, Easter, Whitsun, Michaelmas, Christmas; sowing, campaigning, harvesting, more campaigning, hunting; and it is probable that each of the kings had his own favoured place according to the season and his tastes. King Edmund's fondness for stag-hunting from his palace at Cheddar is well known because of his connection with St Dunstan. In the troubled days late in the reign of the Confessor, in the summer of 1065, Earl Harold spent time and energy setting up a lodge at Portskewett near the mouth of the Wye to which he had intended to invite King Edward. Woodstock and Kirtlington, both known sites of witans, were favoured centres for hunting.[3] Campaigning occasionally brought the Court to the more distant parts of the kingdom, to Chester, to Lincoln and to York. The great Benedictine revival in the Fenlands and East Anglia provided centres where it could stay with some degree of comfort. Yet the overall impression remains that the late Old-English monarchy tended to be based physically very much in the south. Its forages elsewhere, notably to lands north of the Humber, have much the nature of summer campaigning expeditions. In the south itself it may well be that we have tended to underestimate the degree and significance of the urbanization achieved in the last century of Anglo-Saxon rule. The monarchy may have been more clearly linked to that other developing institution, the town, than has been always realized.

England was small enough so that the king was never impossibly remote even if he spent much or nearly all of his time in the south. His physical presence at York was rare, but his chosen ealdormen or earls could and would make the royal presence felt and the royal name feared. The king's council, the *witan*, helped to keep the group of active governors together. For general administration the king relied on his Household.[4] Gaps in evidence make it difficult to reconstruct the Household in detail, but enough has survived to suggest that the organization of the English royal Household resembled Carolingian and Ottonian models and parallels in the tenth century and that strong Danish influence, particularly on the military side with the institution of the housecarls, brought about modifications in the eleventh century. The increased range of the monarchy under Athelstan and his successors involved an increased dignity and more formal ceremonial practice at Court. Witness lists to charters, royal wills, and the occasional hint from glossaries give us valuable clues to the composition of

3 *ASCh*, 1065; F. Liebermann, *The National Assembly in the Anglo-Saxon Period* (Halle, 1913), pp. 45–6.
4 L.M. Larson, *The King's Household in England before the Norman Conquest* (Madison, 1904) although out of date in diplomatic matters, contains much valuable material.

the Court and the Household. The immediate royal family was probably much more influential than the references to the presence of the
queen or æthelings would have us believe: the Court and the Household
were in many respects personal to the king and the ruling kin. Factions
could emerge in them as violently as in the Tudor age, particularly
when for one reason or another succession problems reared their
heads. The prominence of Athelstan's brother, Edmund, in the last
years of Athelstan's reign or of Ethelred's son, Athelstan at one
stage in Ethelred's reign may hint at such emergence of purposeful
faction. The use of the term ætheling to describe such princes of royal
blood close to the reigning king (*æthele* meant 'noble') was not tan-
tamount to the designation of a successor, but the tendency to
associate a single person with the term used as a title (Edward the
Ætheling and then finally Edgar the Ætheling during the Confessor's
reign and after) may suggest special dignity including a specific element of kingworthyness. By and large the ruling kin remained special
and distinct, and the phrase 'ealdormen and thegns' *duces et ministri*
in Latin, remained the common means of describing the members of
the central Court, which was clearly more hierarchical and therefore
more sophisticated than was hitherto supposed. Recent work has
shown beyond shadow of doubt that for long periods there was a
positive pecking order among the great men of the realm in the witness
lists to charters.[5] This is most marked during the reign of Ethelred.
From 993 to 1015, the royal princes, the æthelings, for example,
subscribed in strict order of seniority. Ethelred had eight sons who
subscribed. Athelstan, the eldest, was always first until his death in
1013, followed by Egbert up to 1005, and then by Edmund, ultimate
successor of their father, Ethelred, who tops the witness lists in the last
years of Ethelred's reign. The other sons, almost without exception,
subscribe in due order of seniority whenever they appear on witness
lists. Even more startling is the order of subscription of ealdormen to
charters throughout the reign. From 979 to 983, Ælfhere, ealdorman
of Mercia, headed the lists, from 983 to 990 Æthelwine of East
Anglia, from 993 to 998 Æthelweard of the western shires, from 999
to 1009, Ælfric of Hampshire, and finally (in the lifetime of other
ealdormen who had once been his seniors) Eadric Streona of Mercia in
the last turbulent years of the reign from 1009 or 1012 to 1016. Bishops
and abbots follow a similar order of precedence, not quite as strictly
but firmly enough to show that a clear order of seniority was the
regular understood practice. The thegns or *ministri* also had a more

5 The following paragraphs depend heavily on the work of Simon Keynes, *The Diplomas of
King Æthelred 'the Unready', 978–1016* (Cambridge, 1980); the end-tables relating to
subscriptions to charters are of special value in this context.

complicated but firm order of precedence, and the leading thegns
Æthelmær and Ordulf, for example, were almost invariably first and
second on the list of witnesses between 994 and 1006. This accords
with what one would expect of a Germanic community and may well at
ministerial level be associated with a growth in importance of specific
household offices.

Charter evidence is consistently important, and helps to substan-
tiate the picture given in one document of the greatest importance for
an understanding of tenth-century conditions. King Eadred died in
956, leaving a will which gives clear insight into the organization of the
royal Household.[6] Men who normally appear in charters as simple
ministri (ministers or thegns) were carefully differentiated. Eadred
left the substantial sum of 80 mancuses to each of his accredited
discthegns, hræglthegns, and *birele.* These terms have strong associations with offices that we can recognize in the court of Charles the
Great and his successors on the continent. A 'dishthegn' presumably
originally was an officer who looked after the commissariat. It was
borrowed about this time into Welsh in the form *disteyn* and there took
on the specialized meaning of steward or household steward in much
the same way as the borrowed term *edling* (from ætheling) came to
mean heir to the throne. A *hræglthegn,* a 'raiment-thegn', in origin
meant one who looked after the clothing for the royal Household and
a *birel* was a butler. King Alfred's own mother, Osburh, had been the
daughter of a man of noble birth and proud genealogy, Oslac by
name, who had nevertheless served as butler, *pincerna,* to King
Ethelwulf. Household officers were men of distinguished birth, rank
and lineage but they did not develop in England into the powerful
ministerial dynasties that are to be found in the feudal world. King
Eadred singled out the men who held offices originally associated with
food, clothing and drink for special generosity, but he did not forget
the lesser men. He made a smaller but still substantial bequest of 30
mancuses to each of his stewards (*stigweards*), and they could well still
have been men who had responsibility for the administration and particularly the financial administration of royal estates. There were
also many mass-priests and other priests and men holding a great
variety of offices in the royal Household. King Eadred's will was
written in the vernacular, in Anglo-Saxon, but similar offices appear
spasmodically in the records, particularly in the charters in Latin
form. The term *camerarius* or chamberlain, the one who looked after
the royal chamber, may have been used generally, but could have been
regarded as the equivalent of any of the offices mentioned above, or as

6 F.E. Harmer, *Select English Historical Documents of the Ninth and Tenth Centuries* (Cambridge, 1914), no. xxi, pp. 34-5.

a *burthegn* or even as one responsible for the royal treasure, a *hordere*. Where Latin terms appear in charters, *disciferi, pincernae, cubicularii* or *camerarii,* they often subscribe immediately after the ealdormen and before the bulk of the *ministri*. They suggest the presence of a very strong official element among the thegns who served regularly at the royal Court.[7] Marshals and constables do not assume the special importance in Anglo-Saxon Household administration that they came to assume on the continent; and indeed the failure of England to produce these permanent high-ranking officers, marshals and constables, associated with the organization of a mounted army, may in itself constitute important ancillary evidence concerning the nature of foot-slogging military service itself. Under the Danes the useful word 'staller', a place-man, was employed to describe a man with office in the king's hall or presence.[8] The general impression is given of relative undifferentiation in personnel: stallers, stewards, reeves. King's servants were called on to provide service for the king, thegns increasingly to serve nobly. A similar lack of differentiation existed in function, though gradually divisions became clear between the three principal elements in governmental business, the secretariat in the general sense, the financial offices and judicial business. In all three respects Anglo-Saxon governmental technique was advanced for its age and bears favourable comparison with anything on the continent of Europe.

The king himself needed to be vigorous and active. A Worcester tradition, preserved in the chronicle that we know as Florence of Worcester's work, gave splendid insight into what were reckoned as the special virtues of King Edgar in the following terms:[9]

> In the winter and the spring he used to make progresses through all the provinces of England, and enquire diligently whether the laws of the land and his own ordinances were obeyed, so that the poor might not suffer wrong and be oppressed by the powerful. . . . Thus his enemies on every side were filled with awe, and the love of those who owed him allegiance was secured.

It was taken as an extraordinary manifestation of royal skill that Edgar travelled around his country in the winter and the spring, the most unpropitious seasons. Edgar was also credited with more ambitious schemes, and was said to have assembled a great fleet, year in and year out, which had the task of patrolling the whole circuit of the British Isles, so keeping the shores freer from piracy than they had

7 Keynes, pp. 159-61, provides the best modern account.
8 F.M. Stenton, *Anglo-Saxon England,* pp. 639–40.
9 *Chronicon ex Chronicis,* s.a. 975, ed. B. Thorpe (London, 1848).

been since the early days of the Danish invasions. Even allowing for evident exaggeration it seems likely that some extraordinary personal effort to achieve and maintain peace lies behind these eulogical traditions.

There was a limit of course to what the king could achieve on his own. His preponderance of social interest in the south is an effective reminder of physical limitations, and brings us face to face with one basic fact concerning kingship in this early period. He could not govern closely an area even as relatively compact as England. He had to rely on the cooperation of powerful men in his own Household and elsewhere, especially on the cooperation of ealdormen, bishops, thegns and other dignitaries, ecclesiastical and lay, who in their varying ways controlled the localities. For immediate support in all his ventures, as we have seen, the king depended on his Household, ordered very much on the Carolingian model with its central core of officers with titular duties at stable or at table, marshals, food-attendants, dish-thegns, stewards, and the like.[10] There was also a picked troop of soldiers, thegns near to the king, serving on a carefully arranged rota basis so that some were in constant attendance. A private legal compilation of the early eleventh century tells that it was the duty of all thegns with five hides of land to hold office in the king's hall.[11] The group was amorphous. A hard core was certainly in constant, virtually continuous, attendance, but the larger part of the group would vary in composition from season to season and from area to area as the king made progress throughout the country. The Household and the royal Court in its wider sense constituted the central executive government of the realm.

The Witenagemot

The ultimate test of royal authority is whether it is respected in the localities. It requires some manifestation there, either in the person of the king or of his representative. The Household could provide such representatives, but even more, particularly as the kingdom grew in size, the king had to rely more on the cooperation of men with special authority and responsibility in their own localities, above all on the ealdormen or earls as they came to be known under revived Danish influence in the eleventh century. Contemporary homilists recognized this. Ælfric stated the position fairly when he wrote:

10 L.M. Larson, *The King's Household in England before the Norman Conquest* (Madison, 1904).
11 *EHD* i, no 51, pp. 468–70. Lieb.i., pp. 456–7, Geþyncðo, cl.2

Historians who write about kings tell us that ancient kings in former times considered how they might alleviate their burdens, because a single man cannot be everywhere and sustain all things at once, though he might have sole authority (*anweald*). Then the kings appointed ealdormen under them, as support for themselves, and they often sent them to many battles, as it is written in heathen books and in the Bible; and the ealdormen conquered the attacking enemies, as we shall recount some examples about them from Latin books . . . .[12]

The king relied too, increasingly heavily under Edgar and after Edgar's time, on his bishops and his abbots, and on powerful and wealthy thegns with a strong territorial base in one or more shires, bound by special oaths of loyalty (*hold-oaths*). The support of all these types of man and their continuous cooperation could be ensured to some measure institutionally by attendance at royal councils, meetings which became known generally as witenagemots, meetings of wise men, or witans.

The nineteenth century with its preoccupation with parliamentary institutions had much to say about these witans, which were often interpreted as primitive folk-moots, large assemblies in which the democratic instincts of free Germanic peoples were given full expression. Some scholars, but not the great Liebermann who was much more aware of the full complexities than most, talked of the possibility that all ordinary freemen had the right to be present at such assemblies.[13] These views are no longer tenable. Talk of witenagemots has tended to die away, and in its place scholarly emphasis has been put on the royal nature of the councils. It may be that the reaction has been too extreme. The witan was of course a royal council. Yet it could in moments of crisis acquire not only a dignity but a function of its own. On the death of a king the process of election was carried through in the witan. It is true that this often amounted to no more than formal acquiescence in decisions made elsewhere, but nevertheless the identification of a proper place for such acts was in itself a matter of some significance. Those who acquired the throne by conquest or by physical strength were most careful to gain the general assent of the witan. Promulgation of law codes was carried out in the witan, and the ecclesiastical members present were responsible for framing in writing the results of the deliberations on matters of law. Indeed the responsibility taken on by, for example, Archbishop Wulfstan, in the reigns of Ethelred and Cnut for drawing up in publishable form the dooms decided on in the witan was altogether

---

12 *The Homilies of the Anglo-Saxon Church,* ed. B. Thorpe (London, 1844–6), ii, p. 728.
13 F. Liebermann, *The National Assembly in the Anglo-Saxon Period* (Halle, 1913), p. 39. E.A. Freeman, *The Norman Conquest* (London, 1867-79), i, pp. 105-8 etc.

remarkable. Advice was asked on all important ecclesiastical questions, and it was customary for the bishops and abbots and other prominent members of the ecclesiastical order on occasions to meet apart and to deliberate. Some statements of law such as the second code of Edgar and the first code of Cnut were completely ecclesiastical in content.[14] It must have been difficult to distinguish between the body that drew up these codes and a formal national ecclesiastical synod, but the age found no difficulty here. The king was present, not necessarily at the deliberations but at the moment when the law was declared, and the body of councillors around him constituted a witan. Any governmental act of more than routine significance, such as for example the solemn declaration of a royal will, would take place in a witan. And charters testifying to grants of land to laymen or ecclesiastics would also be authenticated in a witan, and indeed these charters provide an indispensable guide to the very varied composition of the witans. Some of the splendid 'British' assemblies of the reign of Athelstan contained at least a hundred persons, ranging from Welsh kings to humble thegns and priests. The total assembly, when reasonable allowance is made for soldiers, retainers and camp-followers, must have amounted on such occasions to the best part of 500 people. On other occasions, however, only a handful of councillors are known to have been present though the full authority of the king with the consent of his witan was being exercised. The ecclesiastical element, especially in the person of the archbishops, was normally important, though it was possible for a king's council to meet with no ecclesiastical element at all. Sir Frank Stenton concluded in his analysis of the composition of the witan that the one consistent element was the presence of 'noblemen under direct allegiance to the king'.[15] These would include substantial thegns as well as ealdormen and other officers. The witan served in this way to bring what a later age would have recognized as 'a sense of constitutionalism' into the Old-English monarchy.

We know a little of the places at which the witans met, information which is helpful in relation to problems concerning the nature of the monarchy and royal government because it tells in detail of the mobility of the king and his court. Witans were recorded at more than fifty places between 900 and 1066, nearly all of them in the south of England with only isolated examples, as at Nottingham in 934 (on a royal expedition north) or at Lincoln in 1045, to remind us of the wider range of the English monarchy. London was outstandingly the most

---

14   *EHD* i, no. 40, pp. 431-3, Edgar II, and no. 49, pp. 454-5 (part of Cnut I). Lieb. i, pp. 194-201 and 278-307.
15   F.M. Stenton, *Anglo-Saxon England*, pp. 550-51.

favoured spot, especially later in the period, and nine meetings were recorded there between 1044 and 1066. Winchester was also well favoured, but only two meetings were recorded at Gloucester (in 964 and 1051). After the Norman Conquest William the Conqueror chose Winchester, Westminster, and Gloucester as the three regular places to hold his councils at Easter, Whitsun, and Christmas; and it is exceedingly likely that he was generalizing past practice and in typical Norman fashion urbanizing it at the same time. In late Anglo-Saxon England there were many meetings in the West Country, mostly at places that had a direct and immediate association with royal estates, palaces or towns: Axminster, Bath, Calne, Cheddar (in 941, 956, and 968), Chippenham, Cirencester (in 986 and 999), Edington, Malmesbury, Somerton (Penbridge) and Winchcombe were among these places as well as the more distant Exeter. It seems likely that Norman Gloucester served as a more regular meeting place for a West Country witan because it gave reasonable access to men from the midlands and the north along the route of the Severn valley. In the political crisis of 1051 the forces of King Edward and Godwin were in confrontation at Beverstone not far from Gloucester, and the arrival of men from the northern earldoms decided the day in favour of the king who was, as the Anglo-Saxon Chronicler tells us, able to hold a witan at Gloucester.[16] In the same way Winchester in more urbanized Norman fashion served as a centre in place of the numerous meeting places recorded for the witan in the mid-Thames valley and places south, again mostly places with a special royal connection: Abingdon, Amesbury, Andover, Aylesford, Cookham, either or both the Dorchesters, Faversham, King's Enham, Southampton, and Wantage, even Oxford itself (1015, 1035 and 1065), Kirtlington, and Woodstock. London was always *sui generis*, and there are fewer records of meetings at small places within easy reach of London than one might expect; the special role of Westminster reduced and destroyed the prestige that at times seemed to be accruing around Chelsea and Kingston. The political and military situation was alone responsible for the meeting of witans at Olney (in 1016) and at Berkhamstead (in 1066). It seems very likely that the Conqueror gave more rigid institutional form to what had long been royal custom. An itinerary which led the king to consult with his great men in the West Country in winter, in the centre of old Wessex from the Middle Thames to the Solent, from Oxford to Winchester in the spring (at Easter), and at London or Westminster in the summer (at Whitsun) would seem fully in accord with the practice of the Old-English monarchy. The normal itinerary lay in the south where the bulk of royal followers and royal estates

16 *ASCh* 1051, ed. D. Whitelock, pp. 117-19.

were to be found. The major oddity is the apparent weakness of institutional life at this level in the Severn valley, a reminder perhaps of the extraordinary strength of the bishop of Worcester in the western Mercian lands. Witans were held in fact only infrequently outside the bounds of Wessex, the Cotswolds and the Thames valley.

The favoured sites for meeting in late-Saxon England were indeed royal palaces, royal towns, villages and hunting seats. Excavations at Cheddar have helped to give a vivid picture of one such site.[17] A substantial timbered hall, some 78 feet in length and 20 feet at its widest point was surrounded by a whole complex of other timber buildings, chapels, kitchens, mills, smithies and storehouses. This royal palace complex was reorganized in the first half of the tenth century when the great hall was replaced by a new hall, 60 feet in length and 28 to 30 feet in external breadth. Secure defences made it by no means an unsuitable conference centre for the mid-tenth century, and the witan met there at least three times between 941 and 968. By this stage, no matter what the custom in earlier centuries, the witan normally met indoors. Bishops and ealdormen were seated. A graphic entry in the Anglo-Saxon Chronicle for 978 told how disaster overcame the witan at Calne when the floor of an upper storey collapsed.[18] Archbishop Dunstan alone remained completely safe, standing upon a beam, but some were very severely injured there and some did not survive it. The meetings of the king's courts at the high festivals of the ecclesiastical year, Christmas, Easter and Whitsun, were the most convenient occasions for the summons of the witan, although a degree of informality and a great deal of flexibility must be allowed for at this period. Careful distinctions between a royal council and a witan are the product of modern scholarly niceness of argument rather than a reflection of tenth-century political practice. William the Conqueror, as the Anglo-Saxon Chronicle tells us, emphasized the special nature of the witans by wearing his crown at these great festivals.[19] The act may have symbolized more than the setting apart of royalty, and may have signified a readiness to deliver judgement. Proceedings could be lengthy. A witan met at Andover in 980 and then moved leisurely to Winchester for the consecration of the new cathedral. In 997 we know that a witan was moved from Calne to Wantage. In the course of the major crisis of 1051 something not unlike an official adjournment was achieved, the witan transferring itself from Gloucester and reassembling eighteen days later in London.[20] The language used in

17 P. Rahtz 'The Saxon and Medieval Palace at Cheddar, Somerset – an Interim Report', *Medieval Archaeology*, 6–7 (1962), pp. 53–66.
18 *ASCh 978.*
19 *ibid.*, 1087.
20 *ibid.*, 1051, ed. D. Whitelock, pp. 119-20.

4 Meeting places of witenagemots in late Anglo-Saxon England.

discussion was English. Failure to answer summons to the witan could be punished by heavy penalties up to the exaction of a man's wergeld or, in case of contumacious repeated refusal, outlawry. The ecclesiastical element was strong and outstanding prelates, notably St Dunstan, archbishop of Canterbury 960—988, and Wulfstan, archbishop of York 1002—1023, played part of their influential political role in the witan. Business of all types was transacted, general, financial and judicial. Nevertheless it remains true that the essence of the witan's work was deliberative and consultative, and in the field of constitutional development and executive government its part was relatively small.

It has been argued with great force and some accuracy that up to the reign of Alfred the shaping of the constitution came from below, and from Alfred to the Normans and beyond from above.[21] Such a view does scanty justice to the achievements of the early Anglo-Saxon kings, but it has a measure of truth. In the tenth and eleventh centuries the kings were still not technically and in the modern sense law-makers, but wider fields of legal activity were coming to be recognized as their preserve. The concern of Athelstan and Edgar with the sup-pression of theft, and Cnut's use of the process of outlawry, merely to take conspicuous examples, point to a sharper appreciation of the royal duty to preserve peace. Social and economic forces helped to throw the responsibility for order yet more decisively on the shoulders of the monarch. The king, in part because of his religious pre-eminence, became the focus of loyalties of the English communities, the symbol to which they turned for the maintenance of peace. The royal relationship with the Church was clear-cut and in no respect is this more obvious than in relation to the witan. He expected to receive advice from his archbishops and bishops and expected them to be pre-sent. Bishops of the southern province were in regular attendance and at times subscribed to charters in set precedence. In the main the kings were pious, very much the self-conscious defenders of Christendom. There is in many fields a surprising lack of differentiation between lay and spiritual. Bishops were councillors. Important ecclesiastical ap-pointments lay in royal hands. Monks elected their abbots, but the royal approval was all-important before the abbot took office. Carol-ingian theocratic ideals were neatly embodied in much of the institu-tional life of these late Old-English kings and their witenagemots.

The Secretariat

The royal Household provided a permanent source of manpower for active royal government in its three principal fields, general literate administration, finance and the administration of justice. In all three considerable advance was made during the Anglo-Saxon period. We deal first with literate administration, with what may be called (although the term is inadequate) the secretariat or writing office.

The secretariat is the most important aspect of Anglo-Saxon central government to the historian both in its own right and because of the value of the records it produced. Evidence for the existence of elaborate and systematic secretarial work connected with the business of government comes from the survival of a large number of land charters and a smaller number of memoranda, wills, writ-charters, writs and other diplomatic instruments. Royal letters, too, should not be disregarded. From the earliest days it was from time to time

---

21   J.E.A. Joliffe, *The Constitutional History of Medieval England* (Oxford, 1939), p. 100.

necessary for letters to be written in the royal name, to the pope, to Frankish kings, to English missions on the continent and there were always clerks available in the royal Household with the special skills needed to compose and pen such letters. Indeed as early as AD 852 one of these clerks, a Frankish scholar named Felix, was specifically referred to by a Frankish abbot as *secretarius* to King Ethelwulf, Alfred's father. Felix was entrusted with the task of looking after the king's letters.[22] The political conditions of the reign of Alfred and of his son Edward the Elder seem (to say the least) to have slowed developments in the secretariat. Production of permanent record, of charters, was as much part of its duty as the writing of ephemera, but there is a dearth of charters from these reigns, and it is not until the 930s that the series begins again in truly significant numbers, Well over a thousand documents have survived from the last 140 years or so of Anglo-Saxon England, of varying authenticity it is true, but providing a formidable testimony to the use of written record in their sheer bulk. They are unique in the Europe of their day, lacking outward sign of validation, seal, autograph cross or subscription, even lacking the name of the scribe.[23] They nevertheless constituted powerful and precious possessions, and it seems likely that by the end of the tenth century a high proportion of the land of England was held by charter, was indeed 'bookland'.

In the early tenth century to judge from surviving documents, a leading part in the drawing up of landgrants was played by men associated with the *scriptorium* at Winchester under Bishop Ælfheah (d. 951), one of the leading figures in the initiation of the Benedictine revival and teacher of St Dunstan and St Ethelwold. The Winchester *scriptorium* was a great training ground, establishing new standards in handwriting and the presentation of documents, but men trained there did not necessarily remain there. Winchester men throughout the ages have not been slow to seek the lush pastures of government service. As the monastic impulse spread, Glastonbury (in the 950s) and Abingdon (in the 960s) also provided writing centres which the king could use, or which could build up their own archives. According to the oldest life of St Dunstan, written between 995 and 1005, King Eadred (946–956) entrusted to Dunstan at Glastonbury all the best of his goods, namely many title-deeds and the ancient treasures of preceding kings, as well as various precious things he had acquired himself, to be faithfully kept in the security of his monastery. Eadred, feeling that he was

---

22 Lupus of Ferrieres, *MGH*, Epist. vi, p. 22, vs. 13. F.M. Stenton, *The Latin Charters of the Anglo-Saxon Period* (Oxford, 1955), pp. 47–8 and references.
23 N.P. Brooks, 'Anglo-Saxon Charters; the Work of the Last Twenty Years', *Anglo-Saxon England* 3 (Cambridge, 1974), pp. 212-14. P.H. Sawyer, *Anglo-Saxon Charters*, RHS (1968) is indispensable.

about to die and wishing to distribute his precious goods before he died, ordered Dunstan and other keepers of the royal treasures to bring them to him, and Dunstan dutifully assembled the treasure in packs on horseback and brought them to the royal Court.[24] The interest of the passage is that landbooks were reckoned among the treasures of the kingdom, that copies were entrusted to the new monastic houses and that the country was safe enough in the mid tenth century, more so than in early or late, to entrust precious goods to monastic keeping.

Much has been made of the activities of the new monks to underline the fact that there is so little evidence (some say none) to indicate that Anglo-Saxon diplomas were drafted or written in 'what might be called even loosely a central royal secretariat, that is to say in a single organized department staffed with scribes who specialized in royal business.'[25] In fact, evidence at least for some significant central activity is not negligible; and helpful though it has been to stress the role of the beneficiary in the preservation and to some extent the production of surviving diplomas, the pendulum may have swung too far from the centre. An interesting account from the twelfth-century *Liber Eliensis* tells us that from the reign of Edgar until the Norman Conquest the functions of royal chancellor were discharged in rotation by the abbots of St Augustine's Canterbury, Ely and Glastonbury, each acting for four months at a time.[26] This is not likely to be literally true, but it may well reflect reasonable traditions about the way from time to time the secretariat attempted to increase its efficiency. Recruitment from favoured monastic houses and use of local resources must not however disguise the fact that the chief source of secretarial activity continued to be clerks in attendance on the king, some more or less permanent, others organized on a rota basis, and all particularly active at the time of the great councils, the witans.

It is important to remember, however, that acts of government in the tenth century tended to be oral, authenticated by good witness and pledge. Our modern minds lay more emphasis to the written record because such record provides almost the only way we can begin to know what went on in the tenth-century world. This is also true of the legal situation. Dooms (judgements or statements of general rules) were dictated by the king in solemn witans, and nine times out of ten the actual recording in writing was left in a surprisingly casual way to

---

24 *EHD* i, no. 234, p. 900; W. Stubbs, *Memorials of St Dunstan*, RS (1874), pp. 3–52.

25 P. Chaplais, 'The Origin and Authenticity of the Royal Anglo-Saxon Diploma', *J. Soc. Archivists* 3 (1965-69), pp. 48-61, especially pp. 58-61. Also 'The Anglo-Saxon Chancery: from the Dipolma to the Writ,' *ibid.*, pp. 160–76. N.P. Brooks, 'Anglo-Saxon Charters', pp. 215–19 provides an excellent introduction to the problems.

26 *Liber Eliensis*, ed. E.O. Blake (Camden series, RHS, London, 1962), p. 146.

ecclesiastics and to individual or local enterprise. Landbooks (i.e. charters) were more sophisticated and the exact form and method of recording more important. They were held to be among the treasures of the kingdom both as far as the king himself was concerned and as far as the favoured individuals in whose favour the grants were made. It is probable that even now we underestimate the impact of the Benedictine reformation on the whole apparatus of government, and it is in this respect that the Ely traditions are important. The new abbeys, often stoutly built of stone, provided splendid repositories and places where charters and copies of charters could be made. It is understandable that experiments should be made, particularly during the reigns of Eadred and Edgar, with a more systematic drafting of charters and that such experiments should be associated with the new abbeys. Clerks attached to a peripatetic Court would be glad to use the facilities of a *scriptorium,* indeed would be expected to use them and to draw on local help when pressure of business transacted at the witan demanded quick activity. The fact that beneficiaries increasingly came to draw up the written record of landgrants should not be allowed, however, to mask the fact that the mainspring of action still rested with the royal Court, nor should it obscure the fact that a writing office still existed with the power to standardize formulae and rubrics in the charters. From time to time, according to changes in personnel and personal circumstances that we can never hope to recover, it became expedient for royal clerks to remain at a fixed point for a long period. Eadred's will referred to his mass priests whom he had set up in his *reliquium* (i.e. the sanctuary where he kept his relics.)[27] Documents were certainly kept with the relics in the royal sanctuary during the reign of Ethelred, though it is a forged charter which purports to be written *per calamum et atramentum et manum notarii et scrinarii Ethelredi regis Anglorum,* 'by the pen and ink and hand of the notary and *scrinarius* of Ethelred, king of the English.' A *scrinarius* was one who looked after precious religious goods, shrines, as well as writings, and the term could be glossed *cancellarius* by an Anglo-Saxon scribe. Ethelred himself, not altogether unexpectedly when the mass of charter evidence for his reign is considered, was prepared to show favour to his scribes. He made over a substantial grant of land at Brighthampton, Aston Bampton and Lew in Oxfordshire to his *scriptor, Ælfwine,* in 984.[28] The whole secretariat was still

27 Harmer, *Select Documents,* pp. 34–5; *ælcan minra mæssepreosta þe ic gesette hæbbe in to minum reliquium.* They were to receive fifty mancuses of gold and five pounds in silver, in all probability a little less than a half the sum due to each of the bishops, i.e. a long hundred of 120 mancuses of gold.
28 D. Whitelock, *Anglo-Saxon Wills* (Cambridge, 1930), pp. 152 and 164: *Anglo-Saxon Charters,* ed. P. Sawyer, no. 1380; no. 853 (Ælfwine, *scriptor*).

surely fluid as late as the reign of the Confessor, but some of the later familiar institutional moulds were already hardening. Royal treasure, relics, written documents would be kept at Winchester and in the course of time at Westminster. A golden road to preferment to a bishopric lay through the royal chapel, increasingly so in the last half century of Anglo-Saxon England as the initial fervour of the monastic revival eased. Among those clerks at the royal chapel were literate, capable men, well fitted to supervise the work of an active secretariat. The St Albans tradition was by no means foolish and may have been accurate when it claimed that its one time abbot Ælfric, later archbishop of Canterbury, had been King Ethelred's *cancellarius* before he entered the monastic life.[29] Royal control of format, royal custody of documents, the special prestige of royal clerks and priests must outweigh in institutional importance the part played by draftsmen and recorders among beneficiary abbeys and churches. Charters remained important. In a *locus classicus* the archbishop of Canterbury, Lyfing, grumbled that he had many charters, if only they were worth anything.[30] Such grumbles were probably no more significant than those of the modern shareholder who on occasions laments that his paper record of equitable holdings in this or that wealthy financial corporation is not worth the paper it is printed on.

Charters were formal, elaborate and presumably expensive documents. Originally at least, they were not in themselves grants of land, but record of such grants, supplements to the memory of mortal men. The actual physical transmission of land was a matter of oral declaration by the proper authority, king and witan, coupled with a symbolic physical act, the handing over of a twig or the cutting of a sod of earth, or the placing of a knife (or a charter) on an altar. The charter, once drawn up, could then serve as an effective title-deed, and was transferred to the new owner with the estate. New monasteries founded in the late tenth or eleventh centuries could possess charters dating back many generations. Charters were adduced as proof of right. In the Ely records it was stated bluntly that it was more fitting that he who had the charter (cyrograph) should have the estate than he who had not. We hear of men handing over title deeds as completion of a transaction.[31] Land was not given without rights, and a charter

---

29 Keynes, p. 136, fn. 177, comment on similar references to chancellors.

30 F.E. Harmer, *Anglo-Saxon Writs* (Manchester, 1952), pp. 181–2: a writ of King Cnut in which the archbishop was reported to have said of the king that *he freolsas genoge hæfde gyf hi aht forstoden* (he had charters of freedom enough if they were good for anything).

31 Harmer, *Select Documents,* xviii, pp. 60-3; in the great Fonthill dispute, Helmstan was at one stage given the opportunity of bringing the title-deeds (*ðon bocon* – the books) forward in support of his claim and at another stage to have given the writer the title-deed (*ða boc*) to an estate.

also records a grant of immunity, vague but well understood, an immunity from contribution to the foodrent of the king, from the obligation to feed and entertain an ealdorman or royal messenger, from building work or cartage. A charter was an open document, unsealed, though with the cross or mark or sign of the king, the bishops, abbots, ealdormen, thegns and other dignitaries as witness to the transaction. Its importance as a creator of privilege as well as a conveyancing instrument made it unlikely that any powerful king would be willing to allow a *scriptorium* not under his direct control to assume complete responsibility for production.

A good example of a standard Old-English charter occurs in a Worcester document, printed in full in the early eighteenth century, though afterwards destroyed in a fire at Lincoln's Inn in 1752. It is a grant by King Edgar of land at Kineton, Warwickshire in 969.[32] After a short religious proem Edgar grants ten hides at Kineton to his faithful thegn Ælfwald as an eternal inheritance so that he may enjoy it in his lifetime with all its advantages, meadows, pasture and woods, and afterwards leave it unburdened to heirs of his choice. The estate was to be free of all earthly service except the three that were (in fact) always reserved: military service and the restoration of bridges and fortresses. There follows a standard commination (indeed one could almost say fulmination) against anyone presuming to infringe the terms of the grant, threatening excommunication and eternal damnation. Up to this point the document has been in Latin but the substantive part now concludes, an increasingly common practice in the tenth and early eleventh centuries, with a detailed description of the bounds in Anglo-Saxon:

> from Wellesbourne to the gully, from the gully to the ditch, from the ditch on the boundary to the paved road, from the paved road to the *morth-hlaw* (murder mound), from the *morth-hlaw* to the foul pit, from the foul pit to the springs, from the springs to the boundary of the Mercians, from the boundary of the Mercians to *Succan-pit,* from *Succan-pit* to *Grundlinga* brook along the stream, from that stream to Fidestan, from that stone to *Hragra thorn,* from *Hragra thorn* back to Wellesbourne.

Such close detailed local knowledge shows the hand of local men and of the beneficiary. Nevertheless the set form of proem, substance of grant, immunity, reservation of 'three necessities' and commination underline the royal nature of the act and this is further reinforced by the subscriptions which include Edgar, king of the English, with the consent of his advisers, Dunstan, archbishop of Canterbury, six bishops, including Ethelwold of Winchester and Oswald of

32 *EHD* i, no. 113, pp. 563-4.

Worcester, six abbots, six ealdormen and twelve king's thegns. Ælfwald received a similar grant at Apsley in Bedfordshire on the same occasion. The record was preserved because the charters ultimately found their way into the Worcester archive, but it is essentially a secular record. Ecclesiastical preponderance among benefactors in surviving documents is a consequence of methods of preservation and can distort the true picture if we take such preponderance as a sympton of tenurial practice.

The view that the secretariat within the royal Household played an active and important part in the production of charters has been strengthened recently by the work of Dr Simon Keynes.[33] In a series of penetrating studies, based on careful examination of archival practice and of witness lists he has been able to point to two possible conclusions of the utmost importance to the general historian, namely that charters were often (possibly most often) drawn up at meetings of councils, of witenagemots and that where responsibility for the drawing up of charters was delegated there has often remained evidence of the royal interest in the form of a written instrument or reference to a written instrument. The evidence for production at witans during 956 is particularly strong and valuable. The sixty or so diplomas that have survived from that year fall into groups that suggest meetings of the witan in January, February and November with either one or two intermediate sessions. The first group is particularly illuminating since diplomas were produced on a single occasion by a single agency for estates in Berkshire, Hampshire, Somerset and Wiltshire; and these diplomas were preserved in the archives of no fewer than six religious houses. No one would claim absolute uniformity in this matter of charter production, but Dr Keynes's second proposition also points in the direction of central control. Dr Harmer's comment that the delegation of responsibility for production of a landbook in the eleventh century could require the authorization of a royal writ assumes fresh significance in the light of Dr Keynes's enquiries.[34] Close cooperation with the beneficiary was often expedient and indeed often quite indispensable. Absolute reliance on the beneficiary was quite another matter. It may well be that recent convincing and helpful work on the role of the beneficiary has led to some natural confusion between the beneficiary as producer and the beneficiary as repository: the two roles could coincide but did not have to do so. The king needed to have ready access to records concerning the transmission of land. So much depended on the status of landholders and land holding. Military service, the payments of dues and renders could vary

33 S.D. Keynes, *The Diplomas of King Æthelred, 'the Unready', 978–1016.* (Cambridge, 1980).
34 Harmer, *Anglo-Saxon Writs*, pp. 39–41. Keynes, pp. 79–83.

with status: it was important to know what was bookland, especially bookland newly created, and what not. A complete archive was impossible, but it was exceedingly likely that the royal Court would keep some tangible record of major land transactions completed by charter.

Such charters provided good if cumbersome title to land and rights and the custom grew for them to be drawn up in duplicate or in triplicate, the one copy to rest with the beneficiary the other or others to rest ideally with the king and with an impartial bishop or other trustworthy man. The parchment would be cut in an irregular fashion so that it could be seen at a glance by the fit of the separate pieces if the charters were indeed authentic. The documents so divided were known as chirographs, and the cut in the parchment sometimes ran through the word chirograph or cyrograph written along the point of division.[35] Often charters, for convenience in consultation, were endorsed with a brief summary of their contents. An elaborate grant of Cornish lands by Cnut to the bishop of Cornwall has an explanatory paragraph in Old English showing that this was a ratification of arrangements made by Cnut's predecessor Edmund Ironside, and a simple Old-English endorsement:

> This is the title-deed of the lands at Landrake and Tinnel, of the four hides which King Cnut granted by charter to Bishop Burhwold in eternal inheritance.[36]

The history of diplomatic studies in the Old-English period does not, however, deal solely with the great Latin charters. There is also a solid stratum of government activity in the vernacular, and there survives an impressive number of wills, memoranda and allied documents to show some degree of sophistication in the art of authenticating decision and ensuring continuity. Most important and in some senses most complicated of all, is the evolution of the sealed writ, in the eyes of many the supreme Anglo-Saxon achievement in the field of government.

In one sense the history of the writ has been unnecessarily complicated because of the tendency of historians to associate it too closely with the solemn charters, to such an extent that we have grown ac-

---

35 Some good judges believe they may have been an innovation as early as the ninth century in the Anglo-Saxon world: *Anglo-Saxon Wills*, ed. D. Whitelock, pp. 150-1 with references to the work of Bresslau. Æthelred's confirmation of the will of Æthelric (*ibid.*, pp. 46–7) was written and read before the king and council and witnessed by the great men gathered there. Three of the resulting documents (*gewrita*) were kept, one at Christchurch, one in the royal sanctuary, and one by the widow.

36 *EHD* i, no. 131, pp. 597-8: *Anglo-Saxon Charters*, ed. P. Sawyer, no. 951. P. Chaplais, 'The Authenticity of the Royal Anglo-Saxon Diplomas of Exeter', *BIHR* 39 (1966), pp. 21–2 argues for a later date for this document (probably the third quarter of the eleventh century.

customed to referring to a whole class of documents of the eleventh and early twelfth centuries as 'writ-charters'. It is true that the writ came to replace the charter in some instances as the best evidence of good title to land. It was simpler, easier to keep, and more difficult to forge. It did not replace the charter completely, though the use of the solemn landbook (as the charter is often called), with its ponderous set forms and lists of signatures, grew increasingly infrequent until in the course of the twelfth century, save for specialized cases and in specialized instances, it virtually disappeared under the impact of Norman chancery practice. The writ was however both more and less than the charter, strictly complementary to it rather than a substitute. The process of booking land was finite, and once estates had been booked there was no need to repeat the process until or unless the charters wore out. The charter had permanent effect on the status of the land. The writ was different in nature, carrying the authentic stamp of immediate royal authority though at the same time lacking the solemnity of the landbook. It also covered a wider range of governmental activity. Two examples, drawn from Miss Harmer's magnificent collection of writs, will help to illustrate its nature, range and purpose.[37]

The first is taken from a Westminster cartulary, known as the Westminster Domesday. The text has been copied and modernized in the cartulary but it reads:

> King Edward sends friendly greetings to Abbot Edwin and Ælfgæt the sheriff. And I inform you that I have given to Teinfrith my 'church-wright' the land at Shepperton, with sake and with soke, exempt from scot and tax in hundred and in shire. And I will not permit anyone by any means to do him wrong. But let him have infangenetheof and flymenafyrmth.

The second is an immensely important document from a Worcester source. Miss Harmer thought that in its existing form (Brit.Library, Add.Charter 19802) it is an original writ of 1062 that was written (and sealed) by the clerks of King Edward's secretariat. It is a matter for comment that the writ form was considered proper to publicize a matter as central to the political life of the country as the appointment of a bishop of Worcester:

> King Edward sends friendly greetings to Earl Harold and Earl Ælfgar and all the thegns in Worcestershire and Gloucestershire and Warwickshire. And I inform you that I have granted to the monk Wulfstan the bishopric of Worcester with sake and soke, toll and team, within

---

37 Harmer, *Anglo-Saxon Writs*, no. 87 and no. 116.

borough and without, as fully and completely in all things as ever any of his predecessors possessed it. Therefore I will not permit anyone in any matter to do him wrong, or to deprive him of any of the things he ought lawfully to have for his bishopric.

The nature of the writ stands out clearly from these two examples. It was a letter under seal, a notification to the royal officers in the localities that such and such a thing had been done, and by implication a royal order to them to see to what executive action was needed to ensure that the royal will was carried out. The Worcester example was addressed to the two earls, Harold and Ælfgar, who were the most important laymen to have interest in the diocese and in the three shires within the diocese. Writs were in the vernacular, in Anglo-Saxon, and were intended to be read publicly in the shire court as an impressive witness to a governmental act. They contained a threat and exhortation not to do anything contrary to the royal will. Their simple concise standard basic structural form suggests firm and continuous direction from the centre. Some were certainly drawn up by local beneficiaries, but credit must belong to the royal clerks for standardizing what became a principal means of making known the king's will in the localities.

The writ has a long line of descent, certainly from the time of Alfred and probably much earlier. There is an important reference in the Alfredian translation of the Soliloquies of St Augustine to a royal letter delivered under seal, or possibly authenticated by an accompanying seal.[38] The formulæ of extant eleventh-century writs bear a strong verbal resemblance to the opening words of Alfred's preface to his translation of Gregory the Great's Pastoral Care (in which 'he bids greet bishop Wærferth in these words lovingly and in friendly fashion, and bids you make known that . . . '), but these similarities do not necessarily prove a continuous institutional life for the writs as we know them in the eleventh century. Ethelred certainly was accustomed to sending orders, probably verbal orders, to shire moots authenticated by a seal. Cnut also issued verbal orders which were again written down by interested parties. Full proof of the issue of writs under seal does not come until the reign of Edward the Confessor. It was then that writs seem first to have been sealed with what is called a patent seal, that is to say sealed in such fashion that the seal did not have to be broken in order that the letter or order or writ could be read. The result was that the writing itself could be preserved as evidence. Some scholars consider that it was not indeed until after the Conquest that the writ came into its own, largely as a means of proving good title

38 ed. W. Endter, *König Alfreds des Grossen Bearbeitung der Soliloquien des Augustinus*, Bibl. der Ang.-Sächs. Prosa, xi (Hamburg, 1922), p. 24.

to land and rights against the Conqueror.[39] Evolution of the standard written form of the writ is another proof of a certain sophistication in the secretariat. But Dr Harmer was able to print 120 examples in her standard edition and more have been added to the list since then. Only a small fraction of the number issued can have survived. The issue of sealed writs demanded a relatively large permanent staff in the royal Household capable of dealing with business in the vernacular speedily but efficiently, and capable too of the diplomatic practice associated with the sealing of documents and keeping good guard on the royal seal, the mark of authenticity.

Interest in the practice of sealing documents has quickened recently with the discovery at Sittingbourne in Kent of an ivory seal matrix with the portrait of a man brandishing a sword and the inscription *Sigillum Wulfrici*. It resembles other presumably lay seals from Wallingford (ivory) and Weeke in Hampshire (bronze) and has led to the belief that many prominent laymen by the time of Ethelred possessed seals of their own[40] though as Dr Keynes has said, 'to assume that they were used for sealing and authenticating written documents would involve some wishful thinking.' At the royal level possession of means of authenticating the royal will was essential and associated closely with the growing tendency to set the king apart and to emphasize his separate and unique position. Examples of the use of representations of a ruler sitting in majesty and bearing the symbols of royal authority have been traced back into the fourth century AD but in the post-Roman world in the West the German emperors in the late tenth century appear to have been the first to use the *majestas* style. King Cnut may have used a two-faced seal, possibly signifying his double kingdom of England and Denmark, but work on the seal of Edward the Confessor has suggested that it was modelled on contemporary German Imperial prototypes rather than in direct succession to the seal of Cnut. The king is portrayed in full face seated on his throne, crowned, with beard and moustache, dressed in an undertunic. He bears the royal insignia, on the obverse a sceptre, topped with a trefoil, and an orb, on the reverse a long sceptre, topped with a bird, and a sword resting on his left shoulder. The legend on both sides is

'Sigillum Eadwardi Anglorum basilei'.

The seal is large, nearly three inches in diameter, and is two-faced, and

---

39 T.A. Heslop, 'English Seals from the Mid-Ninth Century to 1100', *J. Brit. Arch. Ass.* 133 (1980), p. 11 points out that Edward the Confessor, King William and Odo of Bayeux are the three people mentioned in Domesday Book as issuing writs as evidence of tenure. G. Barraclough, 'The Anglo-Saxon Writ', *History* 39 (1954), pp. 193–215.

40 Keynes, *The Diplomas of King Æthelred*, pp. 138-40. He notes (p. 139 and footnote) that the Sittingbourne seal, described in 1977, may have been out of the ground some time.

was apparently fixed to the lower edge of the document by a strip of parchment cut from the document itself. It is now virtually certain that there was only one Great Seal at the time of the Confessor, and that all others attributed to him were, in fact, falsifications. Edward was the first king to strike a coinage in which he was portrayed seated on his throne, and it has been suggested that the *majestas* coin of Edward and his seal may have been engraved by the same man, possibly by the German, Theoderic, who is known to have been a prominent gold and silversmith at work in England during the reign of the Confessor.[41]

For all the reservations that some scholars make concerning the writ, it remains an impressive testimony to the coherence of late Old-English government. Whereas previous rulers had to content themselves with oral instructions and to rely on oral transmission of orders by trusted individuals, buttressed by the physical reminders of the royal presence embodied in his seal, or a ring or some other recognizable token, it was now possible for a ruler to have drafted for him, normally by royal clerks (though he would not object if local ecclesiastics did the job for him), a writ authenticated by his known and distinctive seal attached to the document. Most of the surviving writs can indeed be described as writ-charters, a term to which we have raised some objection, but it seems quite certain that a large number of writ-mandates were also issued. They have not survived for the simple reason that their purpose was immediate, to convey precise written instructions to men capable of carrying out an order in the localities, and they were presumably destroyed when their purpose was fulfilled. A government capable of maintaining continuous written contact with local shire moots was advanced for its day in Western Europe. As far as can be judged from present evidence (though the fluidity of terminology and the weight given, for example, to some oddities in the glosses, may yet alter the picture) there was no permanent officer about the Court or royal chapel regularly known as a chancellor before 1066 and therefore, it has been argued, in the strict sense no chancery.[42] There was, however, a clerk or group of clerks responsible for the custody and use of the great seal; and there was a writing office capable of initiating set forms of unsealed charter and sealed writ. If much of the routine work was done at the ecclesiastical *scriptoria* of cathedrals and abbeys it would still seem wrong to deny credit to the royal clerks who initiated and succeeded in maintaining a standard form and a continuity in format, type and calligraphy for the charter

---

41 Harmer, *Anglo-Saxon Writs*, pp. 92-103; cf. also *The Facsimiles of English Royal Writs to AD 1100* ed. T.A.M. Bishop and P. Chaplais, (Oxford, 1957).
42 Stenton, *Anglo-Saxon England*, 353; but Keynes assembles powerful evidence in favour of the possibility that the office of *cancellarius* was known in Anglo-Saxon England, *The Diplomas of King Æthelred*, pp. 146-53.

and the writ. Under royal direction, at the court, in cathedrals and in abbeys, an increasing weight of governmental business was ceasing to be oral and was becoming literate.

Financial Organization–Treasury, Taxes and Coinage

Historians hesitate and debate the use of the word 'chancery' in late Anglo-Saxon England and similar hesitations also occur over the use of the term 'treasury'. In a fine phrase a recent writer described the origins of the English treasury as 'mysterious as the migration of eels' and Warren Hollister in a very perceptive essay confessed that there were times when he was tempted to turn from treasury origins to the simpler problem of eel migration[43]! Known facts are few. Chamberlains, men who looked after the king's raiment or his relics, *hordere*, men busy in the Household, in the royal chamber or wardrobe, all can be shown from time to time to have responsibility in financial matters, but there was no officer solely in charge of the royal treasury on a permanent basis at a fixed point before 1066. Some concentration and specialization in financial expertise certainly occurred. Royal treasure was kept at Winchester from at least the early eleventh century, and one of Edward the Confessor's financial officers was known as Odo of Winchester. It was generally believed in the twelfth century that the financial attributes of the Lower Exchequer with its basic function of storing royal money and treasure had its roots deep in the pre-Conquest period. The Court was peripatetic, needed a certain flexibility both in the receipt of revenues, fines and dues, and also in the expenditure of moneys for campaigning or for ordinary routine needs, but also needed a safe store-house or store-houses for surplus treasures. Winchester emerged as the chief of these centres, but one should not expect it to be exclusive. Administration, collection of routine renders and returns was conducted on a shire basis. Strong houses, royal manors, church towers, presumably in some areas the new and thriving Benedictine abbeys, would provide suitable local centres. A surprising amount of silver was in circulation in the eleventh century, capable of being weighed, tested and assayed. It is reasonable to believe that officers capable of carrying out such tasks were present at the royal Court, in the Household or the chamber or settled at Winchester or suitable comparable centres; and that all was not left to the local moneyers at their mints. But until further archaeological evidence turns up to support inference from the numismatic side it would be wrong to suggest that there was more than

---

43 C. Warren Hollister, 'The Origins of the English Treasury', *EHR* 93 (1978), p. 262, quoting Henry Roseveare, *The English Treasury* (London, 1969).

a tendency to concentrate financial business at a fixed centre or centres complementary to the activities and subject to the authority of the still undifferentiated royal Court and Household.

We move to firmer ground when we state that there was a long tradition of financial organization in Anglo-Saxon England. From earliest days, as we have seen, it was customary for renders to be paid to the king according to a well understood system of assessment. In the tenth and eleventh centuries these traditional renders continued to be paid but sink in importance by the side of the increasingly onerous burden of the geld, a tax on land levied according to hidage, a land-tax that worked. The resurgent monarchy of the tenth century evolved its own means and methods of making this imposition efficient. Regional peculiarities persisted. For example in East Anglia, vills paid a stated number of pence as geld when £1 was paid from the hundred as a whole. The vills were further grouped into blocks, known as leets, which represented units of equal or very nearly equal assessment within the hundred. The hundred of Thinghoe in Suffolk was divided into twelve such leets, the town of Sudbury representing three leets or a quarter of that particular hundred: each leet contributed ls. 8d. when the hundred paid £1.[44] Elsewhere for the most part geld was levied territorially. Villages contributed according to their assessed hidage, often in units of five over much of the south and west, that is to say English England, and according to assessed carucage or ploughlands, often in units of six over much of the land settled by the Danes, the Danelaw. This arrangement of assessment according to five-hide units is disguised in our great source, Domesday Book, because of the tenurial feudal pattern imposed on the Domesday material in the Book itself. Villages have to be reconstructed from the entries in several fiefs. Nevertheless five-hide units have been discovered in Middlesex, Hertfordshire, Surrey, Wiltshire, Devon, Berkshire, Buckinghamshire, Oxfordshire, Worcestershire, Bedfordshire, Huntingdonshire, and Northamptonshire. Six-carucate units appeared in Yorkshire, Lincolnshire. the land between Ribble and Mersey, Derbyshire, Nottinghamshire, Leicestershire and Rutland.[45] There were also special terms of assessment in other parts of the country; in Kent, for example, where the unit was not the hide but the *sulung* or double hide, and in Northumbria where elaborate systems based on foodrents and on Celtic customs were practised. Assessment was generally territorial, but for sake of convenience it became customary for geld in many areas to be collected by landlords, and by the end of the period it

44 D.C. Douglas, *The Social Structure of Medieval East Anglia* (Oxford, 1927), especially pp. 209-10, and the introduction to *Feudal Documents from the Abbey of Bury St Edmunds*, Brit. Acad., Records of Social and Economic History, VIII (London, 1932).
45 Round, *Feudal England*, pp. 44-69.

is very difficult to disentangle the original clear pattern of five-hide and six-carucate units. Only in the important, if somewhat isolated, County Hidage and the Northamptonshire Geld Roll is it possible to see what was in the royal servants' minds in the first instance. The County Hidage, a list prepared in the form of a rough governmental memorandum, set out its estimate for the tax on thirteen of the English shires probably relating to a date in the early eleventh century.[46] Six of the estimates correspond exactly with the number of hundreds within the shire at the time of Domesday Book, and eight correspond closely to the recorded hidage in Domesday Book itself. There are discrepancies and variations as well as agreement, and the one certain lesson is that considerable flexibility was possible in the assessment laid on a shire in late Anglo-Saxon England. Northampton provides a particularly illuminating example because of the survival of the Northamptonshire Geld Roll from the early years of the reign of William I.[47] According to the County Hidage Northamptonshire was assessed to the geld at 3,200 hides and yet Domesday Book allowed for considerably less than half that hidage (1,356 hides). The Geld Roll gives information that suggests an initial 3,200 hides for Northamptonshire, though the figure has dropped to 2,663½ in its own account. The waste and devastation caused just before the Conquest probably explains the beneficial terms that were made with the county in the reign of King William. It is clear that responsibility for the apportionment of hidage was transmitted downwards from the shire to the smaller units of the hundreds or wapentakes, and it may be that assessment to tax in terms of hidage was a basic element in mens' minds during the actual process of the creation of those territorial units. It is also likely, as we shall see later, that the decisive steps were taken in this process of territorialization and clarification of financial burdens during the reign of Edward the Elder and steadily extended over the rest of the country as West-Saxon political domination itself extended its range. Further impetus was given to these aspects of financial experience by the grim business of buying-off the Dane. In the 980s Scandinavian attacks, quiescent for a generation, started again, reaching a critical danger point in the early 990s. Byrhtnoth, the ealdorman of Essex, was killed with the greater part of his hearthtroop at the battle of Maldon, and the decision was taken — probably at the instigation of Archbishop Sigeric — to pay the tribute the Danes

46 There is an acute discussion of the County Hidage in P.H. Sawyer, *From Roman Britain to Norman England* (London, 1978), pp. 228-9. He gives evidence to indicate reasons for confidence in the figures of the Hidage, to show examples of shire assessment related to the size of the *burh*, and to illustrate how assessments could be changed.
47 ed. A.J. Robertson, *Anglo-Saxon Charters* (Cambridge, 1939), pp. 230-6; V.H. Galbraith, *Domesday Book, its Place in Administrative History* (Oxford, 1974), pp. 92-5.

demanded in the hope that they would go away.[48] For a period of more than a quarter of a century, culminating in the vast sum levied by the Danish king Cnut in 1018, England paid huge quantities of silver to its Scandinavian attackers. In all £134,000 is recorded by the Anglo-Saxon Chronicle as having passed out of English possession between 991 and 1012. In 1018 when Cnut was firmly in the saddle, £72,000 was exacted from England as tribute, apart from a further £10,500 from London alone.[49] Such exactions were no doubt matters to be lamented, and contemporaries were not slow to make their laments heard. As indices however of the prosperity and of the efficiency of the English community they bear another lesson to the historian. They indicate not only the weight of fluid wealth available in England, but also the capacity to tap it. Machinery for the exaction of Danegeld was assuredly the same as the machinery for the exaction of ordinary geld. There was a further complication when a Danish dynasty ruled in England. From the reign of Cnut to the late 1040s we hear of the payment of a geld, known as heregeld, which constituted payments made for soldiers and sailors. Edward the Confessor in 1049 saved himself a sizeable expense when he paid off most of his ships' crews, threw the burden of naval defence on the Cinque Ports in return for privileges and finally abolished heregeld.[50] It seems highly unlikely that government was sophisticated enough to make subtle distinction between these various gelds. Geld was geld and tax was tax, but the abolition of the specific extra impost for support of ships' crews brought some relief, if possibly at the cost of fatal ultimate weakness. By the last decades of Anglo-Saxon England the geld was almost certainly a regular annual imposition, normally at the rate of 2s. a hide.[51] The system was fluid enough and flexible enough for a practice of beneficial hidation to be established, by which estates, rich in arable and plough-teams, could be assessed at a much lower figure than would normally be considered proper in order to bring special advantage to the owner. To give one extreme example the prosperous estate at Chilcombe in Hampshire, reckoned to be worth all of a hundred hides, was assigned to the bishopric of Winchester and subject to the

---

48 *ASCh*, 991; according to MS C. (D.E.) *þæne rædde geræde Siric arceb. – archbishop Sigeric gave that advice.*
49 *ASCh*, 1018: referred to as *gafol*; tribute.
50 *ASCh* 1050–51: ed. D. Whitelock pp. 115–16: see also below p. 168. The Chronicle (D) is precise about the abolition of *heregeld,* stressing that it had precedence over other taxes and oppressed the people in various ways. It is said to have been instituted by King Ethelred thirty-nine years (Florence of Worcester says 38) before the date of its abolition.
51 V.H. Galbraith, *The Making of Domesday Book* (Oxford, 1961), pp. 97-8: 'I see no reason... to doubt that under William I geld became once more what it had been before 1051, and what it was later, an annual levy which excited notice only when charged at two or three times the usual rate.'

trivial imposition of assessment at the rate of one hide.[52] This privileged assessment has been in force from the days of Ethelred and even possibly as early as the mid-ninth century. The point is important in the history of English government. Land tax, geld, was such a commonplace on the English scene that it could be used in this negative way to benefit favoured individuals or religious houses. Not, of course, that we should extol the assessment system so as to leave the impression that an army of tax collectors was exacting revenue from the whole country in an easy official manner. Sanctions were still primitive. When the men of Worcester failed to pay their taxes in 1041, and killed two of Harthacnut's tax-collectors, the only redress at the king's disposal was to lay waste to all Worcestershire in a savage punitive expedition. According to Florence of Worcester the ravaging which began on 12 November lasted four days and was conducted by the chief earls in the kingdom (including Godwin, Leofric and Siward) and by the royal housecarls. Casualties would have been greater if the citizens and provincials had not shown themselves resolute and won peace from the invaders by a successful defence of a small island in the middle of the Severn.[53] Records in Latin and too-facile generalization sometimes mask the violence that underlay eleventh-century society.

Payment of geld involved the handling of coinage, and it is no coincidence that the well-taxed English should produce the most advanced currency in the Europe of its day — which is one of our best indications of the strength of royal government in England and of the general coherence of the English community. Athelstan in the second quarter of the tenth century decreed that each *burh* should have a mint, and even attempted to limit the number of moneyers:

In Canterbury (there are to be) seven moneyers;
four of the king, two of the bishop, one of the abbot;
in Rochester three, two of the king, one of the bishop; in London eight;
in Winchester six; in Lewes two;
in Hastings one; another at Chichester;
at Southampton two;
at Wareham two; (at Dorchester one); at Exeter two;
at Shaftesbury two; otherwise in the other boroughs one.[54]

Edgar reinforced his uncle's legislation by giving prominence in his own law codes to Athelstan's statement, 'There shall run one coinage

52 ed. M. Biddle, *Winchester in the Early Middle Ages*, pp. 256-8, where the suggestion is made convincingly that the ancient estate of Chilcombe (later known as the manor of Barton) may well have been 'comparable to the *territoria* around certain towns in Gaul in the Merovingian and Carolingian periods.' (p. 257).

53 Florence of Worcester 1041, *MHB*, ed. H. Petrie (London, 1848), p. 600: trs. T. Forester (London 1854), pp. 143–4.

54 *EHD* i, no. 35, p. 420: Lieb. i, p. 158: Ath. 14.2.

throughout the realm,' and Edgar's realm was more extensive than Athelstan's.[55] Legislative activity was brought to a fine point at the time of Ethelred and Cnut when an attempt was made to limit the privilege of possessing more than one moneyer to the chief towns the *summi portus*, and they were to have only three.[56] This attempt failed under pressure of sheer economic circumstance. Reputable moneyers were important men, often possessing rights of private jurisdiction. The king had every reason to limit the number, if it was expedient and sensible so to do, and even more reason to make sure that moneyers were answerable to him in as definite and clearcut relationship as possible. One must think of the moneyer as a member or potential member of the thegnly class.

Numismatists have been able to show that these legislative enactments were no mere idle theories.[57] The only regular current coin was the silver penny, but every effort was made to keep the silver content of high standard and also to introduce genuine artistic talent into the design. The obverse of the coin bore the king's head and his name, the reverse (after Edgar) the name of the mint and the name of the moneyer. Designs on the reverse were at times of considerable symbolic importance and of some subtlety. A series of coins of Edward the Elder struck at Chester carry the picture of town gates. Others concentrate rather on what were to be the standard motifs of long cross and short cross. The most beautiful piece of coin engraving was done during the reign of Ethelred when for special purposes a coin known as the *Agnus Dei* was struck, with the Lamb of God on the one side and the Dove of Peace on the other. Martlets are used as a distinctive design on the reverse of some of the coinage of the Confessor. A decisive moment in the history of the English coinage came during the later years of Edgar, after his solemn coronation at Bath. Reforms were instituted which were to set the pattern of coinage for the following two centuries. The individual coins present the now traditional shape and size of English silver pennies, but the Small Cross type of Edgar inaugurated a period of central control of sequence.[58] New coins were issued and the types changed probably at six-yearly intervals. The number of mints increased, as an integral part of the reform of 973, with the clear-cut object that no man living south of a line drawn from

55 *EHD* i, no. 40, p. 433: Lieb. i, p, 204. III Edgar, 8: *ga an mynet ofer ealne pæs cynges anweald ond pone nan man ne forsace* – and no man is to refuse it.
56 Lieb. i., p. 236. IV Eth. 9: *in omni summo porto III, et in omni alio portu sit unus monetarius.*
57 Much seminal work was brought together in a volume of historical studies presented to Sir Frank Stenton, *Anglo-Saxon Coins*, ed. R.H.M. Dolley (London, 1961). See also R.H.M. Dolley 'The Coins', *The Archaeology of Anglo-Saxon England*, ed. D.M. Wilson (London, 1976), pp. 349-72.
58 R.H.M. Dolley and D.M. Metcalf, 'The Reform of the Coinage under Eadgar', *Anglo-Saxon Coins*, pp. 136-68.

5   Anglo-Saxon mints.

Uncertain mints include *'Eanburgh'* – (Cnut - Dorset?), *'Brygin and Niwan'* – (Edgar and Ethelred II, formerly attributed to Bridgnorth but probably in the Shaftesbury area), *'Wiltu'* – (Ethelred II - East Anglia?), *'Fro'* – (Edward the Confessor – Somerset?), Castle Gotha remains a possible site for *Gothaburh*.

the Humber to the Mersey should be more than fifteen or twenty miles from a mint. Every borough was expected to issue coinage. At its maximum number there were more than sixty mints in operation during the reign of Ethelred, though some of these struck coins for a short time only or for special administrative or political reasons, drawing their moneyers from larger mints in the locality. Some, such as the mint at Cadbury, were no more than temporary, set up at defensible positions in times of invasion and political trouble. In spite of this great diversity in place of issue central control was strictly maintained by the issue of dies from die-cutting offices which remained heavily under royal supervision or under the supervision of the ealdormen who were the principal royal agents. Numismatic evidence is clear at times for the existence of regional die-cutting centres.[59] The high

59 Pauline Stafford, 'Historical Implications of the Regional Production of Dies under Æthelred II', *BNJ 48* (1978), pp. 35–50.

quality of the output of the Norwich mint from 932 has been associated with the dominance of the West-Saxon noble family of Athelstan Half-King who held office as ealdormen in East Anglia. Under Ethelred regional die-cutting was carried on at London, Winchester, Canterbury, Exeter, Chester, York, Lincoln and Norwich, though there was a tendency to concentrate ultimately on one centre at London. Domesday Book has preserved for us information about the procedures in use. The three moneyers of Shrewsbury used to pay for their dies like other moneyers of the country and a further 20s. fifteen days after their return. The moneyers of Hereford paid 18s. when they received their dies and a further 20s. within a month after their return to Hereford.[60] Royal profit also came from a controlled variation in weight from type to type and, if modern subtle analysis can be believed, also within the type sequences. Variation in weight within the same type may well be explained by the regional variations in royal needs. Heavier coins were sometimes struck in areas where royal lands and revenue were concentrated, and lighter coins in areas such as parts of the Danelaw where royal interests would best be met by a minting tax increasing with the flow of coinage rather than on direct supply of silver coins from estates.[61] If the weight of the coinage dropped, and the flow remained constant, royal profit could come in the tangible surplus of silver received: if it rose, it seems likely that profit could also be taken by a careful royal servant by accurate timing of receipts of dues and of geld. The king certainly would not lose over interchange and a vigorous discipline was maintained over the moneyers. Fearsome penalties were inflicted on men who struck false coins, especially on those who worked in workshops up in the hills and away from the main centres.[62] It is possible indeed that profits taken on change of money were less important to the king than the maintenance of the integrity of the coinage, in itself a factor of considerable importance to royal prestige, to commercial prosperity and to the political integrity of England.

Edgar's reforms set the standard and it proved flexible enough to carry the coinage through the recurring political crises of the eleventh century. Under Ethelred there was a tremendous increase in the output of the mints, partly in order to pay the Danegeld. Estimates of the total number of coins issued in any one type vary greatly, but the number of coins in use clearly must be reckoned in millions. The sequence of

---

60 DB i, 252a, (Shrewsbury); DB i, 179a (Hereford).
61 Pauline Stafford comments perceptively that a variable minting fee might account for the variations between heavy and light coins, 'light coins representing a heavy tax on the use of coin', *art. cit*, p. 36.
62 Lieb. I, pp. 234–6; IV Eth. 5–9.

types increased in frequency as the eleventh century progressed. By the reign of Edward the Confessor a three-year cycle was customary, with a reduction to two years at one stage.[63] This was probably as short a period as was manageable in eleventh-century conditions. Good notice had to be given – probably six months – if a currency was to be called in, and there out of necessity had been an allowable period of overlap. Cumbersome though it may appear to be, the system worked. The king and the king alone had the right to strike coins: this right was delegated to no subject, no matter how exalted; and the coinage had no equal in Europe. Scandinavian countries were content to look to England not only for their source of silver and coins, but as their mentor in the arts of striking coins and regulating coinage. It is a tribute to Anglo-Saxon governmental and administrative skill that the system, in advance of anything to be found in the Norman duchy, survived the Conquest successfully.

The King and the Administration of Justice

We have already discussed the importance of the king in the making of the law, in legislative activity. An equal importance, indeed in some respects a greater importance, attaches to his part in the administration of law. In theory his was the final authority as far as the freemen of the community were concerned, saving a possible reserve of rights to the Church and to a man's own lord to whom hold-oaths of loyalty had been sworn. As a last resort, even in these instances, an appeal could be made to the king. Cnut was forced to frame a law to the effect that no appeal should be made to the king unless recourse had earlier been had to the hundred court, a clear indication that appeals to the king were in fact frequent.[64] This was of course the theory, and there is no proof that a weak man could ever succeed in having an appeal heard, let alone successfully upheld. There was much violence, much oppression by headstrong lords who cared little for legal niceties. In everyday affairs reliance on a stout kindred or a strong lord was more likely to be effective than appeal to an often distant court. In the course of the tenth century, however, the royal court began to frame rules and procedures that resulted finally in greater efficiency. The art of definition of offences became more sophisticated. There were certain offences that were to be matters for the king and the king alone. Fuller definition was achieved in the laws of Cnut and in that form

---

63 F. Barlow, *Edward the Confessor* (London), 1970, p. 182, points to the difficulties in attributing exact dates to types.

64 Lieb. i, p. 320, II Cnut, 17, *and ne gesece nan man done cingc, butan he ne mote beon nanes rihtes wyrðe innan his hundrede.*

they were transmitted to the Anglo-Norman lawbooks, notably to the *Leges Henrici Primi*, a private compilation that probably reflected the common practice of the shire court of Hampshire at Winchester in the second decade of the twelfth century. By that time the offences were already referred to as what they long had been in practice, the *dominica placita regis*, or dominical pleas of the king.[65]

Perhaps too much attention has been paid to the existence of these pleas and not enough to their content. The laws of Cnut tell us that payments for violation of the royal *mund*, or violation of royal protection, for attack on men in their own houses (*hamsocn*), for assault (*forsteal*), for the harbouring of fugitives (*flymenafyrmth*), and for neglect of military service (*fyrdwite*) could be granted out as a special favour in Wessex and Mercia and the Danelaw, but such grants were clearly regarded as exceptional. In the Danelaw additional rights were defined as the fine for fighting (*fihtwite*) and an infringement of a more general peace (*griðbryce*). The *Leges Henrici Primi* goes further in definition and consolidates the list of royal pleas (*de iure regis*) as: breach of the king's peace given by his hand or writ; Danegeld; the plea of contempt of his writs or commands; the death or injury of his servants wherever occurring; breach of fealty and treason; any contempt or slander of him; fortifications consisting of three walls (*castellatio trium scannorum*); outlawing; theft punishable by death; murdrum; counterfeiting the coinage; arson; *hamsocn; forsteal; fyrding; flymenafyrmth* (as above in the laws of Cnut); premeditated assault; robbery; *stretbreche*; unlawful appropriation of the king's land or money; treasure-trove; wreck of the sea; things cast up by the sea; rape; abduction; forests; the reliefs of his barons; fighting in the king's dwelling or Household; breach of the peace in the king's troop; failure to perform *burgbot* or *bricgbot* or *firdfare;* receiving and maintaining an excommunicated person or an outlaw; violation of the king's protection; flight in a military or naval battle; false judgement; failure of judgement; violation of the king's law.[66]

This tremendous list probably represents a gallant effort by one who was learned in Anglo-Saxon law and in the practice of early twelfth-century courts, to explain what was happening in the new circumstances of Norman England. It contains the substance of Cnut's rulings, adds the commonplaces of English law (the breach of *borh* and *mund*, failure to perform the *trinoda necessitas*), and mixes it all up with ingredients appropriate to the feudal world of the Norman baronage, fortifications, wrecks, rudimentary flotsam and jetsam,

---

65 Lieb. i, p. 316 *EHD* i, no. 49, p. 456, II Cnut 12–15, *ðis syndon þa gerihta, þe se cingc ah ofer ealle men on Wessexan (Cl.12), Gridbryce* is referred to in Cl.15.
66 *Leges Henrici Primi*, 10, 10, 1; Lieb. i, p. 556: ed. L.J. Downer pp. 108–9 and 323–6.

forest law and feudal law pertaining to the reliefs on entering inheritance. It is a fascinating glimpse of a practising lawyer at work and
an insight, too, into the comparatively slow process at work which
resulted finally in all serious offence reaching the cognizance of the
royal courts. It is not easy now to describe such developments, aware
as we are of the gradations of meaning in terms such as 'offence' and
'cognizance', aware also of variations of meaning, composition and
procedure involved in the simple word 'court'. It was much more difficult for the twelfth-century commentator, but he did his best. It is
interesting and probably vastly significant to note outlawing
(*utlagaria*) entered almost inconspicuously into the list. Concern with
the personal and financial rights of the king in public courts well on the
way to becoming royal, led the author of the *Leges Henrici Primi* to
tell us much of direct relevance to the Anglo-Saxon past as well as to
his Anglo-Norman present.

Outlawry, the formal placing of a man outside the normal protection of the law, was not an exclusive royal prerogative. Shire courts had
the power to declare a man an outlaw if he refused to answer charges
brought against him: this laid him open to private vengeance. In one of
the most famous *causes célèbres* of Anglo-Saxon history, Earl Godwin's eldest son, Sweyn, was declared a *nithing* (one placed outside the
law) after his cowardly murder of his cousin Bjorn in 1049. It is true
that this declaration was made by the act of the king and all the host,
and that it had overtones connected with the special customs of the
housecarls, but its imposition is a reminder of the genuine elements of
folk power to be found in the old English kingdoms. The king could
ask for a sentence of outlawry. He did not by his own will place a
freeman outside the law.

The pleas of the crown represent a definition of a special reserve of
judicial authority. Their existence was made necessary in the general
context of growth of power of private jurisdiction in the course of the
tenth and eleventh centuries, a matter of the utmost complexity to
which we shall have to turn again when we deal with government in the
localities. There can be no doubt about the existence of private courts
in later Anglo-Saxon England, though it is evident that their powers
were limited, their growth fairly vigorously regulated and their
development somewhat belated and circumscribed. Before the tenth
century there is no clear reference to a secular lord holding a formal
court, only ambiguous references to a lord's duty to keep good order
among his retainers. The discipline of a landlord over his estate implied the existence of a petty court; but anything more than that involved the community and then the king. Towards the middle of the
tenth century, however, as part of the general process of clarification
of rights characteristic of the century, it became customary for lords,

ecclesiastical and lay, to receive gifts of jurisdiction from the king. The most common formula used in charters to express these gifts was the phrase 'sake and soke' to which was sometimes appended a string of other more specific rights, quite commonly 'toll, *team* and *infangenetheof*' but capable of extending to as many as a dozen or even more items.[67] Sake and soke itself, cause and suit, implied jurisdiction and control of a court. Individual specific rights involved both government in the localities and private jurisdiction and must be looked at later, but also demand mention here as matters concerning the general theory of royal attitude to administration of justice. For example, *infangenetheof*, the right to take a thief guilty of an offence within an estate presumed the right to possess a gallows. *Team* required supervision of the legal and administrative processes by which a man would prove himself to be in legal possession of goods and chattels. Such rights were profitable, it is true, but they also involved matters of local discipline essential to the health of a community. As such they were the concern of the king, and were not granted lightly. Indeed it cannot be overemphasized that rights of private jurisdiction were delegated rights. Widespread as they undoubtedly were in late Anglo-Saxon England grants of sake and soke emphasized rather than belittled the authority of the king as the source of effective administration of law.

Most private courts dealing with offences of a serious nature seem by the end of the Anglo-Saxon period to have been considered courts of hundreds or groups of hundreds. This is particularly true of ecclesiastical estates, above all in estates attached to the great Benedictine houses, the product of the tenth-century revival in monasticism. Peterborough exercised its jurisdiction over the extensive area in north Cambridgeshire and Northamptonshire known as the Soke of Peterborough. Bury St Edmunds, newly created and endowed in the reign of Cnut, held jurisdiction over 8½ hundreds in Suffolk, and Ely over 5½ hundreds in Suffolk apart from the double hundred at Ely itself. Worcester had special jurisdiction over the triple hundred of Oswaldslaw. The principles behind such grants were not feudal but territorial. The landowners exercised what was essentially an immunity from public courts even though initially the abbots at least may have been more anxious to escape from episcopal rather than from royal control. The actual courts over which in turn he or his ministers presided were not held for his men, his vassals as such, but would be attended by men drawn from the neighbourhood. The right to hold

---

67 A clear and very valuable account of the formulae used appears in Harmer, *Anglo-Saxon Writs*, pp. 61-85.

his own courts was delegated to him by the king: the courts themselves were franchisal.[68]

In the tenth and eleventh centuries there is much evidence throughout Western Europe of a groping towards identity on the part of the various communities. Kingship became the great symbol of identity, but the effectiveness of the monarchy and the ultimate integrity of the community depended on the resources available to permit the king, his advisers, his armies and administrators, to make their will felt in home matters of taxation, administration of justice, exaction of dues, exercise of authority in matters relating to defence and also to material and spiritual welfare. There is much to suggest that in development of central institutions, Household administration, financial capability and legal expertise, England was well advanced for its day. The secretariat with its capacity for issuing charters and writs, the financial offices that dealt with geld and the issue of coinage, the judicial elements from the law-declaring witan to the royal statements and delegation of private justice, testify to growth in the critical fields needed to create permanent government. In spite of political vacillations and occasional disaster, the institutional growth was sound. The balance between resources, potential, and institutional achievement seemed just. Imagery and art, as well as more prosaic laws and writs, bear witness to the increasing veneration felt for the institution of kingship. To talk of central government still bears the smack of anachronism, but the king and the great men of the realm, ealdormen and bishops, exercised authority that can fairly be so described. All public authority was indeed ultimately derived from the Crown. Its effectiveness however depended in large part upon the local situation and upon the means by which the dictates of central authority could be heard and enforced.

---

68 There is need for a new study of the territorial soke along the lines suggested by G.W.S. Barrow, *The Kingdom of the Scots* (London, 1973), pp. 8–27.

6*

Government in the Localities

In the last chapter we touched on many matters concerning finance and the administration of justice that had immediate and powerful impact on the localities, on the regions, the shires and the hundreds. The delicate problems related to private jurisdiction and the delegation of judicial powers by the king cannot be understood without grasp of the general structure of local government. In communities where communications are poor, ceaseless effort is needed to keep the central source of authority in touch with the localities; and for an overwhelming majority of the inhabitants of Anglo-Saxon England administration rarely involved more than the orders of their lords, the reeves of the estate upon which they lived, the demands of the hundredmen, or the commands and exhortations of the local priest. Poverty in communication and relative limitations of resources meant also that there was a danger of overconcentration of wealth and power in the hands of a few aristocratic families. These were some of the difficulties which the expanding authority of the English monarchy in the tenth century met in the regions, shires and hundreds. Under King Alfred the man of highest status in the locality was the ealdorman who was in charge of a single shire; and normally his authority was exercised directly within that shire. As the kingdom extended over the formerly independent kingdoms of Mercia, East Anglia and Northumbria, the tendency grew for some ealdormen to take on greater responsibility. Some of these men were connected with the royal dynasty by blood or marriage, some were not. To judge from the lists of those who subscribed as witnesses to Athelstan's charters, Scan-

---

* Local historians, notably the group built up by H.P.R. Finberg at Leicester, have done much to clarify the situation in late Anglo-Saxon England over the last decades. Uncertainty remains over the exact date and pace of development of the territorial units of government, shires, hundreds, and wapentakes. Evidence from later strictly non-contemporary sources such as parish boundaries or hundred boundaries is often exceedingly helpful. The legal enactments of the later Anglo-Saxon kings remain the essential basic source of evidence, and the work of Helen Cam and Sir Frank Stenton the best and most intelligent guides to the complexities of the social and governmental structures underlying the legal abstractions.

dinavian leaders as well as English were entrusted with authority as *duces* or ealdormen. Welsh princes and princes from Strathclyde were also brought tentatively into the still developing governmental picture.[1] With the stabilization of the territorial position and the creation of the true kingdom of England a group of men emerged whose authority and dignity transcended that of the earlier ealdormen though they still bore the same title. Athelstan 'Half-King', for example, a Wessex landowner close to the ruling dynasty, was ealdorman of East Anglia from 923 to at least 956 and remained a great and influential person throughout his long life. His sons Æthelwold and Æthelwine became ealdormen and Æthelsige a leading Court officer.[2] Byrhtnoth, ealdorman of Essex from 956 to his death at Maldon in 991, Ælfhere, earldorman of Mercia, 956—83, Æthelweard, the translator of the Anglo-Saxon Chronicle into Latin, of royal blood himself and ealdorman of the 'Western Provinces,' 973–998, were all men of the first rank. For some of the period after the early 910s it was customary to find Northumbria under the rule of one ealdorman alone, and it is fully understandable that the Anglo-Scandinavian term *eorl* (later to develop into the familiar English title 'earl') gradually became used in place of the English *ealdorman*. *Eorl* was a term already well known in English usage in poetry and in some set legal phrases, but the Scandinavian equivalent (iarl or jarl) was used more specifically as a title to mark out a man of noble blood and exalted position: and it is with these connotations that it was found useful to denote an ealdorman of special rank and power. In the long reign of Ethelred (978–1016) it was most unusual to find more than four or five ealdormen *(duces)* subscribing to charters and increasingly so as the reign progressed: indeed only one of the twenty-six or so charters that survive with names of ealdormen as witness from 999 to 1016 has more than four ealdormen subscribing. Men of the rank of earl were plentiful, but only few exercised territorial office.[3] The politics of Cnut's reign exaggerated this tendency. The new Danish king, concerned with his Scandinavian interests as well as with England, was content to recognize and regularize the authority of a few great men of earl's rank whose virtually viceregal powers extended over many shires.

---

1 H.R. Loyn. 'England and Wales in the Tenth and Eleventh Centuries', *WHR 10* (1981), pp. 283-301; Scandinavian 'eorls' were present as well as the Welsh *reguli* or *subreguli*.

2 Stenton, *Anglo-Saxon England*, p. 414. C.R. Hart 'Athelstan "half-king" and his family', *Anglo-Saxon England* 2 (Cambridge, 1973), pp. 115-44.

3 The evidence is available in Simon Keynes, *The Diplomas of Æthelred*, table 6: see also pp. 197–8 where the suggestion is made that Ethelred may have tried to break the hold of local families on the office of ealdorman. He showed no hurry to reappoint on the death of an ealdorman, and Dr Keynes draws special attention (p.198, note 165) to the references to *sciresmen*, and to hints at friction between them and ealdormen.

Three principal aristocratic families emerged, those of Godwin in Wessex, Leofric in Mercia and Siward in Northumbria. Their rank and their entitlement to an earl's office were hereditary, though not their right to succeed to office over a particular geographical area. They were appointed by the king and could be removed by him or, in exceptional cases, by pressure from below. They held positions of great privilege, commanded the *fyrd* as the royal representative and took a third of the proceeds of justice from the shire courts, the earl's third penny. They also enjoyed over most English boroughs a third of the royal revenues in customs. The terminological change at this level from ealdorman to *eorl* or earl was not absolute, but in an odd sense it reflects reality. Men such as Eadric Streona in the reign of Ethelred or Harold or Tostig, sons of Godwin, in the reign of the Confessor, were far too exalted to be used for routine work in each and every shire. In the late tenth and early eleventh centuries the records tell increasingly of royal reeves who take over the former ealdorman's function, and it is one of these, the reeve of the shire, the sheriff, who comes to be principally concerned with looking after royal interests in the locality. His function was initially, as his name suggests, to look after the king's estates, or some of the king's estates, within a shire. By 1066 he was the earl's deputy, in practice the chief representative of the king in the shire.

The Shire

The word *scir,* or shire, originally meant no more than a share, a sphere of authority, but it was steadily territorialized. At the end of Alfred's reign it was the normal term used for the subdivisions of the kingdom of Wessex, some of the shires such as Kent and Sussex bearing the shape and name of ancient kingdoms, others such as Hampshire and Wiltshire taking the names from the royal administrative centres, Hamton and Wilton, from which they were governed, and others again probably bearing names which form a link with the early days of settlement-*Sumorsæte and Dornsæte,* the original Saxon settlers in the lands dependent on Somerton and on Dorchester. As the West Saxons extended their lordships at the expense of the Danes it is highly likely that they took their shiring arrangements with them. There are no specific references to the Mercian shires by name until the early eleventh century, but first mention of institutions should not in these centuries be equated with origins of institutions, and the laws of Edgar in the mid-tenth century refer to shires as if they were common to all England. Memories of the older divisions, of course, persisted. A charter of the reign of Edgar, already cited (p. 89) referred in its boundary clause to the boundary between the Mercian and the

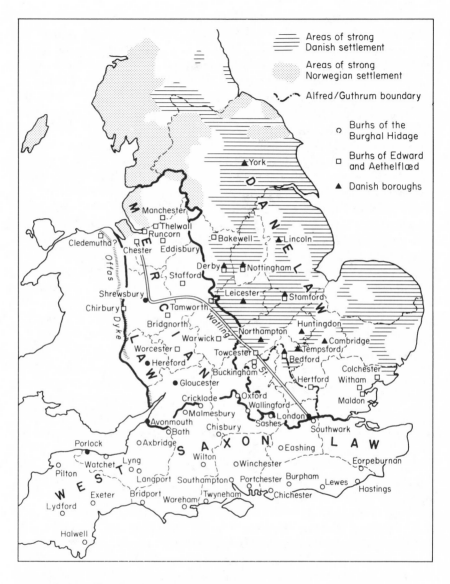

6 Anglo-Scandinavian England in the eleventh century.

The shadings are approximate only and are based on place-name evidence. Among *burhs* still unidentified are *Scergeat* and *Weardbyrig* on the western Mercian border.

Hwicce, and the Anglo-Saxon Chronicle referred to the territory of the Five Boroughs in 942, 1013 and 1015, and to the *Magonsætan* in 1016.[4] The West Saxons should not in any sense be regarded as the conquerors of the other parts of England but their campaigns against the Danes inevitably made them take on the aspect of military redeemers. It is likely that as they restored Christian lordship to the West Mercians as far back as Alfred's reign, to the East Anglians and the Mercians in the reign of Edward the Elder, to the men of the 'Five Boroughs' in the reign of Edmund and to the Northumbrians initially under Athelstan and finally under Eadred, they rearranged the older divisions and planted in the chief centre of each manageable territory officers drawn from the local thegnage who would take a special responsibility for the royal lands and rights. Ealdormen north of the Thames from the early tenth century were entrusted with wider powers and greater endowment than the ealdormen in Wessex. They were comparatively few in number, rarely in Mercia exceeding four or five and exercising authority over areas that corresponded roughly to old provinces such as the territory of the *Magonsætan* or to diocesan boundaries, but this did not mean again that the shiring of Mercia was necessarily late. The active royal officers within what were to be the shires of Mercia were thegns or reeves exercising their authority from borough headquarters, from Chester, Stafford, Shrewsbury, Hereford, Worcester, Warwick, Gloucester, Oxford and Buckingham. It is probable that the active compaigning, defensive and offensive, of the reign of Edward the Elder when his sister Æthelflæd and her husband, the ealdorman Ethelred, governed the Christian Mercians, demanded the presence of more efficient administrative units. The shires are in consequence more artificial than in Wessex, and much more closely linked with the existence of and possibly the creation of military fortified headquarters. All the shires of Western Mercia take their names from boroughs that were newly built, often central geographically to the shire, or newly fortified by Edward or his sister.

The same element of artificiality and reliance on boroughs is evident in the further extension of English royal authority into territories held for a generation or more by the Danes. In the south-east Midlands, Hertford, Bedford, Northampton, Huntingdon and Cambridge had been the fortified headquarters of Danish armies. Essex, an ancient kingdom in its own right, was something of a special case. The prestige of Colchester was great and the borough was fully fortified by Æthelflæd after the vigorous campaign of 917. The

---

4 *ASCh* 1013: *þæt folc of fifburhingan;* in 1015 Prince Edmund went *in to Fifburgum:* the *Magonsætan* were the first to start the flight with the notorious ealdorman Eadric in 1016.

recovery of East Anglia also seems to have been effected on special terms, and the same burghal situation did not apply. Thetford was prominent in the campaign and in the administrative structure thereafter, but the shape of the ancient kingdom with its division into the Northfolk and the Southfolk, Norfolk and Suffolk, persisted and still persists into modern times. The lands of the Five Boroughs by contrast provide a close parallel to the general Mercian situation. They bowed down to Edmund, for fear of the Norwegians further north, in 942, and retained some homogeneity for the following three-quarters of a century. As late as 1015, as we have seen, the Chronicle still refers to the *fifburgingas*, the inhabitants of the Five Boroughs. For administrative purposes it is likely that they were divided early into their constituent units. Nottingham, Derby and Leicester conformed to the regular Midland pattern of shires dependent upon fortified boroughs. The situation in the rest of the Five Boroughs was rather different. The coastline from the Humber to the Wash was a perilous main road for invaders from east over sea, and its defence demanded special efforts. For this reason administrative and military government appears to have been concentrated at the great borough of Lincoln; and Stamford on the southern tip of the modern shire of Lincolnshire, was left without an independent shire organization of its own.[5] When, after 954, Northumbria passed back into English control similar military exigencies demanded a concentrated effort in the north. York was pre-eminent as a fortified position and as the only significant town north of the Humber. Responsibility for defence and administration fell squarely on the borough, and although experiments were undoubtedly made within Yorkshire, as elsewhere in the slowly reconquered north-west, no shire pattern comparable to the compact southern parallels appeared north of the line from Humber to Mersey. Indeed both Yorkshire and Lincolnshire, and especially the former, are best thought of in the late tenth and early eleventh centuries as substantial ealdormanries: it is in the subdivisions, the thridings or ridings, that the nearest resemblance to normal shires can be found.

Elsewhere the shire patterns were from time to time modified before settling by the reign of the Confessor into their familiar permanent moulds. Problems of estuarine defence caused modifications in the structure of the shire of Gloucestershire and as late as the early years of the eleventh century a separate shire of Winchcombeshire was in existence.[6] Tenurial complications, associated with convenient en-

5 *The Making of Stamford*, ed. A. Rogers (Leicester, 1965): H.R. Loyn 'Anglo-Saxon Stamford', pp. 15-33.
6 H.P.R. Finberg, 'The Ancient Shire of Winchcombe', *The Early Charters of the West Midlands* (2nd edn, Leicester, 1972), pp. 228–35.

dowments for the royal ladies, forced the creation of the anomalous shire of Rutland from the territories that fringed Stamford and the Soke of the great abbey of Peterborough.[7] By and large the shape of the English shires was however determined in the processes of reconquest and recovery that filled the campaigns of Edward the Elder and Athelstan. Ethelred ruled an England where the normal territorial subdivision was the shire.

By the time of Domesday Book the shire was treated as the basic unit of administration for many purposes, above all in finance. From early in the eleventh century it had been customary to attribute a fixed number of hides to each shire, 1,200 to Worcestershire and to Bedfordshire, 3,200 to Northamptonshire. Detailed working out of responsibility for payment of geld according to these hides of assessment was hammered out in the hundred court. There is one curious phenomenon which can be teased out of Domesday Book, figures that provide a clue to the development of the shire. The number of hundreds or wapentakes within the shires varied considerably, but by exercising a little ingenuity it is possible to reconstitute from a simple grouping of shires larger units of 120 hundreds. Hampshire, Wiltshire, Berkshire and Surrey, the heart of historic Wessex, contained 120 hundreds; and those four shires also constituted the area covered by the bishoprics of Winchester and Ramsbury after Edward the Elder's reorganization. Kent and Sussex together also contained 120 hundreds. The shires of the south-west, including Cornwall made up some 140 hundreds, but when the special defensive needs and possible over-assessment in Devon are taken into account we may be back to another 120 hundreds in pre-Athelstan days. The phenomenon is not confined to Wessex. In the West Midlands the shires that exist within the ancient bishoprics of Hereford, Worcester and Lichfield yield a similar tally. The East Midlands is more complex with some small and peculiar units such as Rutland and the Isle of Ely, but even so the area south of the 'Five Boroughs' and west of East Anglia can be seen without undue distortion to contain 120 hundreds, a grouping which may have connections with the ancient see of Dorchester in Oxfordshire. East Anglia itself contained 60 hundreds. The situation in Essex (probably 20 hundreds in 1066), Middlesex, and parts of Hertfordshire is too complicated by proximity to London for plausible reconstruction in larger groupings, and it must be remembered that this evidence from the later eleventh century, fascinating though it may be, gives no conclusive proof of earlier pat-

7 C. Phythian-Adams, 'Rutland Reconsidered', *Mercian Studies* ed. A. Dornier (Leicester, 1977), pp. 63-84 suggests that Rutland itself represents a very ancient territorial unit: see also C.R. Hart, *The Hidation of Northamptonshire* (Leicester, 1970).

terns. The hundred was a somewhat volatile territorial unit. It seems reasonable nevertheless to associate the 120 hundred groups with the levy of Danegeld in the reign of Ethelred (often assessed in units of £12,000) or even with the shape of tenth-century ealdormanries. Those who favour a very late date (perhaps as late as the early eleventh century) for the shiring of Mercia are also tempted to take the existence of the larger units as supporting evidence. Such argument does not seem to take firmly enough into account the basic fact that the groups themselves are made up of shires nor that they are to be found both in Wessex (a land incontestably of early shiring) and in Mercia both sides of Watling Street. It is quite in keeping with what we know of Edward the Elder and Athelstan that the older *regiones* and tribal divisions should be split up and rearranged for judicial and administrative purposes. If, as seems possible, the severe gelds of Ethelred's reign forced administrative reform on the community, that reform was more likely to be associated with a sharpening of the sheriff's function and a regrouping of the hundreds rather than with a virtual creation of the shires themselves out of larger ealdormanries of 120 hundreds apiece. Indeed, misled by our own ingenuity, it may well be that we have neglected the force of the existence of round numbers of hundreds in individual shires or within two adjacent shires in our search for more complicated patterns.[8]

The shire possessed a court, apart from the monarchy perhaps the most important institution in Anglo-Saxon England. This court remained unspecialized, a folk-court, the shire or the *comitatus* in action. Suit of court, that is attendance, was owed nominally at least by all freemen in the shire, though sheer necessity and common sense demanded a limitation on the actual presence of men, and the obligation to attend, as distinct from the right to be present, fell increasingly on parcels of land. The court possessed a tremendous variety of functions including the procedures in outlawry. Its jurisdiction appears to have been limitless, saving possible rights of the king, but shire courts did not develop into full royal courts until royal judges were foisted on them by Henry I and Henry II.

---

8 H.M. Chadwick, *Studies on Anglo-Saxon Institutions* (Cambridge, 1905) pp. 209-10, and W.J. Corbett, *Cambridge Medieval History,* vol. iii, pp. 366-7 provide essential introductions to the problem. At some stage it seems pretty clear that in the south-west, for example, there were 40 hundreds in Wiltshire, 40 in Dorset, 60 in Somerset, and probably 40 in a combined group of Devon (33) and Cornwall (7). It may be much more significant that Oxford and Buckinghamshire contained 40 hundreds (22 plus 18) than that they made part of a 120-hundred group, or that Middlesex, Hertfordshire, and Cambridgeshire (5½ plus 9½ plus 15) made a 30-hundred group, than that they made part of a still larger grouping. Much probably depended on the strength of the local king's thegn in effective charge of royal interests in the locality at the time of the creation of the shires.

It was customary for the shire court to meet no more than twice a year in late Anglo-Saxon England, normally about Easter and Michaelmas. The meetings of the courts were public events, social as well as legal occasions. There was no judge present in the modern sense of the word. Earls and bishops, or their direct representatives, presided, and decisions were arrived at by the suitors who declared the law. The suitors gave judgement, after which proof was adduced by ordeal or by compurgation. Much business essential to the smooth running of the community and of the monarchy was transacted in the shire court. Assessments to public burdens in service or in payment had to be decided, and arrangements for the collection of geld and other royal dues had to be made. It was heavily in the interest of all land-owners to be present or to be represented and to no one did this apply more heavily than the king himself. We have already seen how his reeves and particularly one among them who became known as the shire-reeve or shire-man came in many areas to be recognized as chief executive royal officer for routine business within the shire. It would be wrong to talk in terms of formal appointments, duties and procedures at this stage. Not until Norman times was the full potential power of the office of sheriff realized. In late Anglo-Saxon England sheriffs were important men, mostly presumably of thegnly rank, but they moved with the great men of the shire as representatives of the royal interest, sometimes uneasily, sometimes in situations where they could be overborne by bishops, ealdormen, great magnates or wealthy thegns when local politics or the local land situation demanded it. There has survived in a Hereford gospel book a revealing document from the reign of Cnut which shows a shire court in action.[9] A dispute was settled concerning a parcel of land at Wellington and Cradley. Edwin, the son of Enniaun (modern Welsh Einion) brought a suit against his own mother, a kinswoman of Leofflæd, wife of the powerful Thurkil the White. Strong family feelings ran behind the dispute. Before worthy witnesses of high rank the mother declared that her son held no rights in the land and that after her death all land and possession, gold, clothing and all, should go to Leofflæd and not to Edwin. This arrangement was to all appearance carried through, and Thurkil was named in Domesday Book as the pre-Conquest holder of Wellington. Of equal interest with the social content of the document, the suggestion of intermarriage of Welsh and English of landowning rank, the testamentary power of a woman, is the procedural. We are told that there were present at the shire court the bishop (Athelstan of Hereford), the ealdorman Raning, Edwin (the brother of ealdorman Leofwine), Leofwine, son of Wulfsige and

9 *EHD* i, no. 135, pp. 602-3. A.J.Robertson, *Anglo-Saxon Charters*, no. 78.

Thurkil himself. The influential Tofi the Proud, a figure of national importance, founder of the first church at Waltham, was present expressly on the king's business. Bryning the sheriff *(scirgerefa),* Æthelgeard and Leofwine of Frome, and Godric of Stoke were also there and all the thegns of Herefordshire. This was no group of petty provincial rustics. Bishop Athelstan took the initiative once the charge had been brought by Edwin and asked who was to represent the mother. Thurkil spoke up, but with the apparently technical reservation that he was willing to do so 'if he knew the case' *(gif he þa talu cuðe).* He did not, and so the meeting, that is the shire court itself, appointed three thegns, Leofwine of Frome, Æthelsige the Red, and Wynsige the shipman, to ride to her to hear her case. She denied her son's rights publicly, became exceedingly angry, summoned Leofflæd to her and declared her testamentary intentions to leave everything to Leofflæd. In a phrase which rings true she exhorted the three witnesses to 'act well like thegns' and to carry the message back to the court. They did so, Thurkil then took over, stood up in court, asked that his wife's interests be cleared of Edwin's claim, and rode with the permission and witness of all present to the minster at Hereford where he had the record entered in the gospel book. A careful man, Thurkil the White, he took anxious care for his wife's inheritance. We can guess that Wellington and Cradley were no more than the tip of the landed iceberg: the declared will was the central issue. But the record preserves for us indirectly splendid evidence of the importance of these regular meetings of the shire. We are not far from our familiar central medieval institution, the *comitatus* in the territorial sense in action. Leofwine of Frome, Godric of Stoke and Thurkil himself were worthy predecessors of our knights of the shire.

The Hundred and the Tithing

Meetings of the shire courts were special occasions; the mass of routine business in the localities in England was transacted through the hundred court. The origins of the hundred, both as a territorial divison and as a court, are obscure. There is no mention of a hundred court by name until the mid-tenth century when one of the strong West-Saxon kings, either Edmund or Edgar in the earliest years of his reign, issued an ordinance that dealt comprehensively with the function of a hundred. It is nevertheless highly probable that some sort of more or less formal meeting in a territorial unit smaller than a shire was already established custom in England at a much earlier stage.[10] It

10 P.H. Sawyer, *From Roman Britain to Norman England* (London, 1978), pp. 197-200 and references.

could indeed be argued that as soon as regular tribute or taxation was imposed by a king, perhaps as far back as the seventh and certainly by the eighth century, a division into regular taxation units was essential. Many see the origin of the hundreds in such assessment arrangements: to divide the ancient *provinciae* and *regiones* of Wessex and other kingdoms into units assessed at a hundred hides each would be an obvious and sensible course for an overlord to follow. Others have stressed military reasons in accounting for its origins on analogy with continental practice, and others again judicial reasons in the sense that a small and manageable community needed to band itself together formally to take effective precautions against theft and violence.

Certainly in the early years of the tenth century, as Edward the Elder and Æthelflæd gained control of England, efforts were made to stabilize institutional life in the localities so that justice, according to the principles of folk-right, would not be lacking to anyone because of faults of procedure or lack of true witness. Edward relied on his servants, his reeves, as principal agents in his attempts to establish effective royal supervision of folklaw. At Exeter towards the end of his reign he laid down a set of decrees that were meant to apply to the whole of his realm, East Anglia and even Northumbria, as well as Mercia and Wessex. His final statement was that each reeve was to hold a meeting (a *gemot*) every four weeks, and to see to it that every man was worthy of his folkright and that each lawsuit was to have a day appointed for hearing and settlement.[11] These meetings, and we are well justified in referring to them as courts, were not specifically termed hundred courts, but in practice they probably developed in the course of the succeeding generation into hundred courts. They were to meet monthly, to allot precise days for the hearing and settling of disputes, and also to insist on the law-worthiness of the suitors at court – all characteristics of the later hundred. Faced with the specific problem of cattle-theft and the more general problem of establishing a general peace over a wide area of diverse traditions, Edward ordered his chosen servants to regularize district meeting in convenient territorial divisions (in Mercia often assessed at 100 hides) to ensure that each man could obtain his folkright. In practice the existence of these regular meetings would give the impression that many hundreds were districts grouped around a royal manor adminstered by a reeve. We have perhaps been too hesitant in failing to see here the true origin of the continuous institutional life of the English hundred.

---

11 Lieb. i, pp. 140–45; I Edw., cl.8, *ælc gerefa hæbbe gemot a ymbe feower wucan; ond gedon, þæt ælc man sy folcrihtes wyrðe ond þæt ælc spræc hæbbe ende ond andagan, hwænne hit forðcume.* H.R. Loyn, 'The Hundred in the Tenth and Early Eleventh Centuries', *British Government and Administration*, ed. H. Hearder and H.R. Loyn (Cardiff, 1974), pp. 1–15.

Edward's successors continued to legislate as if the presence of permanent courts at this level was universal. In the Danish part of England the term wapentake (derived from the ON *vapnatak,* the taking up of weapons at the end of an assembly or the brandishing of weapons to signify assent) was used, but the principle was the same; lawyers facing the odd term 'wapentake' in the twelfth century, had no hesitation in saying bluntly that a wapentake was a hundred. [12] It is hard to see how good witness could be obtained, oaths assessed and the royal peace proclaimed without their existence. Athelstan was particularly zealous in his attempts to encourage active voluntary peace-guilds that would protect local communities against cattle-theft. The grouping of freemen into companies of ten, tithings, responsible for the overall good behaviour of the group, also indicates how clearer definition was helping the royal demands for better local peace. [13] It is not until the mid-tenth century Hundred Ordinance itself, however, that we have the first unambiguous glimpse of the hundred at work. [14] The Ordinance decreed that the hundred was to meet every four weeks, and that each man should do justice to other men there. Great concern was shown over theft: the value of stolen property was to be given to the owner on recovery, and the rest of the offender's property was to be divided into two parts, half for the hundred and half for the lord. Any proved opposition to the hundred was to be punished by a graded series of financial penalties. Special officers, hundredmen, and men at the head of tithings had responsibility for supervising good witness. The hundredman was especially enjoined to follow the trail of a thief and neglect was punishable by a heavy fine. Folkright was to be enforced in every suit and a day to be appointed for all hearings. Royal authority was firm and essential both in the issuing of the Ordinance and in the supporting disciplinary sanctions. The penalty of outlawry could be imposed for non-compliance in the activities of the hundred.

Legislation in the last century of Anglo-Saxon England reinforced the Hundred Ordinance. King Edgar's gift for systematization was especially important. He described three main types of court in the localities, shire courts that were to meet twice a year, borough courts that were to meet three times a year, and hundred courts that were to meet as previously arranged, that is to say once every four weeks. [15] An

---

12 Lieb. i, p. 652: *Leges Edw. Conf.* 30.1; *quod Angli vocant hundredum, supradicti comitatus vocant wapentagium* (the aforesaid shires (Cl. 30) were Yorkshire, Lincolnshire, Nottinghamshire, Leicestershire, Northamptonshire up to Watling Street and eight miles beyond Watling Street under English law).

13 Lieb. i, pp. 173-83, *EHD* i, no 37, pp. 423-7; VI Ath: ordinance of the bishops and reeves of the London district.

14 *The Hundred Ordinance 939–c961*; Lieb i, pp. 192–6 (I Edgar—*Hundredgemot*); *EHD* i, no. 39, pp. 429–30.

15 Lieb, i, p. 202, III Edg. cl. 5-*swa hit ær geset wæs EHD* i, no. 40, pp. 431–3.

important function of all courts was the provision of a place where good witness could be obtained; panels of 36 witnesses in each borough, twelve in each small borough, and twelve in each hundred, were universally to be established. Hundredmen were entrusted with a great deal of executive responsibility to see that legitimate trading was encouraged and cattle-theft actively discouraged. If a village failed to report suspicious movements of cattle the hundredmen could see to it that the herdsmen were flogged. Financial penalties could pass to the hundred corporately. Edgar's regulations that took special pains to support the hundredmen and the hundreds (and wapentakes) in their struggle against theft were widely disseminated. The greatest ealdormen of the realm, Oslac of Northumbria with all his army, Ælfhere, earl of Mercia, and Æthelwine of East Anglia were expressly commanded to give full support.

The regularity and frequency of the hundredal meetings, coupled with their involvement in practical business concerning theft and provision of good witness, led to a rational extension of function. The laws of Ethelred and of Cnut make frequent reference to the hundreds. Under Ethelred emphasis was placed on the importance of hundreds in the process of oath-taking, of compurgation within one or more hundreds. Under Cnut the situation was reached whereby no one was to appeal to the king unless he had previously failed to obtain justice within the hundred.[16] Strenuous efforts were made to ensure that suitors attended the court, and stringent penalties were imposed on those who did not. Much, though not all, ecclesiastical judicial business was heard at the hundred and the bishop or his representative as well as the ealdorman or his was expected to attend. In some areas lords of the hundred, men of thegnly rank, or their bailiffs and four good men and a parish priest from each vill were the men expected normally to be present at the court. A special peace protected those who were travelling to the court. With a multiplicity of business involving what we would afterwards call civil and criminal cases, land-transfer, tort, and disputes over boundaries, seisin, or ownership, much money changed hands and had to be guarded and much financial advantage was lost and won at the hundred courts. By the end of the Anglo-Saxon period the king, the Church, and landlords with interests in the district found it essential to establish and maintain a presence in the hundred where much of the routine legal business connected with their affairs would be conducted. As for the court itself, it remained a communal court, often meeting at traditional spots, 'moot-stows', which could have had ancient and very remote religious and social associations, an ancient barrow, an earth mound,

16 Lieb. i, p. 320, II Cnut 17, see above p. 126.

or, to give a tangible and well-known example, the cemetery at the north porch of the church at Ely.[17] Many hundred names refer to a prominent point, a hill or a standing stone or a tree, which would have served equally well as a meeting place in pagan days as a site for a regular assembly in the tenth century. The size of hundreds varied greatly and the boundaries of many were fluid. In some areas it was common for the court to be held at a central point in the hundred, and at others – particularly where grouping of hundreds was customary – at a point on the fringe of the hundred. Courts were normally held in the open air, but not invariably: common sense demanded some shelter from winter rains and snow, and the presence of place-name elements such as *sceamol* (bench) in hundred names in Kent, Essex and Cambridgeshire may imply some covered structure with indoor seating.[18]

There was no institutional difference between the hundred and the wapentake, and the use of the one term rather than the other was entirely a matter of linguistic predominance. In the territory of the Five Boroughs and in large parts of Yorkshire, the strength of the Scandinavian or Anglo-Scandinavian language was enough to ensure the retention of wapentake. In procedural matters there was probably little, if any, significant difference though it may be that the traditional litigious nature of the Scandinavian population led to some precocious experiments in the wapentakes of the Danelaw. In a code issued at Wantage and addressed to the men of the Five Boroughs, Ethelred and his councillors made arrangements for the establishment of the peace in the various wapentakes.[19] Provision was made for what many regard as the direct ancestor of the jury of presentment. At a meeting held in each wapentake twelve of the leading thegns together with the king's reeve were to come forward and to swear on relics that they would accuse no innocent man nor conceal any guilty one. They were then to seize the men who had been frequently accused and against whom the reeve was taking action. The number 'twelve' in itself may indicate Scandinavian influence, and in other parts of Anglo-Scandinavian England such as Chester and York, there is indication of similar special selection of lawmen or deemsters who took on specific legal functions and responsibilities.

Proof of guilt or innocence continued to rest with the traditional methods of compurgation or ordeal, but the thegns of the Wantage

17 ed. E.O. Blake, *Liber Eliensis*, RHS (London, 1962), p. 91. *De Wicceford*: interea venit Aegelwinus alderman ad Hely et infra cimiterium ad aquilonalem portam monasterii tenuit placitum cum toto hundreto ibique causam sive litum, que erat inter abbatem et Sumerlede, finivit sic....

18 P. Hunter Blair, *An Introduction to Anglo-Saxon England* (2nd edn Cambridge, 1978), p. 238. The whole section on the hundred (pp. 232-9) gives a valuable introduction to the topic.

19 Lieb. i, pp. 228-33 III Eth. 3i; *EHD* i, no. 43, pp. 439-42.

code were no mere emergency posse of lawmen summoned to perform an executive function only. They exercised judgement in the full sense and were expected to reach a unanimous verdict. If they failed to do so, a majority of eight out of the twelve was deemed sufficient, but the minority was expected then to pay the quite considerable sum of six half-marks each.[20] This is the first statement in English law to recognize the force of a majority verdict. The exaction of penalties and of fines implies a high degree of financial administration connected with the wapentakes and hundreds. The ealdorman or king's reeve would have taken a high share of the responsibiltiy in these financial matters, and again the concern of these who framed the lawcodes to deal with mints and minting rights becomes fully intelligible.

Hundreds and wapentakes extended over virtually all of England except the northern border lands where bailiwicks or wards became the common accredited terms for administrative units larger than ecclesiastical parishes. In parts of the country, notably in the vast shires of Yorkshire and Lincolnshire, administrative divisions smaller than a shire, but larger than a hundred or a wapentake came into being. The ridings of Yorkshire and of Lincolnshire are the best known of these and bear clear analogies with Scandinavian practice elsewhere in Britain, in Orkney and in the Isle of Man. It is not certain that they performed any routine administrative functions in Anglo-Saxon England, but exceedingly likely that they represent convenient divisions for military and financial purposes within which the royal reeves and ealdormen could exercise their administrative functions, perhaps when the army was called out or in any legal case of more than usual complexity. In the twelfth century the ridings were regarded essentially as groupings of hundreds over which a royal reeve would preside. The *Leges Edwardi Confessoris* (written in the reign of Henry I) regard such reeves (*predinggrefes*) as possessing legal authority, receiving causes which could not be settled in wapentakes and transmitting them to the shires if they could not be settled in the ridings; but this is probably a reflection of twelfth-century conditions. The same author's definition of riding is beautifully clear: 'what is termed in English three of four or more hundreds they (in the Danelaw) call a riding.'[21] Within English England the lathes of Kent, representing a very ancient stratum in English administrative history, fulfilled at times the function of a double hundred, and the rapes of Sussex, clearly pre-Conquest in origin, also served as an intermediate unit between the simple hundred and the shire.[22] In essentials,

20 III Eth. 13.2.
21 Lieb. i, p. 653, E.Cf. 31 and 31a.
22 J.E.A. Jolliffe, *Pre-feudal England: the Jutes* (Oxford, 1933, reprinted 1962); J.F.A. Mason, *William I and the Sussex Rapes*, (Historical Association, London, 1966).

however, financial, legal and military, the hundred or the wapentake provided the unit of administration of most immediate moment and consequence to the bulk of the population of England.

Below the hundreds were the vills or townships, the territorial units often treated as legal entities in their own right and the much more complex and difficult institutions, known as tithings. There are great mysteries about the origin of the tithings and great legal complications in the story of their development. Tithings were clearly linked with the hundred and it is probably safe to see this link as a vital part of the general growth in the administrative competence of the king's government in late Anglo-Saxon England. Two legal texts help us to understand the development. Under King Athelstan an elaborate ordinance, to which we have already given passing reference (p. 142), was drawn up by the bishops and reeves of the London district, intended as a practical supplement to the more formal statutes set up by the king and the council at Grately, at Exeter and at Thunderfield.[23] The main purpose of the ordinance was to take effective steps against theft, especially theft of cattle. It had full official support and sanction, but has to be read in a context of voluntary self-help, of rural peace-guilds brought into being to protect property and life. Detailed arrangements were set up for grouping the active free population into tithings and into hundreds. Each tithing was to have a senior person, a tithingman, in charge of the other nine and responsible for the collection of their dues. A hundredman was appointed and he, together with the ten senior tithingmen, was to control the money of the hundred. The group (the ordinance say twelve where one would have expected eleven, but there may have been a statutory cleric!) was to meet once a month, if they had the leisure. There was a social as well as a legal dimension to business as their meeting was to be 'at the time of the filling of the butts' or some other convenient occasion so that they could dine together and supply themselves, and distribute what was left after all their transactions 'for God's sake'.[24] An interesting feature is the direct order given by Athelstan to his ealdormen and reeves to support what looks much like a piece of calculated self-help initiated by bishops with a taste for administration and finance, and anxious to ensure protection against cattle-rustling and other forms of theft. In following the trail of a thief one man was to be selected from each tithing in sparsely populated areas, one man from two tithings in a more heavily populated district. The second vital legal text is even more important when it comes to tracing the continuous history of the tithing. Cnut's great secular code set out consciously to frame accep-

---

23 Lieb. i, pp. 173-83, VI Ath. *EHD* i, No 37, pp. 423-7.
24 *EHD* i, p. 425, VI Ath. 8.1.

table laws in conformity with the general custom of the community. A man's social position and his standing in law depended upon his right to deliver an oath in the public courts, the value of which was assessed according to his status, and his right to wergeld or bloodprice to be paid in case of injury or death. The code now stated that these basic rights of a freeman, the right of exculpation and the right to wergeld were to be denied if the man (over the age of twelve) was not brought into a tithing or a hundred.[25] The statement demanded commentary and the code provided it. Entry into a tithing was associated directly with the age-old protection of group or lord to man, with *borh* and mund, and it is this quality of *borh,* or surety, that was now mentioned specifically in the commentary. Everyone, whether possessing a home of his own or in the following or another, was to be brought into a hundred or under surety, and it was this surety or *borh,* the tithing itself, that was responsible for bringing him to his every legal duty, The tithing system, still under Athelstan an aspect of intelligent self-help, had developed under direct royal initiative to the point where it became a principal means of ensuring good behaviour at the very grass roots of the community. The ten tithings of a hundred people had folded in rather inelegantly to the notion of the territorial hundred and the disciplinary procedures of the hundred court. The tithing took responsibility for a man's deeds, and could be held responsible and fined in the hundred court if he failed to present himself or make amends. Supervision of the tithings became an obligation, a burden for which financial return would be expected. It is likely (certainly thirteenth-century suitors at court believed this to be so) that the tithings did not extend to Northumbria nor to some at least of the Welsh border shires, but by 1066 over most of the country it had become customary for the chief royal representative, ultimately the sheriff, to make sure that the tithings were full and in good order.[26] He did so at two extraordinary meetings of the hundred court which were known after the Conquest as the sheriff's *tourn.* At these meetings a reeve and four men from each vill presented themselves to undergo a searching examination by the sheriff about the state of the vill, the question of theft and the presentation of offenders. The sheriff also collected his dues, the tithing pennies, which came to him from his inspection of the tithings. In the Norman feudal world, supervision of the tithings evolved easily into that most tenacious and characteristic of customs, the view of frankpledge.

---

25 Lieb. i, p. 322; *EHD.* i, no. 49, p. 457, II Cnut 20 (a man was not entitled to the rights of a freeman if he were not in a hundred or a tithing).
26 F. Pollock and F.W. Maitland, *History of English Law* (2nd edn reissued 1968), vol. i, pp. 568–71.

Tithings, hundreds and wapentakes, rapes, lathes and ridings provided a firm territorial sub-structure for Anglo-Saxon England. The main structure depended on the shire organization, and indeed the shire with its courts, officers and traditions was to prove among the most lasting attributes passed on from the Anglo-Saxon world. Although the shiring process was still incomplete, especially in the north and north-west, in 1066 England provided a general pattern of ordered territorial government that had great potential for future growth and development. Many thegns in the tenth and eleventh centuries exercised functions that would not have been utterly strange to the knights of the shire in the central medieval period.

The Borough

The boroughs in the later Anglo-Saxon period deserve particular attention, partly because there used to be a distinct tendency among scholars to underestimate their importance. The image and stereotype of Anglo-Saxon peasant, Norman lord, Anglo-Saxon countryman, Anglo-Norman urban dweller, was so strong that it was difficult to recognize the continuous growth of town life which is now the commonplace of most historical analyses of the last century and a half of Anglo-Saxon England. Careful examination of the currency and of the minting laws has helped to bring about this reappraisal. From the reign of Edgar no borough was without its mint and some of the boroughs were already showing their importance in the commercial world by the issue of a voluminous coinage from the hands of a dozen or so active moneyers. London was prominent but Winchester, York and Lincoln were also substantial towns and minting places by 1066. There was also a group of substantial towns of the middle rank which flourished intermittently sometimes for military and administrative as well as for commercial reasons. Chester, Exeter, Oxford and (as the eleventh century progressed) Bristol, ranked high in this riddle group. Also in the eleventh century, and again possibly because of a genuine commercial revival which attended the creation of Cnut's empire and the resulting increased use of the North Sea by peaceful traders we find a momentum of urban growth sustained in the easterly parts of England. The old Danish headquarters of the Five Boroughs − Leicester, Nottingham, Derby, Stamford as well as Lincoln itself − took on a new lease of life. The boroughs of East Anglia and the Fens country flourished, notably Norwich, Thetford and Cambridge. In Kent at the time of Edward the Confessor the boroughs later to be known as the Cinque Ports gained special privileges in return for taking on responsibility for naval defence. Throughout historic Wessex there was a multitude of small boroughs, many of them in direct line of descent from the Alfredian *burhs*. Mercian towns grew with the shire organization they embodied and symbolized. Many of the episcopal sees were still rural, but Canterbury, Winchester, Worcester, London and Rochester indicated the shape of things to come. Already by 1050 the episcopal see of the south-west had been moved from rural Crediton to urban Exeter.

These urban centres in all their variety and multiplicity give evidence of the prosperity of the trading classes in late Old-English life. References abound to Anglo-Saxon merchants throughout Western Europe from Iceland to Rome. There was also an intense internal trade, especially in wool and cloth and iron and salt. Attempts were made by the kings to confine trading to recognized boroughs, and it was only under sheer pressure of business that these attempts failed. Ethelred and Cnut had to recognize that trade *up on lande* as well as in boroughs was legitimate – but only if conducted with good witness.[27] The whole concern with safety for traders and provision of good witness testifies to the vitality of trading life in late Anglo-Saxon England. Good witness, it was recognized, could be provided in the hundred court, but over most of England the borough court could provide an equivalent that was quite as effective and which indeed in many areas took over the functions of a court over one or two hundreds. The boroughs were also keyed in to the local communities not by territorial legal ties but by tenurial ties. Town houses were frequently attached to local manors, and the charge and obligation to contribute to the defence of the town walls laid fair and square on the surrounding countryside. Within the towns — and this applied to small towns like Abbotsbury and Bedwyn as well as to great boroughs such as Cambridge — merchants were organized into guilds which provided rudimentary safeguards on distant journeys and some security communally for the guild brethren.[28]

An outstanding and altogether remarkable feature of the Anglo-Saxon boroughs is their royal nature. Worcester was substantially an episcopal town from the days of Alfred. Some of the smaller boroughs of Kent were mediatized, Sandwich to Christ Church, Canterbury, and Fordwich to St Augustine's, but the overwhelming majority of the English boroughs were royal. The borough was in nine cases out of ten a royal creation, and in some of them there is early evidence of royal plantation and deliberate royal creation of uniform plots of land to attract settlers. Mintage rights were, as we have seen, completely regalian. The sharing of borough revenues and customs between the

27 *EHD* i, no.49, p.458, II Cn. 24: no one was to buy anything, livestock nor goods, worth more than fourpence without the trustworthy witness of four men, whether in the borough or up country.
28 *EHD* i, nos. 136-9, pp. 603-7.

king and the earl, two-thirds to the king and one-third to the earl, became a characteristic of most Anglo-Saxon boroughs, but the existence of this so-called 'earl's third penny' (often and apparently easily resumed by the early Norman kings) must not obscure the overriding reserve of royal authority. Profits came too from the borough courts. Here again the influence of the king and his officers was of paramount importance though the situation in the larger boroughs could be far from simple. Indeed the shire courts in much of England often came to meet in the boroughs, and there was an inevitable mingling of jurisdictions. This is not to deny the existence of private jurisdiction within the bigger towns. There was a positive network of jurisdiction within London, though the general pattern of one great court which was the equivalent of a shire court and a multitude of hustings was clear enough and simple enough. Complications grow when it is realized that many enclaves existed, perhaps groups of half-a-dozen houses or so, where great men exercised their jurisdiction or soke. Towns of the size of Winchester and York enclosed many such enclaves. Even in a comparatively small town like Hereford the moneyers enjoyed sake and soke, presumably over their mints, and over a small complex of dependants' houses. For the most part, however, the thriving boroughs of Anglo-Saxon England need to be seen in their proper royal context. Deliberately fostered and encouraged by the kings and their advisers, they represent a successful element in the royal aim of achieving an ordered settled society. Potentially the towns of 1066 offered opportunity for extension in the interests of a centralized monarchy, and it is to the credit of the Normans that they exploited this potential to the full.

There remain shadowy and difficult lines of distinction between town and country which are difficult to draw. The last century of Anglo-Saxon England saw a fluid, developing society and hard and fast legal distinctions are not always appropriate. The community itself drew a clear line between landright and boroughright in the general sense,[29] but it could not always have been possible to disentangle, for example, the standing and status of a shire court held in a borough or of a court representing a hundred or a group of hundreds held in a town. Modern scholars are right to stress economic and social realities and the needs that sprang from them. Up to the reign of Alfred the military element in the *burh* predominated; after Alfred with the extension of West-Saxon peace came increased trading and,

---

29 Lieb. i, 477, *Episcopus 6*: ge *burhriht ge landriht*. A bishop was to cooperate with secular judges, to see that false measures and weights were not used, and generally to act in the interests of justice. The fact that a bishop is so instructed is further indication of the complexity and indeed confusion of courts in existence.

conspicuously at the end of the tenth and the beginning of the eleventh centuries, increased international trading. The complexities involved in such transactions, protection of mobile traders, provision for rudimentary insurance on persons and valuable property, arrangements for community action (under royal direction) to build and maintain walls or earthworks demanded some specialist organization different from that applicable to the substantially stationary and immobile rural population of vill or of manor.

The narrative sources of the period make it quite plain that towns came to play an increasingly important part in affairs. London in particular achieved a special prominence during the Ethelredan wars, and Winchester in the south and York in the north occupied positions of special weight. Archaeological evidence, coupled with judicious use of immediate post-Conquest literary sources is helping us to understand something of the physical nature and also of the administrative complexity of these large towns. James Tait, in his masterly and fundamental survey of the medieval borough, rightly selected four characteristics which one would expect to find in a pre-Conquest borough, not necessarily all at the same time, not all essential before the term 'borough' can legitimately be employed. These were a mint, a court, a special tenure bearing resemblance to medieval burgage tenure, and a characteristic to which he gave the ugly but informative designation 'heterogeneity of tenure'.[30] London was naturally a special case. With a population well in excess of 10,000 by 1066 it was the largest town in England and exhibited a corresponding administrative complexity. It was the largest mintage centre and was developing into the die-cutting centre for the whole realm. It had more moneyers at work than any other borough. The complexity of court organization was unique. There was a large popular assembly, a folk-moot which met in the open air on the highest ground in the city, immediately to the north-east of St Paul's, not far from the site of the present Museum of London. It bore some of the characteristics we associate with borough courts and some that seem more typical of shire courts. The right to declare a man an outlaw rested with this court. A network of lesser courts existed — ward-moots, over which aldermen would preside, for the settlement of minor offences and hustings or weekly meetings (house-things of Anglo-Danish origin) initially for the settlement of trading matters and disputes arising from trade. Burgage tenure is implied in the existence and regulation of thegns' guilds within London and heterogeneity of tenure is absolute and unmistakeable. There were men of many lords within London and

---

30 J. Tait, *The Medieval English Borough* (Manchester, 1936).

the resulting complications led in time to the multiplication of special jurisdiction or sokes within the city.[31]

Winchester is now, thanks to the productive and skilful excavations of the decade 1961–1971 the best known among the other greater Anglo-Saxon towns.[32] From the administrative point of view it was of importance on the national as well as on the burghal scale, acting certainly by the end of the period as the chief repository of the royal treasure and fulfilling, as Martin Biddle put it, 'for the Anglo-Saxon state all the requirements of an early capital'.[33] The sequence of its development in the later Anglo-Saxon period is securely established. Refounded in the 880s under the inspiration of King Alfred, with a regular rectilinear street system and refurbished defences, suburban development outside the five principal gates of the city reinforced the strength of Winchester as a centre of population and of commercial and institutional activity. It became the largest of the Wessex boroughs in area, 143.8 acres as opposed to the 100 acres or so of Wallingford and Chichester, the next largest in size. By the reign of the Confessor its street plan filled the entire walled area. A strong royal palace and a most impressive set of ecclesiastical and monastic buildings in the south-east corner of the town provided a centre without equal for training, schooling and exercise of administrators. As a mint it ranked high in the hierarchy of English coin production, well behind London but vying with, and on occasions equalling, the output of the two other major mints at York and Lincoln. Its structure of legal courts was much simpler than that of London, and the royal reeves occupied key positions in the administration of justice. Division into wards, as in London, was a pre-Conquest feature and again aldermen, as they were called, were the officers in charge of these units, possibly in Winchester consisting of individual streets. Citizens enjoyed access to at least four associations in guilds (social or neighbourhood units in many essentials) with their guildhalls. There was also a guild for priests and deacons. Special burgage tenure was a consistent element in Winchester history presumably from the planned Alfredian foundation and heterogeneity of tenure certainly existed although the strong presence of the royal house and of the great religious foundations helped in some measure to distort and to simplify the tenurial scene. By 1057, the probable date of the survey

31 C.N.L. Brooke and Gillian Keir, *London 800-1216: The Shaping of a City* (London, 1975), especially pp. 155-7.

32 ed. M. Biddle, *Winchester in the Early Middle Ages* (Oxford, 1976).

33 M. Biddle, 'Winchester: The development of an early capital'. *Vor- und frühformen der europäischen Stadt im Mittelalter*, t.1, ed. H. Jankuhn, W. Schlesinger, Hecko Steuer (Gottingen, 1973), p. 261.

used in the *Liber Winton,* Winchester was large, populous, and owned substantially by the king and six great churches.

York alone of the northern towns, though Lincoln comes near to challenging it, stands out as an example of urban administrative complexity in the later Anglo-Saxon period. Again recent detailed archaeological investigation has brought out the nature of this bustling northern city, truly Anglo-Danish rather than just simply Anglo-Saxon.[34] Its importance as a commercial centre was of European as well as of British dimension. As a mint York ranked consistently as second in volume of output behind London and probably in population too, though exaggerated contemporary claims that it possessed some 30,000 adult inhabitants clearly have to be discounted. Its court structure seemed close to the Winchester model though its wards (or shires) were fewer and more compact. The archbishop possessed full rights under the king over one of the seven 'shires' into which the city was divided, and the king depended heavily on the archbishop to see to it that royal rights were enjoyed and royal servants respected. The presence of standard burgage tenements can be fairly inferred from immediate post-Conquest evidence and there were men of many lands living in this complex thriving metropolis of the north in 1066. The sheer volume of work demanded for successful government of York, as for London and Winchester, reminds us of the number of men, for the most part unchronicled and unnamed, who must have been busy in humdrum routine administrative matters in late Anglo-Saxon England.

It is harder to speak with certainty of the middling and lesser boroughs, though there again plentiful evidence exists for the period immediately before 1066 of the complexities of communities such as those at Chester, Lincoln, Hereford, Norwich, Exeter, Oxford and the Kentish boroughs. Guild regulations have survived from the last generation before the Conquest from four of these less distinguished boroughs, from Cambridge, Exeter, Bedwyn and Abbotsbury, and it is helpful to consider the administrative implications of these documents.[35] The Cambridge regulations concern a guild of thegns and significantly deal largely with the protection given to members, to guild-brothers, in matters relating to the feud and vengeance for injury. There was an element of basic insurance involved; a guild-

---

34 A.G. Dickens, 'York Before the Norman Conquest', *VCH The City of York* (1961), pp. 2-24. Also A.P. Smyth, *Scandinavian York and Dublin, I and II* (Dublin, 1975 and 1979). P.V. Addyman, 'Excavations in York, 1972-73'. *Antiquaries Journal* 54 (1975), pp. 200-31, and later reports in the *Antiquaries Journal.*

35 Good translations of the regulations for Cambridge, Exeter, Bedwyn, and Abbotsbury appear in *EHD* i, nos. 136-9, pp. 603-7.

brother if he died or was taken ill, was to be brought home, dead or alive, by his brethren. The Exeter statutes were more religious in tone and dealt with arrangements for pilgrimage, including pilgrimage to Rome. Only a fragment of the Bedwyn Guild statutes survive, enough however to show that they conformed to what seems a set pattern, payment on death, payment and recompense at the burning of a house and reconciliation and peace-keeping among the brethren. It is the little new borough of Abbotsbury that gives the best insight into this not altogether familiar aspect of Anglo-Saxon life. A prominent Danish housecarl of Cnut, Urki by name, gave in the 1040s the guildhall and the site at Abbotsbury to the guildship, presumably associated with the new little abbey at Abbotsbury. They drew up regulations, the first section of which dealt with alms to the church. There followed social regulations to keep the group together, a good brewing or forfeiture of entrance fee if the brewing should prove unsatisfactory and regulations for keeping the peace among the brethren. Finally, and in great detail, approved by eloquent religious sanction, rules were laid down to ensure safety in sickness or decent burial after death.

> And if any one of us becomes ill within 60 miles we are then to find 15 men to fetch him − 30 if he be dead − and these are to bring him to the place which he desired in his life; and if he dies in the neighbourhood, the steward is to be informed to what place the body ought to be taken, and the steward is then to inform the guild-brothers, as many as he can possibly ride to or send to, that they are to come there and worthily attend the body and bring it to the minster, and pray earnestly for the soul.[36]

The intrinsic interest of the passage has sometimes concealed the importance of the incidental value of the evidence for eleventh-century conditions. Abbotsbury was a new monastery and a new borough. There was nevertheless the calm assumption that enough funds and manpower would be available to fulfil basic social obligations within a radius of sixty miles from the Dorset coast.

The Church

The prominence of the Church and churchmen in royal government and general administration is one of the outstanding feature of late Old-English society. The bishops were great men, active in society, natural advisers to the king in the witan. They were also for the most part wealthy men, responsible for the administration of extensive estates that belonged to the see or technically to the saint to whom their

36 *EHD* i, no. 139, p. 607.

cathedral church was dedicated. Some of them held firmly lands of their own, and they tended to be drawn from the wealthier land-owning classes of society. The endowments and resources directly under a bishop's control represented in microcosm what royal estates represented on the larger scene, the means of sustaining a household with peculiar rights and duties and also the means of fulfilling public obligations. The separation of specifically episcopal lands from lands held by the chapters of the greater churches added a fresh complica-tion to the scene, particularly after the Benedictine reforms of Edgar's reign which brought into being in some of the greater of the churches the characteristic English institution, the monastic cathedral chapter. Possession of extensive estates held by charter, bookland, brought immunity from basic payments to support the king or his officers, but the obligations of exercising the resulting lordships remained onerous. Defence and the keeping open of communications, bridge-service and the upkeep of fortifications could not be escaped. Much must have depended on temperament. Warlike bishops, such as Leofgar of Hereford, for example, who was killed on an expedition against the Welsh in 1056, would play an active part in the actual fighting. All bishops had to look to the military capacity of their lands and to see that proper steps were taken to ensure peace from outside barbarians or from cattle raiders and other disturbers of the peace. The increasing tendency during the last century of Anglo-Saxon England for bishops and abbots to take over prime responsibility for the running of many hundred courts, brought about further involvement in the judicial and administrative business of the community.

The literacy of the bishops and of the clergy in general is one of those simple truths it is only too easy to neglect. Permanence in government demanded record and the clerks were the people able to provide it. Bishops were by and large appointed by the king or at the least (in the case especially of the monastic chapters) approved by him. Such was the custom of the community, and there is little evidence of scandal or of simony in any serious sense. At the royal court itself there existed, sometimes in identifiable form over many years, a body of clerks, useful men about the place, who provided a reserve of literate help to the king. The influence of this clerical element on royal government and administration can scarcely be exaggerated. Advice on the formulation of statements of law was freely given and freely accepted. Dunstan is said to have influenced Edgar in putting forward laws with a moral tone,[37] and we have already seen examples from the reigns of Edgar, Ethelred and Cnut of an interpenetration of secular

---

37 *Memorials of St Dunstan, archbishop of Canterbury*, ed. W. Stubbs, RS, 63 (London, 1874), p. 110.

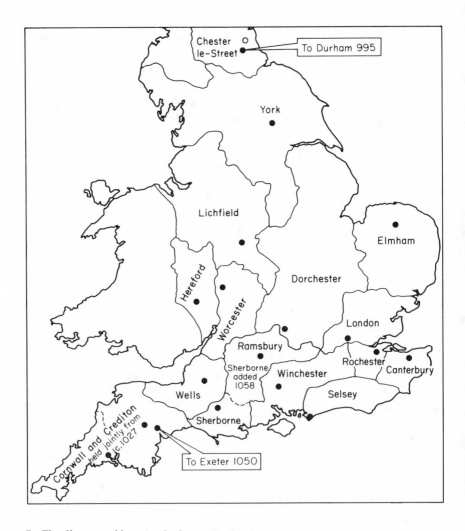

Chester le-Street ⊙ ● — To Durham 995

York ●

Lichfield ●

Elmham ●

Hereford ●

Worcester ●

Dorchester

Ramsbury ●

London ●

Rochester ● ● Canterbury

Sherborne added 1058

Winchester ●

Wells ●

Selsey

Cornwall and Crediton held jointly from c.1027 ●

Sherborne ●

To Exeter 1050

7   The dioceses of late Anglo-Saxon England.

Cornwall and Crediton were held jointly first by Lyfing (c.1027–46) and then by Leofric (1046–72) who moved the centre of the see to Exeter in 1050. Ramsbury and Sherborne were joined together by Herman in 1058 (ultimately in post-Conquest days it became the diocese of Salisbury). The extensive diocese of Dorchester was created out of earlier dioceses of Lindsey and Leicester after the troubles caused by the Scandinavian invasions (ultimately in post-Conquest days it became the diocese of Lincoln).

and ecclesiastical, of rules for the world and rules for God's Church. Royal authority and the authority of earls and thegns was vital for the successful practical application of general rules. Churches had to be protected and the financial interests of churches, the collection of dues, safeguarded. The liturgical year was also the social year, and matters concerning the proper observance of festivals and fasts needed secular power in support. A moral code implied moral penalties with force in reserve to make such penalties significant against criminous clerks, vagrant monks, loss of chastity, even reversion to heathen practices. The clergy had a prominent part to play in sanctifying oaths at ordeal or compurgation; failure to play such a part led to fines and penalties. At the shire court and the hundred court the bishop or his representative must have been among the busiest of people. Yet in a curious sense such action in the public courts did not necessarily weaken the integrity of the Church as a separate institution. There was a special reserve of jurisdictory power, notably in the bishop. The lack of clear definitions in the clerical situation helped to avoid later open quarrels and possible tensions over the justiciability of criminous clerks. The laws of Cnut, a deliberate and successful general statement drawn up under the inspiration of a great archbishop for a Danish conqueror, give us a good example. It was the bishop who was to direct the amends that priests should provide to God and to man if they were found guilty of breaking their oaths, or giving false witness, or stealing, or acting in concert with thieves. If greater crimes, even homicide, were in question, a triple penalty was exacted: the priest was to lose his priestly rank, he was to be banished and to seek the Pope in order to receive penance. For the greatest crimes of all, presumably those that were passing into the category of pleas of the Crown, a curious compromise seems to have been reached. Such guilty priests were to be passed to the bishop for final judgement according to the nature of the deed.[38]

Side by side therefore with the public courts and apparatus of justice with which they themselves were intimately bound, there also existed a powerful age-old tradition of episcopal jurisdiction that was indeed intensified in the course of the tenth century as knowledge of Carolingian-Frankish modifications of canon law became better known. There was an area of doubt and hesitation and overlap between the shire court at which the bishop could preside and the bishop's court. Attempts were made, notably by Archbishop Wulfstan of

---

38 Lieb. i, pp. 287-9, 340 and 42 I Cn. 5, 3; II Cn. 41 and 43: *EHD* i, no 49, p. 461: the difficult phrase *forwyrce mid deaðscylde* is used in clause 43, translated in the *Quadripartitus* as *se forisfaciat in morte plectendis actibus* and more succinctly in the *Consiliatio Cnuti* as *se forisfaciat crimine mortali.*

York, to make known procedure relating to public penance, and to regularize and bring up to date a full penitential system, based on Frankish precedents; these attempts deserve notice as evidence of ecclesiastical authority over its proper disciplinary field.[39]

Finally one aspect of Church life must receive some attention in relation to administrative problems, and that is the straightforward question of territorial organization. In the early Anglo-Saxon period the Church provided something of a precocious example to influence and to modify the political groupings of the early kings. For the later period the roles at times appear reversed with the kings taking the initiative and with the diocesan arrangements, for example, subject to radical modification in the interests of politics. In Church as in State men from the south were often appointed to positions of trust in the more remote and hostile north.[40] It proved expedient for secular reasons as much as for spiritual to combine the impoverished archiepiscopal see of York with the wealthy see of Worcester under one bishop, and indeed,it took a special effort on the part of the reformed papacy to break up this liaison. Pope Nicholas II at first refused the pallium to Ealdred for moving to York without giving up his old see at Worcester; and it was only after agreement was made to separate the sees that papal consent was obtained. There were seventeen dioceses in all in the last phase of Anglo-Saxon England. South of the Thames the correspondence between secular and ecclesiastical administrative units remained close. The two ancient dioceses of Rochester and Canterbury looked after the interests of west Kent and east Kent, of the men of Kent and the Kentishmen. Selsey provided a see for the men of Sussex, the South Saxons. Shire boundaries corresponded for the most part with diocesan in historic Wessex, Winchester for the two prosperous shires of Hampshire and Surrey, Ramsbury for Wiltshire and Berkshire, Sherborne for Dorset, Wells for Somerset, Crediton and then after 1050 Exeter for Devon, and St Germans for part of the period for Cornwall. Edward the Elder had been chiefly responsible for this systematic arrangement in Wessex, showing his administrative skill in ecclesiastical as well as in secular matters. After the death of Denewulf, bishop of Winchester, in 908 and of Asser of Sherborne in the following year he saw to it that three extra sees were endowed at Ramsbury, Wells and Crediton, though it appears that the endowments of roughly 300 hides proved ultimately inadequate. In the reign of Athelstan St Germans was set up as the see for Cornwall

---

39 *A Wulfstan Manuscript*, ed. H.R. Loyn, Early English Manuscripts in Facsimile (Copenhagen, 1971), pp. 53-4.

40 D. Whitelock, 'The Dealings of the Kings of England with Northumbria in the Tenth and Eleventh Centuries', *The Anglo-Saxons*, ed. P. Clemoes (London, 1959), pp. 70–88.

though again inadequate funding caused difficulty, Cornwall passing under the control of the bishop for Devon before the end of the period. Such a concentration on shire boundaries was not possible in English Mercia. Shiring was late and artificial, and the dioceses tended to maintain the outlines of ancient tribal divisions, Hereford for the *Magonsætan,* Worcester for the *Hwicce,* and Lichfield for the complex of folk who dwelt in the north-west of Mercia. On the far side of Watling Street within the Danelaw there was a situation of great uncertainty and it was not really until the 950s after the flight of Eric Bloodaxe from York that diocesan boundaries were clarified. Viking attacks and settlement had played havoc with the diocesan boundaries of eastern Mercia. Lindsey and Leicester had disappeared as episcopal sees and the huge residual complex from Humber to Thames depended on the bishop of Dorchester whose own territorial wealth and interests tended to be solidly south in Oxfordshire, Buckinghamshire and to some extent Huntingdonshire and Bedfordshire. The see of London kept its old bounds of Essex, Middlesex and Hertfordshire; but East Anglia had to be content with a single diocese with its cathedral centre of Elmham. North of the Humber the Viking presence had led to a massive simplification with the large diocese of York and, after 995, the see of St Cuthbert which settled at Durham. Many of the diocesan centres where the bishop had his cathedral were proving too rural and remote, though archaeological investigation is now teaching us belatedly not to underrate the greatest Old-English churches, so many of which were swept away to make room for the Norman innovator and builder.

The cathedral was the bishop's centre of administration, but the situation was complicated in many dioceses by the presence of great monasteries of the tenth-century reformation, in some areas such as East Anglia and the Fenlands wealthier and more prestigious than the diocesan centres themselves. The Normans were in a position after the Conquest to rationalize and clarify the situation, and we still have in our see of Bath and Wells indications of the permanence of one such move where the endowment and wealth of a Benedictine abbey helped to sustain the diminishing resources of the see for Somersetshire at Wells. Similar schemes were suggested, but came to nothing in relation to the abbey of Bury St Edmunds in Suffolk. Apart from the great churches, there was a recognized hierarchy of ecclesiastical institutions, expressed legally in the laws of Ethelred which recognized the existence of four principal types of church, chief minsters, smaller minsters, smaller ones still where there was still a cemetery with presumably profitable burial rights, and what were described as field churches. Violation of sanctuary in the church was to vary according to its status: £5 in English law for a chief minster, 120s. for the rather smaller variety, 60s. for one smaller again, and 30s. for a field church.[41] The more substantial of the minsters were clearly special establishments and in areas bordering on the Celtic communities may well have resembled the *clas* churches of Wales, more or less the physical property at times of recognized kindreds, and serving a large geographical area from a centre which might provide the base for a small community of priests. Elsewhere in varying sizes and with amazing variety in wealth a multitude of churches existed, some approximating to large parish churches, others little more than territorial churches adjacent to a lord's estate, and others again probably little more than a churchyard area with rough buildings attached. For spiritual purposes the Anglo-Saxon bishops succeeded in the main in retaining their rights with all that implied over these varieties of church, but lordship over the temporalities was a very different matter. Again for the most part the English Church avoided the worst abuses to be found elsewhere and it was clearly exceedingly rare for a priest not to be free. The only known specific example indeed occurs in the relatively recently discovered Will of Æthelgifu.[42] Property was another matter. All churches were subject to a lord, and that lord whether layman or cleric expected to make a profit out of them. Control of tithe and churchscot rested clearly with the minsters. Some ecclesiastical customs, plough alms, burial rights and so on could be treated as appurtenances of a manor.

To govern the dioceses, particularly large dioceses such as Dorchester, a bishop needed much assistance. Coadjutor bishops are occasionally to be found and it has been suggested that the presence of such *chorepiscopi* may be taken as a rebuttal of the old view that in Anglo-Saxon England there were no ranks between the bishop and the priest.[43] Archdeacons were employed especially in the complex of Worcester and York under Oswald and his successors. Historically these men were in Western Europe the bishop's chief executive agents, especially his chief legal servants. In England there is evidence at Canterbury as early as the ninth century for a chief deacon singled out from the cathedral clergy to be the principal active servant in the episcopal household. At least one archbishop, Wulfred (805–832), had been an archdeacon.[44] No territorial subdivision of the dioceses in England appears to have been attempted, and even at Canterbury the

---

41 Lieb. i, pp. 264 and 282; *EHD* i, no 46., p. 449, VIII Eth. 5.1; 1 Cn. 3.2.
42 *The Will of Æthelgifu*, trs. and examined D. Whitelock, Neil Ker, Lord Rennell of Rodd, Roxburghe Club (Oxford, 1968), pp. 32–3. Edwin the priest was to be freed and to have the church for his lifetime on condition he keep it in repair, and he was to be given a man.
43 F. Barlow, *The English Church, 1000–1066*, (London, 1963), pp. 246–7.
44 Margaret Deanesly, *Sidelights on the Anglo-Saxon Church* (London, 1962), pp. 150-1: there is a valuable section on 'archdeacons and deans', pp. 165–70.

periods when a single archdeacon predominated were followed by periods when there were many. The deacons and the archdeacons were men who had not proceeded to higher spiritual orders, probably because of a feeling that they were involved too closely in worldly affairs. In the vast diocese of York the need for activity on the part of men who could serve in the bishop's name may have led to some pre-Conquest clarification of the archdeacon's position. A complex document known as the 'Law of the Northumbrian Priests' has survived from the first quarter of the eleventh century, in which the archdeacon appears as a man with considerable disciplinary and legal authority over the lesser clergy. If a priest neglected the bishop's summons he was to pay 20 *oras* normally equivalent to 16 pence an *ora*, but he was to pay 12 *oras* if he neglected the archdeacon's. If a priest committed an offence and celebrated mass in spite of the bishop's prohibition he was to pay 20 oras for disregard of the prohibition and to make amends for the offence he had previously committed. The archdeacon's prohibition was protected in a similar fashion, subject to penalty of 12 *oras*.[45] It was not until after the Norman Conquest, however, that archdeacons came into their own as the bishop's right-hand man in all dioceses. Organized rural deaneries were also a matter for the future, although men holding the title *decanus* (dean) were prominent among those helping in various ways with the running of the complex ecclesiastical institutions, regular and secular, that we recognize through the fragmentary evidence. The tenth-century Benedictine reformation increased the popularity of the term 'dean' to describe the chief monk after the abbot in a community, especially as the monastic movement spread deeply into the secular channel with the institution of monastic chapters at the great cathedral of Christ Church, the Old Minster at Winchester, and Worcester. Simplification in function if not in terminology – for provost and prior remained terms that were acceptable if not always precise – came with the Normans. The brunt of the administrative burden continued to be borne by the bishop and his household: and his deacons were his principal administrative agents.

Private Jurisdiction

Much of the richness and subtlety of the administrative and legal situation is lost of we fail to realize that in the last century of Anglo-Saxon England, private jurisdiction was also achieving close definition and growing along lines parallel to and sometimes overlapping with the recognized jurisdiction of a hundred court or other public tribunal,

45 Lieb. i, pp. 380-3: *EHD* i, no. 52, p. 472, *North. Pr. Law*, cls. 3,4,6,7.

territorial or burghal. There was a reserve of judicial authority implicit in the inner nature of lordship, secular and ecclesiastical. Earl or bishop, thegn or abbot, the lord was held responsible for the good behaviour of his household and immediate followers, and such responsibility involved an exercise in judgement which could easily be formalized into the giving of judgements. The strength of the monarchy and the nature of the political moves against the Danes resulting in the unification of England, enabled the worst abuses of private jurisdiction to be avoided, and surviving records suggest considerable emphasis on the franchisal nature of all such jurisdiction as the tenth century progressed. The most frequently specified juridicial rights (see above, pp. 129–30) were sake and soke and toll and *team* and *infangenetheof*. Sake and soke developed into a convenient composite term in its own right, signifying jurisdiction in general, but the other terms are more specific. Toll referred to the right to take toll on goods sold within an estate, and also to hear questions of dispute over such toll. There is no evidence to support the view that it involved the right to impose a levy on goods in transit. *Team* signified the valuable right to supervise the process known as vouching to warranty, that is the presentation of convincing evidence that goods offered for sale truly belonged to the vendor. *Infangenetheof,* or the right to hang a thief caught red-handed within the estate with the goods on him, was an important legal right invoking a right to gallows. Constrained by our awareness that such formulae became conventional in charters dealing with rural estates, we have perhaps failed to recognize the purpose of such grants which amounted in essence to the grant of rights over a market with effective powers of discipline to ensure fair trading and effective, if arbitrary, punishment of thieves who would be only too likely to congregate at such assemblies.[46]

By the end of the period and in many areas grant of soke and sake clearly involved grants of rights over a hundred court. This has led many scholars to suggest that all such grants involved the grant of rights, financial as much as judicial, within the framework of public courts. Such an interpretation does not take proper account of the fluidity of the judicial situation; we are dealing with a period of growth and development both in the public and in the private exercise of jurisdiction. Rights over a hundred would involve substantial financial advantages, the privilege of appointing or approving the hundredman, and the duty as lord of a hundred to ensure that police functions as well as social and commercial functions were properly exercised. The coincidence with grants of soke and sake over an estate was complete though the effects were magnified, even more so when

46 Harmer, *Anglo-Saxon Writs*, pp. 73-85.

groups of hundreds were in question as at Peterborough, Ely, Bury St Edmunds and the triple hundred of the Oswaldslaw at Worcester.[47] A lord with the right to supervise good witness, exact tolls, and hang a thief, was well on his way to controlling the territorial area in which his sphere of jurisdiction lay. Survivals into the modern period of names such as the 'Soke of Peterborough' and Thorpe-le-soke illustrate one facet of this process of territorialization. The confusion of franchisal rights with private duties led to much anomaly, and it is no wonder that the boundaries of hundreds in particular became much more unstable than is customary with such territorial divisions. The sheer convenience of associating separate hundreds together under the same lordship made for variations and change. It has been estimated that no fewer than 130 hundreds and wapentakes, not far from a third of the total number in England, were in private hands by 1086.[48] Executive strength alone, personified in the person of the sheriff with his financial prerequisites, prevented the hundred from degenerating into a dominical institution.

Military Organization

Reference has already been made to important financial aspects of military organization. Evidence unfortunately tends to be negative in detail, more concerned with penalties for failing to perform military service rather than with what is involved in practice with its performance. For a nobleman, as early as the reign of Ine of Wessex (688–725) forfeiture of land and a heavy penalty (120s.) was the penalty for neglecting proper military service, and graded penalties were also exacted from noblemen owning no land (60s.) and from ordinary freemen (*ceorls*) 30s. for such offences.[49] Prominent among the standardized penalties known to the later Anglo-Saxon laws was *fyrdwite,* the fine taken for failure to serve in the *fyrd,* in the national defence force. Under the stress of the Danish invasions at the time of Ethelred, attempts were made to frame general regulations that would conform to accepted principle, but would be applicable to the special circumstances of threats by sea. People were instructed to be zealous about the maintenance of the peace, about the improvement of the

47 Fundamental lines of enquiry were opened by Helen Cam in 'Manorium cum Hundredo: the Hundred and the Hundredal Manor', *EHR* 47 (1932), and 'Early Groups of Hundreds', *Historical Essays in Honour of James Tait (Manchester 1933).* reprinted *Liberties and Communities in Medieval England* (Cambridge, 1966), pp. 64-105. See above, pp. 140–8.

48 *Liberties and Communities*, pp. 59–60, where in an essay on 'Suitors and Scabini', *Speculum* 10 (1935), Miss Cam agreed that there is a stron presumption of the existence of at least 130 private hundreds by 1066.

49 *EHD* i, no 32, 404, Ine 51. See also above pp. 32 and 48.

roads everywhere in the country, about the repair of fortifications and bridges, and also about military service, doing whatever was decreed whenever it was necessary. Specific orders were given about the supplying of ships, each to be ready equipped after Easter every year. Damage to a warship of the people (*folces fyrdscip*) was punishable by a fine payable to the king for breach of his protection (*mund*) and if the warship were damaged irreparably, then the full value was to be paid together with the *mundbryce*.[50] Desertion from the army when the king himself was present was subject to the most severe penalties, the offender to be placed in peril of his life and the loss of wergeld or all his property. Other deserters where the king himself was not present, were subject to the stiff fine of 120s.[51] There is an abstract quality to these statements of law which nevertheless does not detract from their importance as an index to contemporary opinion. They fit in perfectly with a period when, as the Anglo-Saxon chronicler tells us, the king ordered (in 1008) 'that ships should be built unremittingly over all England, namely a warship from 310 hides and a helmet and corselet from eight hides' and when the present of 'his best ship', fully equipped with sailing tackle, and sixty helmets and sixty coats of mail was regarded as a seemly gift to be bequeathed by an archbishop to the king under the terms of a will which also made provision for the gift of a ship to the people of Kent and another to Wiltshire.[52] The chronicler tells us that the naval force so collected was of no more use to the country than it had been on many previous occasions. The administrative capacity to raise the resources to provide it is nevertheless assumed; and the association in law between national defence and the fine for the infringement of royal protection is absolute and explicit.

Great changes took place between the death of King Alfred and the Norman Conquest in the organization of the defence of the kingdom as indeed in all other spheres of govenment but some basic principles remained constant. To be capable of taking part in the defence of the community was a mark of the free man, and the obligation to do so virtually a function of freedom. In theory always and in practice more often than not, a free man owned weapons, some of which came to be specified in law, and he would be expected to use them in defence of his home and his neighbours. The king's overall duty was to provide leadership for the free men in arms and in a basic sense the *fyrd* provided such a national army and *fyrdwite* was indeed the penalty exacted as a matter of course for failure to perform service in such an

50 Lieb. i, p. 242; *EHD* i, no. 44, p.445 V Eth. 27; Lieb. i, p. 254 VI Eth. 33-4.
51 Lieb. i, p. 244, V. Eth. 28, 28 i; *EHD* i, no. 44, pp. 445-6.
52 *ASCh* 1008-09, ed. D. Whitelock, pp. 88-9; D. Whitelock, *Anglo-Saxon Wills*, no. 18; *EHD* i, no. 126., pp. 589-90.

army. This basic obligation to military service grew more extensive and complex between 899 and 1066. Groupings of men into tithings and hundreds on a voluntary basis for protection against theft and violence both coincided with and differed from national obligations to service at *fyrd*, fortifications, and bridges. Ealdormen (later earls) and thegns were the most prominent men in the fighting forces, and grew increasingly prominent, as landlords, in the organization, the summons and the assembling of those forces. Landlords, ecclesiastical as well as lay, were involved vitally in the financial and personal organization essential to ensure that competent levies appeared to perform military duties on behalf of their estates. The personal obligation of the freeman to serve remained firm, but tended to fall into the background in face of military needs and social pressures, and it became unusual for a *fyrd* to serve beyond its own recognized field of immediate command, its shire. For defensive campaigning it was right, proper and expedient that all freemen should be called out to defend a finite area, a shire or a group of hundreds, in effect their own hearths and homes. Tenth and eleventh-century campaigning on the contrary, often involved considerable mobility against a principal enemy, the Scandinavians, known for their mobility. It was understandable in England as in Carolingian Europe and post-Carolingian Europe generally, that a more selective force should be called on for campaigns and royal expeditions in defence of an increasingly complex realm. Grouping of estates into five-hide units or six-carucate units became commonplace, and it is highly probable that the customs that are brought to light in Domesday Book whereby one soldier would be sent with full sustenance and resources from five hides 'if the king took an army anywhere' indicate the general trend in the country throughout the last century of Anglo-Saxon England.[53] The so-called 'select fyrd' existed side by side with the great fyrd and some variation in the fines exacted for *fyrdwite*, particularly on the Welsh border, is probably associated with the varying service demanded at select fyrd or a great fyrd.[54]

Over and above the general levy of troops there existed the age-old institutions which provided leadership to the army, the hearthtroop, or picked body of retainers surrounding the king and the great men of the realm. These men could be maintained completely in a lord's household, but increasingly it became common to settle them on land. The growth of a territorial thegnage is a characteristic of late Old-

53 DB i, 56b. This entry from the Berkshire folios emphasizes that one soldier only is to serve from five hides: *tantum unus miles ibat*.
54 C.W. Hollister, *Anglo-Saxon Military Institutions* (Oxford, 1962), especially Ch.III pp. 38–58 'The Select Fyrd and the Five-Hide Unit'.

English society, providing the basis of social conventions upon which the Norman feudal structure could easily be erected. At the royal level the importance of the hearthtroop was intensified rather than diminished by the Danish Conquest. A new term, that of 'housecarl', was introduced to England to describe the household troops, because such they were initially even if they tended to become absorbed into the territorial aristocracy. Later Scandinavian historians equated them with the crews of the forty ships who remained with Cnut in England in 1018, a formidable force of some 2,000 men or so.[55] There is evidence to suggest that they retained their identity as a corps d'elite, particularly in naval warfare, into the reign of Edward the Confessor, but they never developed into a Norman baronage, assimilating rather to the native thegnage, especially in English England where the spoils were greater than in the Danelaw. Each great earl's retinue provided the heart of his own contingent, and a heavy charge on his resources and administrative capacity. In the political crisis of 1051 Edward the Confessor relied on the picked men brought down from the north and from the midlands by his two loyal earls, Siward and Leofric, who were able to send back to their earldoms for a great army, called out to help their lord after they had learned how things were in the south.[56]

Legal texts from the early eleventh century help to illustrate the complexities of the military situation. The men who drafted Cnut's laws were especially concerned with what one may call the officer class in this respect, the earls and the thegns. In personal terms the health of the kingdom depended in large part on the way in which the king was able to exercise his authority over these people, and one sure indication of authority was the exaction of a right known as heriot, that is the insistence that stated payments or returns should be made to a lord, in this instance the king, on the death of his man. The term 'heriot' (*heregeat*) meant originally 'war-gear' or 'war-equipment' and came in feudal days to be equated with the *relevamentum* or relief paid by an heir to enter his ancestor's inheritance. An earl's heriot was substantial, eight horses, four saddled and four unsaddled, four helmets, four coats of mail, eight spears, eight shields, four swords and no less than 200 mancuses of gold. The king's thegns who were nearest to him paid less, but the amount was still great: four horses, two saddled and two unsaddled, two swords, four spears and shields, one helmet, a coat of mail and 50 mancuses of gold. For a lesser thegn a heriot consisted of a horse and its trappings, his weapons or his *healsfang* in Wessex (i.e. a tenth of his wergeld, 600 pence or £2½), or £2 in Mercia, or £2 in East Anglia. Among the Danes who had rights of

---

55 *ASCh*. 1018, ed. D. Whitelock, p. 97. F.M. Stenton, *Anglo-Saxon England*, p. 412.
56. *ASCh* 1051, ed. D. Whitelock, p. 118.

jurisdiction £4 was expected. If he (presumably the Danish thegn) was closer to the king, two horses, one saddled and one unsaddled, a sword, two spears and shields, and 50 mancuses of gold were to be received; from one of lower position £2.[57] There are some doubts and ambiguities over interpretation and it is not to be believed that the system was as tidy in practice as in legal theory. The basic impression, however, is clear and sound. Earls and thegns were men magnificently equipped for the warfare of the age.

This impression is reinforced by one other precious legal glimpse that has survived of mens' status from the same age. Some anonymous writers were concerned with mobility in society, showing proper anxiety over the position of ceorls, who prospered so that they could aspire to thegnhood. One of these writers, describing what he calls the law of the North People (Norðleoda) has a revealing comment to make. He agreed that if the *ceorl* had five hides of land on which he discharged the king's dues his blood price or *wergeld* should be that of a thegn, Possession of the five hides of land was the vital social fact and without it he remained a *ceorl* even if he possessed a helmet, a coat of mail and a gold-plated sword.[58] Anglo-Saxon wills support this legal comment. Fine weapons were precious goods and also a symbol of status and function in the community but they did not carry the weight of landed wealth, the true determinant of social rank and position.

Service in war was the mark of the freeman and leadership in war the mark of the man of exalted status developing fast into a nobleman by birth and class as well as by function. Poetic accounts emphasized the division as we have already seen in the case of the poem on the Battle of Maldon and the Bayeux Tapestry preserves in fine pictorial form representations of well-armed and resolute warriors, quite distinct from the ceorlish militia who occasionally intrude on the scene. The Anglo-Saxon Chronicle itself does not give much detail of military equipment nor indeed of military engagements, but the twelfth-century writer who drew on a now-lost version to construct the history we know as that of Florence or John of Worcester, had a special interest in such affairs and helps us to understand some of the administrative procedures that were needed to keep and equip the formidable English armies. At a critical and hard-fought battle at Sherston in Wiltshire during his campaigns against Cnut in 1016, Edmund is said to have drawn up his men, posting all the best troops in the first line, placing the next in reserve, exhorting them to defend their country, their families and their homes. The king himself fought

---

57 Lieb. i, pp. 356-8; *EHD* i, no. 49, p. 465 Cnut II, 71-71.5.
58 Lieb. i, p. 460, Norðleoda laga, 9–10.

hard at close quarters, performing the duties of a brave soldier as well as an able general. Florence of Worcester showed similar interest in the Welsh campaigns of the 1050s, making the valuable comment on the Hereford disaster that the English had been instructed, contrary to their custom, to fight on horseback, clearly indicating that this was at the least a contributory cause of the disaster.[59] At its best, as it showed at Stamford Bridge, the English army could meet and defeat very powerful traditional military opposition. Transport by horse but battle on foot was their rule: but as experienced and well-trained foot-soldiers they ranked high.

A word needs finally to be said specifically of naval matters. Of all the matters connected with defence the building and manning and deployment of ships demanded the most sustained administrative skills. Alfred had attempted to defeat the Scandinavians in their own element, building longships manned by 60 oarsmen and more. Edgar placed great reliance on his fleet and Ethelred's most far-sighted, though unsuccessful, efforts were directed towards the provision of an effective naval force. Cnut knew the position well from the other side of the fence, and the forty ships that stayed with him in 1018 may well have formed the nucleus of his standing fleet in support of which heregeld was paid and for the provisioning and renewal of which modifications seem to have been made in inland, as well as in coastline shires for the grouping of assessment units into 300 hides, in places known as shipsokes. When Earl Godwin wished to win the favour of Cnut's son Hardicnut, in 1041, he presented him with a fine ship of admirable workmanship with a gilded figure-head, rigged with the best materials and manned with eighty chosen soldiers splendidly armed. If Florence of Worcester can be believed, each of these soldiers wore on each arm a golden bracelet, six ounces in weight, a triple coat of mail and a helmet partly gilt, and a sword with gilded hilt, a Danish battle-axe inlaid with gold, and a shield, the boss and studs of which were gilt. Each also carried a lance, an *ætgar* (*atgeiar* in Old Norse).[60] Maintenance of a fleet was indeed expensive and Edward the Confessor's standing fleet had shrunk to only fourteen vessels by the end of 1049. Even this proved too much. By the end of the year nine crews had been paid off and by the end of 1050 the five remaining crews had also been honourably retired. The country was not left defenceless. Although some portion of the geld, specifically referred to as heregeld, was abolished this action on King Edward's part was accompanied by a set of bargains with the ports of the south-east

59 Florence of Worcester. 1055; *MHB*, p. 607: *Anglos contra morem in equis pugnare iussit.*
  It was the *timidus dux*, Ralph, nephew of the Confessor, who gave the orders.
60 Florence of Worcester. 1040, *MHB*, p. 600: trs. T. Forester, p. 143.

under the terms of which the ports guaranteed a number of ships and seamen for naval defence in return for the profits of justice in their courts. Sandwich, Dover, Fordwich and Romney reached such agreement, and Hythe and Hastings may well have followed suit. From this curious arrangement, as a substitute to the provision of a specifically royal fleet, there grew up that most English of institutions known as the Cinque Ports.[61]

Conclusion

There is a sense in which the historian who attempts to ask the basic questions about late Anglo-Saxon England is attempting the impossible. Was England a well-governed land in 1066, was it a much-governed land, was it rather a land with potential for government, a potential soon to be realized with no holds barred by the new Norman masters? The easy way out, and all of us at times are tempted to take it or actually take it, is to sprinkle our analysis liberally with words such as comparative or reasonable. By the side of feudal France royal England retained full integrity in matters of government; though even in these respects some doubt exists over the nature of the earldoms in mid-eleventh century. By the side of imperial Germany, England presented a simple task to the administrator, a relatively small geographical area, prosperous and capable of easy exploitation given the technical agrarian resources of the day. There is another tack, too, that it is only too easy to follow. For long, indeed from the first generation after the Norman Conquest, it was fashionable among many to denigrate the achievements of the Anglo-Saxons. They were the losers and the Conquest was readily interpreted as a judgement upon the unworthy. The implications of this line of thought for the administrative historian are complicated. For the believers in the existence of and virtues of primitive Germanic democracy this signified no more than that the breaking point had been reached by the mid-eleventh century, and that liberty had indeed degenerated into license and freedom into anarchy. Such believers are no longer to be found among serious historians, but the idea of degeneration lingers on. It is universally recognized that the personalities of the kings were facts of great importance and some of the doubts and hesitations about the administrative potential of the kingdom are reflected in attitudes to the kings. Edgar and Cnut retain their reputation as powerful rulers under whose guidance England was both well-governed and much-

---

61 F.M. Stenton, *Anglo-Saxon England*, pp. 430-2; C.W. Hollister, *Anglo-Saxon Military Institutions*, pp. 116-23.

governed. Ethelred, subject to massive revaluation and speculation, is more difficult to assess and shown to have been energetic and constructive in some fields just as he was a disaster in others; and it is the paradox of the record of sound administration, laws, charters and coins, coupled with appalling narrative accounts of his reign that has led to some revaluation. The biggest puzzle has been over the person of Edward the Confessor. In the happy days when Edward could be dismissed as a pious nincompoop, the historians who regarded William the Conqueror as a judgement on the incompetent and hope for the future had no problems. Modern investigation, again most fruitful on administrative matters, has destroyed this simple picture.[62] Edward the Confessor has emerged as an intelligent ruler, capable of balancing disparate forces within his kingdom and of maintaining diplomatic equilibrium outside. The dominant modern view rejects the inbuilt tendencies to anarchy, stresses the continuity in basic administrative and social growth in the last century of Anglo-Saxon England and interprets William's achievements as the successful running of a monarchy at full power that had already moulded the English community into governable shape.

It was the great legal historian, F.W. Maitland, who instructed us by precept and example to work from the known to the unknown.[63] Since the example that he put before us was Domesday Book and the unknown behind it was Anglo-Saxon England we have always interpreted his dictum along chronological lines. There is another sense in which the precept is true. After nine hundred years and more only a limited amount of evidence has survived and only a limited amount of inference is strictly permissible. Yet a great deal of legitimate difference of opinion comes from judgement, not idle speculation but honest judgement, over the significance of surviving material in relation to that which has not survived. Miss Harmer in her authoritative edition of Anglo-Saxon writs printed 121 writs from 25 different places of origin. She added two later and it is possible that the tally could be further increased by some relaxation of critical method to perhaps as many as 150.[64] Are we or are we not justified in placing the emphasis that we do on the writ in the light of this relatively small number? The answer here must be yes; the nature of the writ, the necessarily ephemeral nature of some of the orders contained in it, add extra weight to the survivors. And the multiplicity of written forms

62 F. Barlow, *Edward the Confessor*, (London, 1970). Barlow comments (p. 268) shrewdly that a close examination of Edward's problems and behaviour reveals 'his intelligence and resourcefulness if not good judgement and wisdom'.

63 F.W. Maitland, *Domesday Book and Beyond* (Cambridge, 2nd edn, 1960).

64 Harmer, *Anglo-Saxon Writs*; also 'A Bromfield and a Coventry Writ of King Edward the Confessor', *The Anglo-Saxons* ed. P. Clemoes (London, 1959), pp. 89-103.

that do survive, wills, memoranda, inventories of estates, may be held, and probably should be held, to have an importance in evidential value relating to Anglo-Saxon administration disproportionate to their number. Similar arguments can be adduced to strengthen the picture of an organized community. The continuous existence of what became virtually permanent territorial administrative divisions is an outstanding case in point. The structure of English local government, shire, hundred, wapentake and vill was fully formed by 1066, and the effective court systems complete. The mintage system, coinage and currency, was advanced and sophisticated. One final reservation remains to be made. Much of the evidence for order and system comes inevitably from the institutions whose business it was to promote order and system, namely the monarchy and the Church. But social historians argue that in the tenth and eleventh centuries a third partner was active and central to the process of creating peaceful ordered society and that was the person of the secular lord. Our earls and thegns and shire-reeves and drengs as they appear in royal writs, themselves held rights and jurisdictions over other freemen. We have seen how exercise of the rights of *sake and soke* could be synonymous with or develop into the exercise of rights over a hundred court. Royal rights and royal administration personified by the shire-reeve with his financial interest in the hundred, prevented further degeneration into institutionalized dominical tyranny, but to lose sight of the clearer definition of the authority and rights of the secular lord is to miss one of the most difficult yet significant strands in the administrative history of late Anglo-Saxon England. In a great tract on the duties of a discriminating reeve, an Anglo-Saxon writer stated wisely that a good reeve should know the right his lord had in the land as well as the rights of the people.[65] With royal and ecclesiastical strands added these two threads of lordship right and folk rights run in complex pattern through the whole fabric of late Old-English society. It is a great tribute to the kings, ealdormen and bishops of the age that in spite of political turbulence, the fabric of such an ordered society was preserved substantially strengthened.

---

65 Lieb. i, p. 453: *se sceadwis gerefa sceal æg ðer witan ge hlafordes landriht ge folces gerihtu*

Part III
The Norman Conquest

7*

Norman Government in the Early Stages of Conquest and Settlement

The preceding six chapters have shown how the government in England was conducted and developed over six centuries. By 1066 England was a much-governed and on occasion a well-governed kingdom, though at times there was a sad gap between ideal and reality when the monarch failed to live up to his office and to his responsibilities. In 1066 the kingdom was conquered by a new and foreign dynasty and aristocracy. The reasons for this conquest have been much debated, as the last chapter has indicated, and the same is true of its consequences. How far did it destroy or revitalize Anglo-Saxon government?

Generations of historians have attempted to present a balanced view of the contributions of the Normans to the permanent shape of government and administration in England, and only too often have succeeded merely in expounding their own beliefs about the state of their own contemporary world. Some have looked on the Conquest as a judgement or a disaster brought upon an enfeebled people, laid low by their own inadequacies, moral as well as political. Others have interpreted the Conquest as a happy event, bringing needed discipline to a wealthy community where liberty was giving way to license and freedom to anarchy. There is a tendency in our days with a strong economic strand to interpretation to read the Conquest as a giant and highly successful take-over bid. Others with memories of world wars still vivid stress the universality of the basic Norman problem, a problem in conquest and occupation technique. When we read that a

* The work of J. Le Patourel is vital to an understanding of the complexities of royal government in both England and Normandy, especially his chapter on 'The Dynamic and the Mechanics of Norman Expansion' *The Norman Empire* (Oxford, 1976). Much valuable up-to-date comment appears regularly in the proceedings of the *Battle Conference* 1978 etc., ed. R. Allen Brown. Domesday Book is the outstanding primary source and good guides to it are to be found in the work of V.H. Galbraith, S. Harvey, and R. Welldon Finn. Introduction to most of the other available material is to be found in *EHD* (vol. ii) and in the *Regesta Regum Anglo-Normannorum* (vol. i) ed. H.W.C. Davis.

heavy fine, the so-called *murdrum* fine, of 46 marks was laid on the whole hundred if a slayer of a Norman was not apprehended, analogies with twentieth-century occupying forces come inevitably to mind. Others again with the amalgam of political, social and economic strands that characterizes some of the best of modern work, emphasize the element of colonization that surely followed Norman success. All commentators are drawn legitimately by the nature of available evidence to say something of the curious combination of English and Norman elements that went to the making of a recognizably Anglo-Norman kingdom.

The first thing that needs to be said is trite and yet important. England before the Normans came was a monarchy with all that implied, and even in the worst of moments the royal Court remained an active centre of royal government. The Christian king governed according to law. Regalian rights were not exclusive, but tended to be overriding and on some matters absolute. There was a network of courts which in theory guaranteed the rights of the freemen. The structure of local government in the pattern of shire, hundred or wapentake, tithing and vill was fully formulated in characteristic medieval shape. By the side of this solid institutional achievement the Norman contribution appears at first sight to be slender. Yet many good critics isolate English vernacular culture and Norman executive skill as two of the principal original contributions to the life of Western Europe in the eleventh and twelfth centuries; and it is helpful to attempt to assess the worth of the specifically Norman contribution to English government.

William I was a conqueror, a harsh master, stern beyond all measure to those who dared oppose his will, and yet, conqueror as he was, he strove to preserve and if necessary to assume continuity with the Anglo-Saxon past. He ruled as the legal and legitimate successor to the last royal representative of the Saxon ruling house, Edward the Confessor, who happened to be William's great-aunt's son. There was a tendency in some Norman circles virtually to ignore Harold II, Harold Godwinson, and only by accident is he accorded the royal title in the whole length of Domesday Book where his normal designation is 'Earl Harold' (*Haroldus comes*). The official Norman view of Harold as an oath-breaker and usurper was indeed firm among the ruling group. William was the true heir who had successfully asserted his lawful rights at Hastings. Norman respect for law was profitable to the Normans, but was not the only reason for their emphasis on legality of succession. When innovation was needed there was little hesitation on William's part. If land had to be placed under special law to protect game for the royal hunt existing rights could be ridden over roughshod. Forest law became an intelligible symbol for much of the arbitrary elements in Norman rule. Perhaps we treat such actions too glibly as exceptional. But for the most part this stern new master of an ancient kingdom found much to his taste in English precedent. In the early years of his reign he directed a writ in Anglo-Saxon to William, bishop of London, and Gosfrith the portreeve, and all the burgesses of London, enjoining them to be worthy of all laws that they were worthy of in King Edward's day and assuring them that each child should be his father's heir after his father's day. He offered them protection stating that he would not suffer any man to do them wrong. There is no reason to think the sentiments were not typical; and in return William expected to enjoy the fruits of legitimate kingship.

One outstanding characteristic that the Normans were able to bring to the task of government was their confidence. This is a strange psychological phenomenon which the historian can record, but cannot truly explain. For some reason for more than a century, say from the arrival of the Hauteville family in the South of Italy in the 1030s and the battle of Val-ès-Dunes in the mid-1040s to the deaths of Roger of Sicily and Stephen of England in the early 1150s, the relatively small but newly prosperous and flourishing duchy of Normandy, technically a fief of the Capetian kingdom of France, produced a race of men who were to play a dominant part in the shaping of Western Europe. The two best-organized kingdoms in Europe, England and Sicily, came under Norman control. Norman skill in war became a by-word, and Norman valour at Civitate and Hastings, Palermo and Antioch added permanent chapters to European military history and legend. From the Scottish border (and beyond as we move into the twelfth century) to Apulia, Capua, Calabria and Sicily over to Corfu and the Greek mainland, to Constantinople and Antioch, Norman names were renowned. There was one sense in which these enterprises were more close-knit than English historians have always realized. The conquest and settlement of England was a tremendous achievement, but it was only one among many of this people whose ambitions were boundless. William Fitzosbern, one of the key men in the English settlement, Earl of Hereford and vicegerent in William's absence from England in 1067, died in 1071 contending for the county of Flanders. William Rufus himself, not content with effective control of the Conqueror's heritage, was planning a move on Aquitaine at the time of his death in 1100. The Montgomery-Bellême family at the height of its power and influence possessed enormous territories within the Anglo-Norman world and limitless ambitions outside it. Robert of Normandy himself married a great-niece of Robert Guiscard the principal moulder of the Hauteville inheritance in the south of Italy. The Tosny family from as early as 1015-16 fought in Italy and Spain and in later generations was prominent in the English Settlement. The Crispin family made impact on the history of Spain, England and the eastern empire. Robert of

Rhuddlan and Hugh I of Grandmesnil were prominent in the Anglo-Norman world: their close kinsfolk played important parts in the Norman settlement of Calabria and South Italy. The Grandmesnil family was especially active in diplomatic negotiations with the eastern empire later in the eleventh century and in the First Crusade itself even though their reputation as fighting men suffered heavily in the fighting around Antioch.[1]

Modern investigation is right to stress that there is an artificiality about the suggested unity of Norman endeavour and achievement, that much of the certainty of identity comes from their own eloquence and from the writings of their own historians, that there was indeed a Norman myth propounded and refined by a formidable group of historians from Dudo of Saint Quentin in the early eleventh century to Ordericus Vitalis, William of Malmesbury, Henry of Huntingdon and their successors in the first half of the twelfth.[2] Those on the receiving end of Norman activity were inclined to dismiss them all as French. Yet it would seem hard not to accept a unity of spirit behind so many of their enterprises in the troubled and creative century c. 1050 – 1150, and not to recognize that an element accurately described as Norman was an identifiable feature of that unity. Architecture reveals the unity better than any other medium. Support of reform in the Church was a characteristic feature of the Normans, better expressed in the solid Romanesque achievements proper to Benedictine abbeys than in the more intangible, vexed and tortuous support given to the Hildebrandine reforms, *milites Christi* though these Normans professed to be. At Jumièges and Westminster, at Durham and Bayeux, Lessay and Palermo the same spirit was at work, massive, splendid and built to endure. There are analogies in the political world. The Norman kings of England did not consider themselves solely kings of England. They were also dukes or potential dukes of Normandy and heirs to multiform enterprise in Wales, Maine, Scotland and the Vexin. They were aware of their Norman cousins in Italy and the Holy Land. To the English they might all be French: among themselves they remained Norman. Yet in spite of all the complications this brought in its train they governed England as Normans came to govern Sicily – as a kingdom in their own right. If at the same time they or their kinsfolk controlled the Norman duchies of Normandy itself or of Apulia, adjustments and modifications would naturally be made to the native systems. The historian can bear this range in mind, and yet still may

---

1 D.C. Douglas, *The Norman Achievement* (London, 1969), pp. 122-9.
2 This view is ably expressed by R.H.C. Davis, *The Normans and their Myth* (London, 1976). G.A. Loud neatly places the idea of a *gens Normannorum* in the wider context of eleventh-century political thought in the *Gens Normannorum* – Myth or Reality, *Proceedings of the Battle Conference 1981*, iv (Bury St Edmunds, 1982), pp. 104-16.

properly examine Norman government in the kingdom of England alone.

Modifications appear most dramatically at the top level. The kings were also for the greater part of the period king-dukes. The combination made for increased business and also demanded a means of delegation to principal subordinates as great if not greater though different in type from that which had been forced on English kings in the imperial days of Cnut. At various times during the reign of the Conqueror, his half-brother Odo bishop of Bayeux and earl of Kent, William Fitzosbern, Geoffrey, bishop of Coutances (consistently in legal matters) and Archbishop Lanfranc took on virtually viceregal roles when the king was in Normandy. Preoccupation with Norman affairs and a fondness for life in the duchy in fact kept the Conqueror there for nearly half his reign, some months in most years and a whole three years between 1077–80. Not that we should overemphasize his absence. Communications were simpler between Rouen and Winchester or London than between either of the English cities and York. Royal government remained royal government. The Court and the Household were itinerant. The king-duke had 'one chancellor, one writing-office, one chamber and it seems one treasurer'; and indeed it seems that writs sped freely in either direction across the Channel.[3] The king also possessed one great seal, representing the king seated in majesty on the one side and on horseback on the other. The inscriptions on the seal reflect political reality. They run together to make continuous sense of a double hexameter:

Hoc Normannorum Willelmum nosce patronum si
Hoc Anglis Regem Signo Fatearis eundem

Men were to recognize by the seal that he was patron to the Normans and a king to the English.[4]

One phrase seems to sum up the nature of the realization of potential of the English monarchy: increased centralization and increased efficiency. Part of the reason for this may be sought in the nature of the Conquest. An astonishingly small number of men benefited politically from the Conquest. At a rough estimate something like a quarter of the landed wealth of England in 1086 was held by no more than twelve men, most of whom were bound to the king by close bonds of blood or personal loyalty or both.[5] Even if the range is extended

---

3 C.H. Haskins *Norman Institutions*, (New York, 1918, reprinted 1960), p. 54.

4 F.E. Harmer, *Anglo-Saxon Writs* (Manchester, 1952), pp. 94-101.

5 There are various means of bringing out this concentration of wealth. For example D.C. Douglas, *EHD*, ii (London, 1953), p. 22 points out that about half the land held by lay tenure from the king had after the Conquest been granted to only ten men. See also H.R. Loyn, *The Norman Conquest* (3rd edn London, 1982), pp. 116–24.

wide to cover substantial tenants-in-chief there were no more than 180 men of what was later to be considered baronial wealth mentioned in Domesday Book, that is to say men holding land worth more than £100 a year. Concentration of wealth on this scale involved also concentration of political power. Virtually all these men were new men, most of them Normans with some Bretons among them; and they were separated off from the native inhabitants by that most powerful social index, language, by social attitudes, by the possession of strong fortified residences and, above all, by function in the Conqueror's England. Centralization is a meaningless phrase unless it is applied to those twin and essential bases of social strength and military service.

The Conquest in so many ways simplified the structure of English society. In no respect was this more evident than in relation to tenure. In Anglo-Saxon England there were three principal forms of tenure, folkland or land held under the law by a freeman subject to customary rights of the kindred, bookland or land held by charter and normally alienable, and *laenland* or land held on conditional lease. There was also alodial land, or land held in absolute proprietorship. Royal rights (or perhaps it might be truer to say communal folk rights enforced by recourse to the king) were powerful over all land, but the idea that all land was held by the king was new to English society. The Norman Conqueror had no inhibitions on such matters. William's first action after his coronation was to sequester land from all those who had stood in array against him, the rightful lord of England. He also saw to it that all landowners in England bought their land back from him, so recognizing that all land was royal. This important principle was asserted with no difficulty whatsoever: it was an essential clarification. The king enjoyed lordship over every parcel of land in his kingdom no matter how many intermediate tenants there might be; and there can be no doubt but that all jurisdictions were in the eyes of contemporaries annexed to the Crown. The implications for military service were even more significant.

William brought with him from Normandy notions of military service that are best described as feudal. In return for his benefice or fief a royal vassal would promise his lord, the king, specific military service assessed in terms of the number of knights he would bring to the royal host to fight on the king's behalf without pay for an agreed number of days a year. Details might vary but the heart of the matter rested there, and the great Norman barons, as they received their fiefs, promised to perform that service. Knights' fees, the grouping of fees in parcels of five or ten knights' service and the overlord's reserve of authority expressed in late-Carolingian terms as a special use of the arrière-ban or *retrobannus,* became a characteristic of much that was known as the Norman world. In the very earliest days of the Conquest it is likely that the terms of service were relatively vague, dependent on the basic obligation of a man to help his lord with his person, his sword and his purse. Systematic allotment of knight service would not be possible nor would it be desirable until a reasonably permanent and secure land settlement had been made. By 1072 with the defeat of the great rebellions in the north, and in the Fenlands, and with the settlement at Abernethy with the Scottish king, such a moment had been reached. The Church, its reorganization ensured by the election of Lanfranc to Canterbury and his successful assertion of authority over his fellow metropolitan at York, could also be firmly brought into the picture. It is probably then or very shortly afterwards that William proceeded to one of his master administrative strokes — the allotment of quotas to his tenants-in-chief. Our best evidence comes from the great monastic houses, which preserved their written documents well, and we know for example that at some stage between 1072 and 1076 a writ was issued to the formidable Anglo-Saxon Æthelwig, abbot of Evesham, enjoining him to attend the king at Clarendon with his own quota of five knights, and to see to it that the other tenants-in-chief in the West Midlands also obeyed the royal summons.[6] Allotment of the quota was a matter to be decided between the king and his tenants-in-chief. It was personal and not based directly on the value of the land nor indeed on favour. Local conditions and personal inclinations seemed to determine whether or not the service was light or heavy. The abbot of Bury St Edmunds, close to the king though he was, owed the heavy service of 40 knights. His was the fourth best-endowed of the eleventh-century monasteries with an estimated income of nearly £640, but St Augustine's Canterbury, only marginally poorer (£635), was responsible for the service of only fifteen. Peterborough, which had been out of favour, now possessed a warlike Norman abbot, and was in a position of considerable military danger, yet its quota reached 60 knights, though its estimated income (admittedly high at £323) was lower than Ramsey's (£358) which owed only four knights' service. Tavistock, a poor house, was nevertheless in a very exposed position in the south-west, and again had a tradition of military service. An imposition of 15 knights service was laid on it. Significantly there is no mention of knight service in Domesday Book, although in so many other respects that great record bears many of the characteristics of a feodary. The Domesday commissioners were anxious to clarify the land-holding situation, the basic source of wealth in a feudal world. Service in the unique conditions of the Norman Conquest was only indirectly connected with the landed wealth of the tenants-in-chief,

---

6 *EHD* ii, p. 859; J.H. Round, *Feudal England* (London 1895), and also (with commentary) in the many editions of W. Stubbs, *Select Charters*.

ecclesiastical and lay. We must remember too that promises of knight service were only an element, though a very important one, in a tenant's military obligation. If the archbishop of Canterbury may be taken as an example it was the custom quite early in the Norman period for the barons, the most important of the tenants-in-chief, to surround themselves with more knights than the number they owed to the king. A survey of the archbishop's barony, taken in the 1090s, showed that he was owed the service of close on 100 knights, ranging from ten from the bishop of Rochester to a group of some twenty tenants (some with English names) who owed mere fractions of a knight's fee, a half or a quarter. English barons did not go to the lengths of some Norman bishops who established a large superplus, as it was called.: in the twelfth century, for example, the bishop of Bayeux owed twenty knights to royal service, but had enfeoffed 120 knights. Common sense demanded some flexibility.[7]

At this top level of feudal society no great administrative machine was needed to ensure that military service was effectively performed. Writs of summons to key people such as the abbot of Evesham were enough. Detailed arrangements within the fiefs were a matter primarily for baronial concern. The king could occasionally introduce a loyal fighting man into a subordinate fief. He could certainly bring military discipline to bear if for any reason the feudal quota was not up to strength or quality. Within the larger fiefs a similar process of delegation seems to have been effected. A class of so-called 'honorial barons', men responsible for the provision of five, ten or even more knights to the quota, gradually emerged, a class vital to the health and success of the feudal settlement. Feudal service was a matter basic to the political and personal success of the early Norman kings, but it should not be over-stressed on the governmental and administrative side. Indeed even in military matters non-feudal service continued to be of great importance. From time to time English forces levied in traditional English fashion played an important part in William's campaigns. English soldiers were summoned to fight for their new king as early as 1068 when he led a force against Exeter. Men from Bristol, also in 1068, repelled the sons of Harold who were indulging in piratical raids on the north Somerset coast. Lanfranc relied heavily on local levies to defeat the rebellion of the earls in 1075. Englishmen were also used in warfare on the continent, against Maine in 1073, and in 1079 when an English thegn saved William's life in the course of his campaign around Gerberoi. William also employed mercenaries,

7 Dom David Knowles, *The Monastic Order in England* (Cambridge, 1950), appendix xv, p. 712. Also D.C. Douglas, *Domesday Monachorum of Christ Church, Canterbury* (London, 1944), p. 105 and F.M. Stenton, *The First Century of English Feudalism* (Oxford, 1932, 2nd edn 1961), pp. 7-40 and pp. 145-8.

financed in large part from the spoils of England. The development of money-fiefs and the increased exaction of scutage or shield money in lieu of personal service hint at the complexities of the military situation in early Norman England. The Norman kings aimed at the exploitation of all resources, feudal and non-feudal.

William certainly tried to use existing English institutions to the full. His solemn great courts, held often at the three principal ecclesiastical festivals of Easter, Whitsun and Christmas, were also feudalized. They were attended by the greater tenants-in-chief, and it has been estimated that attendance varied between 50 and 75. Curial organization was by no means negligible. The abbot of Battle, William's new great foundation on the site of the battle of Hastings, was authorized to come to court at Easter, Whitsun and Christmas; and special arrangements were made for provisions to be available there for him and two attendants during his stay.[8] The function of the great tenants was to give counsel, to act as a court, and also as a political sounding board. Ecclesiastical and secular matters would be discussed and indeed our fullest and most informative accounts of the *magnum concilium* in action concern ecclesiastical matters such as, for example, the quarrel relating to the bishopric and castle of the bishop of Durham in the early years of William Rufus's reign, or the contentious debate over Anselm's position in 1095. The Normans were not great legislators, but it was customary for the king to obtain the counsel and by implication the consent of the *magnum concilium* before initiating change in the good old laws of King Edward's day.

Administration as such remained a matter for the king, his Household, and his close advisers. Full continuity was maintained with the general practices and customs of the Old-English monarchy, and yet in some respects modifications that were to lead to dramatic growth quickly became necessary. The frequent absences of William I overseas in his duchy of Normandy demanded delegation, normally to one or more of his barons who had shown special skill in government. On three occasions this delegation appears to have assumed something of a formal institutional element, though one that was to be considered more in the political than in the legal or administrative context. When William returned to Normandy early in 1067 his brother Odo, bishop of Bayeux, and the trusted William Fitzosbern assumed a lordship over England that was military and political. During William's absence in 1075 when the rebellion of the earls momentarily threatened the Norman settlement it was Lanfranc, archbishop of

---

8 *Regesta Regum Anglo-Normannorum, 1066-1154*, vol. i., ed. H.W.C. Davis (Oxford, 1913), no. 60, p. 16: the rations were two simnel loaves (*de dominico*), another two (*de communi*), and wine; and of fish or whatever there might be, three dishes for himself and three for his monks; and two wax candles and ten candle ends.

8 The Norman Settlement

Canterbury ably assisted in the West Midlands by Æthelwig, abbot of Evesham, who suppressed the rebellion. Lanfranc's more or less official despatches to William and his powerful letters of exhortation to Roger, earl of Hereford, suggest an almost jealous safeguarding of viceregal authority on the archbishop's part.[9] In the three years of royal absence from 1077 to 1080, Odo of Baeyeux seems for the greater part of the period to have been the chief repository of royal delegated authority. As precedents these extraordinary acts of delegation may have remained in mens' minds and may have had a bearing on the later development of the powerful office of justiciar, the chief *exactor* of the royal will in the person of Ranulf Flambard under William Rufus, and in the person of Roger of Salisbury, chief justiciar under Henry I; but such developments were matter for the future. Under the Conqueror reliance was placed on a small group of great magnates, none of whom was called a justiciar by contemporaries. Lanfranc ranked high if not chief among these, and later Norman tradition recognized him as *custos Angliae* and one of the principal architects of the English settlement. William Fitzosbern until his death in 1071 and Odo of Bayeux until his disgrace in 1082 were prominent within the group, but so also (and most interesting in some respects) was Geoffrey, bishop of Coutances, founder of the great Mowbray inheritance, who acted consistently and zealously in the king's name, presiding over great land pleas and generally exercising administrative and judicial functions. It is Geoffrey rather than the other greater political figures who seems most akin to the later justiciars. In the second generation of the Conquest, under William Rufus, there were signs that a justiciarship might develop into a permanent office. The ministerial Ranulf Flambard, later to be bishop of Durham, was not drawn from among the great barons, but seemed set fair to initiate a new office of head of the royal administration, though still subordinate and subject to the royal will. In fact this did not come about, but he and his successors in the early Norman period serve to remind us of the growing complexity of government and administration in the late eleventh century.

Developments that were to prove permanent in their effects also took place within the royal Household. Regenbald, who had been the chief of the king's clerks under Edward the Confessor, continued in office under William and writs were issued early in William's reign safeguarding his possessions. Current opinion is again turning to the view that he may well have been known as chancellor *eo nomine* even before the Conquest.[10] His successor Herfast, who became bishop of

9 *The Letters of Lanfranc, Archbishop of Canterbury*, ed. Helen Clover and Margaret Gibson (Oxford, 1979), particularly nos. 34-6, pp. 124-5.
10 Simon Keynes, *The Diplomas of King Æthelred 'the Unready', 978–1016* (Cambridge, 1980), pp. 149–53. *EHD*ii, pp.430–1 for the writs of 1067 addressed to the Saxon authorities.

Elmham or East Anglia in 1070, was most certainly known as chancellor. Herfast had long been a chaplain in Normandy as late as 1069 by which time he was firmly established in his English office. The office of chancellor grew in importance in the course of the succeeding generation when charter evidence enables us to see the main lines of succession, allowing for some possibility of overlap or alternation. Osbern, who became bishop of Exeter in 1072, succeeded Herfast and he in turn was succeeded by Osmund under whom the language of business tended to become Latin in place of the mixture of Latin and vernacular English which characterized the late Old-English scene. Osmund became bishop of Salisbury in 1078, but may have continued as chancellor for some years before Maurice took office. Maurice himself became bishop of London in 1085 and before the Conqueror's death Robert Bloet had assumed the role of chancellor. It was Robert Bloet who crossed to England with the vital letter to Lanfranc in which was laid out the Conqueror's wishes about the disposition of the kingdom and the duchy. At this stage the chancellors were still very much Household officers with responsibility for clerical, administrative and inevitably some financial functions: their great judicial future lay in front of them.[11] It is highly significant indeed that in these early days men were chancellors before they gained high office in the Church: by the twelfth century bishops were content to become chancellor and indeed to regard the office as significant promotion. To be head of the royal secretariat was to be the greatest administrator in the realm. The chancellor was in ultimate charge of the king's seal and so responsible for authenticating all royal acts of government, the issue of charters, writ-charters and general written mandates to justices, sheriffs, hundredmen and reeves. He had a skilled staff dependent on him. The most famous — and best hated — administrator of the late eleventh century, Ranulf Flambard himself, had been a clerk in the chancery of William I, the *custos* of the royal seal, that is to say presumably the man with the immediate responsibility for its physical safety. The chancellor himself was a Household man, peripatetic with the king. A proportion of his staff accompanied him, and a proportion settled at a fixed place, at Winchester, at Westminster or in the Tower of London. We must beware against applying too rigid a definition to functions and a tendency to make the chancellor and the chancery too exclusive a secretariat. Functions in fact overlapped between the secretarial and the financial side of administration. Specialization was not a prominent feature in eleventh-century administration.

11 The introduction to the *Regesta* vol. i ed. H.W.C. Davis, remains the essential authority on this theme, especially pp. xv-xviii.

The outstanding achievement of the secretariat in the early Norman period was undoubtedly the production of Domesday Book. Recent careful investigation of the processes by which the survey was conducted and Domesday Book created has brought a sharper awareness of the competence and complexity of the administrative machinery inherited from Anglo-Saxon England and brought to a fine point of performance under powerful Norman direction. At his great council over Christmas 1085 King William consulted deeply with his principal advisers and decided to set the machinery for the Domesday inquest into motion. It is highly probable — and increasingly obvious from internal evidence in Domesday itself and in the surviving associated documents, the so-called satellites — that the great tenants-in-chief played an active part in collecting the information needed about the land, its value, the nature of the men and chattels on the land, and the number of beasts, mills, fishponds, and the extent of pasture, meadow and woodland. It is also certain that there was a greater wealth of written information available about geld liability and indeed about ordinary manorial composition and contents than had hitherto been suspected. Administrative literacy in Latin and in Anglo-Saxon was relatively high in late eleventh-century England. At the Christmas Council England was divided into seven or just possibly into nine circuits and the royal commissioners set out on their travels.[12] These commissioners were men of the highest rank, probably three to each circuit, and including at least one cleric, bishop or abbot, among their numbers. Their functions were not simple and were reminiscent to some extent of the functions of the *Missi Dominici* in the empire of Charlemagne. They had the status of judges, were empowered to hear pleas relating to land tenure and in some instances settled then and there matters in dispute. More often, it is true, they referred such disputes directly to the royal court. They had financial directions, and kept a wary eye on the fundamental problem of assessment to the geld. They were feudal magnates, for the most part dealing with regions in which they had little or no direct landed interest; and it is to be believed that they satisfied well their own as well as their royal master's curiosity about the wealth and the extent of baronial landed possessions. Preparation for their coming and preparation for the formal meetings that they held in each shire court was intense. A mass of written evidence relating to the royal demesne, to the lands of the ecclesiastical and lay tenants-in-chief, and to intimate manorial detail awaited them at each shire centre. They were the key men in one of the greatest administrative exercises undertaken in pre-industrial

---

12 H.R. Loyn 'Domesday Book', *Proceedings of the Battle Conference* 1 1978, ed. R.A. Brown (Ipswich, 1979), pp. 121–30, especially p. 124.

England. The evidence that was collected under their supervision was shaped, to some considerable extent as it was being collected, into a form fit and manageable for final incorporation in Domesday Book.[13]

The administrative drive that brought the whole enterprise to fruition came from the royal Court itself. Domesday Book consists of two volumes. The first volume is the true finished product, and we can be sure that the master (and, alas, anonymous) administrator who was in charge of the preparation intended that the format of the first volume should be extended to the whole of England. As it stands it covers the greater part of England apart form the three eastern shires of Norfolk, Suffolk and Essex. These eastern shires form the subject matter of the second volume of Domesday Book. It is probable that the death of King William in 1087, combined with the intrinsic difficulty of reducing the complicated tenures of the east to standard and systematic order prevented the completion of the huge task, and thus left us with the long penultimate draft which constitutes the second volume of Domesday Book. Volume II in fact contains much more information than its sister volume, including masses of detailed information about the number of beasts on each manor, but lacks the compressed elegance of Volume I. The first volume achieves an astonishing degree of purposeful uniformity in its entries, even though regional variations which themselves betray the spheres of activity of the Domesday commissioners can on occasion be discerned. The basic administrative unit was the shire and in that sense Domesday Book was a territorial record. Within the shire the substance of the survey was, however, divided according to the holdings of their tenants-in-chief, and in that sense Domesday Book was a feudal record, an account of the wealth and property of the king and of the royal tenants-in-chief. In a typical Domesday shire one meets first an account of the shire-town, and then an index to those holding land in chief within a shire. In Buckinghamshire, for example, an entry relating to the town of Buckingham is followed by a list of no fewer than 57 names: the king, the archbishop of Canterbury, eight prelates, the canons of Oxford, Raenbald the priest, and forty-five lay tenants-in-chief ranging from the king's half-brother, Robert of Mortain, Hugh, earl of Chester, Walter Gifford, and William of Warenne to king's thegns and beneficiaries holding modest parcels of land.[14] The king held the great manor of Wendover, and its description serves as an example of the type of entry to be found throughout Domesday Book, standardized and yet often providing points of special and peculiar interest:

---

13 V.H. Galbraith, *The Making of Domesday Book* (Oxford, 1961), and *Domesday Book, its place in administrative history* (Oxford, 1974), provide the essential guides.

14 DB i; 143r.

A manor. Wendover was always assessed at 24 hides. There is land there for 26 ploughs. There are three ploughs in demesne. There are 26 villeins with six bordars possessing 17 ploughs, and there could be another 6. There are two mills yielding 10 shillings. Pasture of four ploughlands and 20 shillings from the remainder. Wood for 2,000 pigs. In all it is worth and renders per annum £38 of weighed and assayed money. At the time of King Edward it rendered £25 in counted coins. In this manor there are two sokemen holding 1½ hides. They did not lie there at the time of King Edward.[15]

To informed contemporaries the survey itself was prompted by royal curiosity, especially in finance, and the object of the exercise was seen as an inquiry into how many hundred hides there were in the shire, what land or property the king had there and what dues he should have every year, into the lands of the archbishops, bishops, and tenants-in-chief, and indeed into the land and property and what it was worth of all landowning men of any account in England. The survey was also something of an extraordinary and monstrous imposition. 'It is a shame to relate,' wrote the Anglo-Saxon chronicler, 'but he found it no shame to do;' and the chronicler with mounting dismay tells us that King William so surveyed the land that not a hide nor a yardland, not a single ox nor a cow nor a pig was left out, but all was set down in writings, and the writings were afterwards brought to him.[16]

A document preserved by the great abbey of Ely, the *Inquisicio Eliensis,* records what must have surely been the standard form of query made by the commissioners on their circuits.[17] They asked: what was the manor *(mansio)* called, who held it at the time of King Edward, who holds it now, how many hides, how many ploughs in demesne, how many belonging to the men, how many villeins, cottars, slaves, freemen, sokemen, how much woodland, meadow, pasture, how many mills and fisheries, what had been added to or taken away from it, what it is worth now, how much each freeman or sokeman had or has. All this was to be recorded in triplicate, namely at the time of King Edward, and when King William gave it, and as it is now; and if more can be obtained from it than is being obtained. Ely in common with other great ecclesiastical houses and (we suspect) many leading lay tenants also took the opportunity of this vast administrative exercise to establish for themselves a permanent record of their lands, revenues, rights and obligations. Documents relating to this activity survive from Christ Church, Canterbury, from St Augustine's, Canterbury, Rochester and other Kentish houses, Exeter, Bury St Edmunds, Peterborough, Bath and Evesham. Record of part of the

15 DBi, 143v.
16 *ASCh*, 1085, ed. D. Whitelock, pp. 161–2.
17 DB iv, pp. 459-528, especially pp. 495-8; *EHD* ii, pp. 881-2.

proceedings at the shire court has survived from Cambridgeshire.[18] The shire court was attended by men, French and English, represen- ting the hundreds and the vills within the hundred. They gave their evidence on oath, evidence which clearly amounted in most instances to formal attestation of written documents already before the court. Significant numbers of literate administrators must have been active in the background preparations for Domesday Book. For each of the great circuits the evidence must have been collected in book form, and the so-called Exeter Domesday Book, still preserved after close on 900 years at the cathedral at Exeter, is the sole surviving exemplar of this stage in the elaborate administrative processes of the Domesday Survey.[19] Fair copies were then made of the circuit books (vol. II relating to the eastern shires was one of these); and the fair copies were finally sent to Winchester. From them the master administrator who was the controlling mind behind the whole project, constructed the first volume of Domesday Book. Winchester remained its place of be- ing throughout the twelfth century. It was known as the Book of Win- chester or (because of its financial importance) the Book of the Ex- chequer or finally as Domesday Book because there were no appeals from its findings.

Domesday Book represents an extraordinary achievement and pays direct tribute to the efficiency of the administration. We have evidence too of increased efficiency in ordinary administrative processes. The secretariat grew more professional and more static. By 1080 Latin had virtually ousted Anglo-Saxon from its place as a language for im- mediate written governmental business. Financial methods inherited from Anglo-Saxon England were kept in being. Methods of assess- ment to geld were modified to the royal advantage. The Chronicle complained insistently of the heavy gelds that were laid on the com- munity. Domesday Book, though not a geld book, enabled the king and the royal officers to determine how much geldable land lay in the possession of each of the principal tenants-in-chief. The survey itself, as has been well said, gave an opportunity to improve, 'by revision or replacement, routine administrative records damaged or destroyed during the Norman Conquest or become obsolete through the passage of time or through the drastic changes in the ownership of the land which had followed on the invasion.'[20] We are increasingly aware that written administrative records were not rare in eleventh-century England and that a system accustomed to land-tax demanded up-to- date survey.

18 *Inquisitio Comitatus Cantabrigiensis*, ed. N.E.S.A. Hamilton (London, 1876); *EHD ii, pp. 879-81.*

19 DB iv, pp. 1-491. R. Welldon Finn, *The Liber Exoniensis* (London, 1964).

20 V.H. Galbraith (note by Miss Clementi), *The Making of Domesday Book*, pp. 55-8.

Evidence concerning written records no longer surviving but lying behind Domesday Book as we know it, has received careful attention from several scholars in recent years, notably from Miss Sally Harvey in a series of perceptive articles. Drawing from the material contained in Domesday Book itself and from a multiplicity of references in contemporary or near contemporary sources she was able to show beyond shadow of a doubt that written records containing tenurial and fiscal information in feudal form, but recorded by hundreds, were already part of the normal fiscal machinery by the early 1080s and also that Domesday's order was based on existing fiscal documents, some of Edwardian origin.[21] Without overstating her case she is able to show convincingly that it was quite unthinkable that the inquiry which led to the production of Domesday Book would have been initiated, let along brought to a successful and speedy conclusion, had not William and his advisers been perfectly aware that the basic administrative machinery was there. Sets of treasury documents dealing with fiscal liability, lists that gave information in tenurial form and also in hundredal form were already in existence. Such conclusions are of great moment to the administrative historian. Credit for the drive, energy and enterprise that put such machinery to practical use goes properly to the new controlling Norman group. It seems increasingly probable that the great *descriptio* was indeed, as James Campbell suggested, 'the fruit of a strong administrative tradition continuously maintained from Carolingian times'.[22] It also seems likely that we should accept his further suggestion that the home for such a tradition in the century before 1086 was more probably England than Normandy.

One detailed administrative matter demands attention before we turn away from Domesday Book. Evidence was given on oath at the shire court before the royal commissioners according to the Ely Inquest by the sheriff, by all the barons and their Frenchmen and by the whole hundred court, the priest, reeve and six villeins from each village.[23] The pattern varied according to locality, but the main principle remained constant. The Domesday inquiry depended upon the taking of information given on oath from representative inhabitants of a locality. The names of many of these jurors survive. In Cheveley hundred, for example, in the county of Cambridge, the following gave sworn evidence: Richard, the reeve of the hundred; Edward the man of

21 Sally Harvey, 'Royal Revenue and Domesday Terminology', *Econ. HR* 20 (1967), pp. 221–8; 'Domesday Book and its Predecessors', *EHR* 86 (1971), pp. 753–73; 'Domesday Book and Anglo-Norman Governance', *TRHS* 25 (1975), pp 175–93: the comments in *EHR*, 1971, pp. 756 and 763 are especially valuable.

22 James Campbell, 'Observations on English Government from the Tenth to the Twelfth Century', *TRHS* 25 (1975), p. 51.

23 DB iv, p. 498: *per sacramentum vicecomitis scire et omnium baronum et eorum francigenarum et tocius centuriatus presbyteri, praepositi, vi villani uniuscuiusque ville.*

Aubrey of Ver; Ralph de Hotot; William de Mara; Stanhard of Silverley; Frawin of Kirthling; Charles of Cheveley; Ulmar, the man of Wighen.[24] Great interest has naturally been aroused by the existence of the sworn inquest, the jury used administratively to decide matters of fact, and in was for long the custom to see this institution as a Norman importation, an introduction by the consequences of continental practice based on Frankish Carolingian precedents. Better appreciation of late Anglo-Saxon legal enactments, as we have seen, makes the idea of innovation unacceptable, notably the rules laid down by Ethelred concerning the duty of the reeve and twelve senior thegns of a hundred or wapentake to present information on oath relating to criminals. Delicate and close examination of records such as the code known as Ethelred IV. and of documents dealing with the dues owed to the bishop of Winchester at Taunton and to the church at Lambourne strengthen the claims for a pre-Conquest use of the inquest procedure by the Crown.[25] It is likely that much of the material that was collected from our great estates (and not only royal estates) in the last century of Anglo-Saxon England was put together in a written form in the vernacular capable of receiving formal testimonial sanction at the local courts. We may consistently have underestimated the capabilities and function of the reeves of great estates, those busy men whose job it was to know the capacity of their lands from legal rights to arable potential and stock in hand, from ploughs to mousetraps. When they were charged to know both the lord's rights and the custom of the community we can deduce fairly that such information might easily be subject to rigorous testing on oath in the local court.[26]

The system of geld assessment and geld collection is perhaps our clearest indication of the relative sophistication of the financial inheritance from Anglo-Saxon days. Such a system could not have been run from the traditional box under the bed. Succeeding generations in the twelfth century were well aware of the strength of this inheritance. A full account has survived of the working of the Exchequer in the twelfth century. The author of the tract, Richard fitzNigel, treasurer of the Exchequer and bishop of London, was rightly proud of the Exchequer, anxious to stress its efficiency and up-to-date character,

---

24 *EHD* ii, p. 882.
25 James Campbell, *TRHS*, pp. 50–1. Sally Harvey, *ibid.,* pp.178–9 makes a strong and convincing case in favour of the existence of records connected with fixed charges, farms, and miscellaneous dues from boroughs and royal estates and further wisely reminds us that royal records in use before Domesday continued in use long after.
26 Lieb. i., pp. 453–5; discussed in H.R. Loyn, *Anglo-Saxon England and the Norman Conquest*, pp. 193–4. Pauline Stafford 'The Farm of One Night and the Organization of King Edward's Estates in Domesday Book, *Econ. HR* 33 (1980), pp. 491–502 comments accurately on the dynamic management of royal resources in late Anglo-Saxon England, and on the flexibility and relative sophistication of an organization capable of coping with a variety of local situations.

positively patronizing towards the financial institutions of the rude days of William I and *a fortiori* of the native kings before 1066. Even so enough emerges to suggest that the inheritance was not negligible.[27] The elaborate apparatus of the upper Exchequer with its devices and checks to constitute an advanced scheme of accountancy and record was of course new. But in the workings of the lower Exchequer with its apparatus for storing and preserving treasure there are plentiful signs of continuity with the Anglo-Saxon past. Interest has been shown and continues to be shown in the most tangible of all aspects of financial arrangements, that is to say in the coins themselves. Great profits came from royal management of the currency, and fluctuations in weight of the coinage between types and even possibly on occasion within types were associated with accounting devices that made sure the king would not lose control of bullion reserves. For example payments from royal estates and also from boroughs and from lands that had passed temporarily into the king's hand seem to have been adjusted so as to take variations of weight of silver in the coins into account.[28] Flexibility in the exaction of revenue by weight of silver or by number of coins and flexibility also in the ratio of coins to units of account such as the *ora* could also be used to royal advantage. Payments were made according to Domesday Book at the rate of 20d to the *ora* on occasion as well as at the traditional and accurate 16d an *ora*. The Norman Conquest had initially little effect on the methods of making and issuing coinage.[29] A tendency to centralize and to reduce the number of mints in effective operation had been apparent late in the Anglo-Saxon period and this tendency was encouraged. Some Normans were introduced into the system to their own considerable financial advantage. The business of die-making, a most lucrative affair, was placed under the control of Odo, the goldsmith, together with handsome estates in Essex and Suffolk. Waleran, the son of Rannulf, representative of a family already deeply involved in moneyers' work in Normandy, extended his operations to England to such good effect that he came to hold lands in Cambridgeshire, Suffolk, Essex and Hertfordshire together with a home at Wood Street in London.[30] The weight of the Norman pennies appears to have been standardized and the resulting lack of variation in silver content with the consequent reduction of opportunity for resourceful governmen-

27 A. Hughes, C.G. Crump, and C. Johnson, *The Dialogue of the Exchequer* (Oxford, 1902).
28 Sally Harvey, 'Royal Revenue and Domesday Terminology', *Econ.HR* 20 (1967), p. 226.
29 *ibid,* p. 228 where Miss Harvey demonstrates the the '20d *ora*' was an accounting device, R.H.M Dolley, *The Norman Conquest and the English Coinage* (London, 1966) provides the best short guide.
30 D.C. Douglas, *William the Conqueror* (London, 1964), p. 304; H.W.C. Davis, introduction to *Regesta Regum Anglo-Normannorum*, p. xxxiv stresses the importance of the custom of permitting private mints.

tal profit-taking may well have led to the institution of a new impost, on town and on country, known as the *monetagium*. In his coronation charter of 1100 Henry I, while reiterating legal rulings against moneyers or anyone else taken with false money in their possession, utterly forbade the exaction of *monetagium* which he described as an innovation, taken from towns and shires, since the days of Edward the Confessor.[31] In essentials the coinage persisted in its Anglo-Saxon forms and numismatists and historians alike look a century later to the reign of Henry II for major modifications.

Similar institutional continuity is to be found in the more specifically legal field as well as in the secretarial and financial. The Norman *curia regis* was under William the Conqueror a feudal court, but in its wider dimension as the court of the king of England it provided a reserve of trusted manpower by means of which the king's will over the ancient legal institutions of the community could be exercised. No feature of legal administration is more characteristic of William's reign than the holding of great pleas to hear and decide matters of dispute over ownership of land. Records have survived, some in great detail, of disputes involving Lanfranc and Odo of Bayeux, of the lands and rights of the great abbey of Ely, of disputes between Worcester and Evesham and in less detail of lands concerning many of the great new tenants-in-chief. The procedures adopted paid more than lip-service to English tradition. A royal commissioner, often Geoffrey of Coutances, would preside and the appointment of such commissioners foreshadows the use of itinerant justices which becomes such a feature of Norman and Angevin government. The pleas were held, however, in the most English of institutions, the courts of the shire or of a group of shires where the sheriff and the officers of the court played a prominent part and where testimony would be given by jurors on oath who would act in accord with the customary rights of the neighbourhood. At one famous plea, at a trial held at Pinnenden Heath near Maidstone to settle the dispute between Lanfranc and Odo, the aged bishop of Chichester, Ægelric (appointed in 1057), a man very learned in the law of the land, was by the king's command brought to the trial in a waggon so that he could expound the ancient practice of the laws.[32] Full respect was paid to ancient institutions.

In ecclesiastical affairs the outstanding reputation of Lanfranc and the new bishops and abbots who surrounded him inevitably exag-

---

31 *EHD* ii, p. 401: Lieb. i, pp. 521-23: cl. 5, p. 522 – *monetagium commune quod capiebatur per civitates et comitatus, quod non fuit tempore regis Eadwardi, hoc ne amodo sit, omnino defendo. Si quis captus fuerit, sive monetarius sive alius, cum falsa moneta, iusticia recta inde fiat.*
32 *EHD* ii, p. 451

gerates the changes that were brought about after the Conquest. The successful assertion of the supremacy of Canterbury over York, the holding of effective synods, the closer definition of ecclesiastical causes and the withdrawal of pleas relating to episcopal laws by bishops and archdeacons from the hundred court all helped to sharpen the identity of the Norman Church. On the wider political scene the firm refusal of William to pay fealty to the pope, accompanied it is true by willingness to pay the arrears of Peter's Pence hints at a somewhat old fashioned attitude in full accord with Carolingian and Old-English practice. A systematic urbanization of bishoprics points firmly to a Norman love of order and systematic central control. From the administrative point of view it is possible that we have accepted too uncritically the consequences of the increased use of the Latin language, just as we may in the past have underestimated the capacity of the Old-English State in the field of written government. The Benedictine Reformation of the tenth century was no mere ecclesiastical incident, but a movement of great social and educative moment. No monastic movement has been in fact so little withdrawn from society. The result of its educative efforts, the creation of a laity reasonably experienced in the use of written evidence in the vernacular, had great effect on administration in ecclesiastical as well as in local government matters. Such administrative skill persisted even if obscured by the more dramatic Latinate achievements of the newcomers.

Local government itself, in shire and town, retained Old-English forms even when driven to more intense activity by Norman enterprise. The sheriff quickly became a dominant often an overbearing officer in the shire. Initially William naturally relied on the survivors when they had not fought against him in the array at Hastings and writs were issued to men such as Eadric, the shire-reeve in Wiltshire, or Tofi of Somerset. A great changeover appears to have taken place in State as in Church in the earliest years of the 1070s and men of the first order of importance in the new feudal order take over office, men such as Haimo *dapifer* in Kent, Geoffrey of Mandeville in Middlesex, Hugh of Port-en-Bessin in Hampshire, Urse of Abetot in Worcester, or the Malets and Bigots in East Anglia. Some of the greatest of the feudal families owed the origin of their fortunes to ancestors who exercised the office of sheriff under the Conqueror.[33] Complaints against their depredations become commonplace and as early as 1077 William empowered his chief advisers to summon the sheriffs and to see to it that they made restitution to bishops and abbots of lands which they had

---

33 D.C. Douglas, *William the Conqueror*, pp. 297-9. Also W.A. Morris *The Medieval English Sheriff to 1300* (Manchester, 1927), pp. 41ff.

seized by violence or which had been yielded to them either through carelessness or fear or greed.[34] As executive head of the judicial system in the shire means for exploitation were vast. The sheriff and his assistants could make profit from insistence on regular summons to hundred as well as to shire and on an even more zealous insistence on fines for absence. View of frankpledge, systematic enforcement of the proper keeping of the tithings, proper reference of specified cases to the king's court gave plentiful opportunity for exploitation and personal enrichment. At times the sheriff could be commissioned to act as a judge on analogy with the Norman *vicomtes*, though more often other agents might be entrusted with judicial powers, and resident justices in the shire became known in the reigns of the early Norman kings. Military activities, the building and supervision of building new castles, guardianship of the person of the king, even on occasion though by no means universally, functions connected with the custodianship of castles and the provision of castle guard provided profitable sources of revenue for the conscientious as well as for the arbitrary officer. The removal of the Saxon earls left Norman sheriffs with great opportunites for action and profit. Government orders, royal mandates, were directed to them. We have seen already how prominent the sheriff tended to be in fiscal matters. Annual farms of the shire, geld collection, jurisdictional profit from the pleas of the hundreds or boroughs, proceeds from the new fines or feudal dues often passed through the sheriff's hands. The forest law added a fresh dimension to his responsibility and to the profitability of office. Even the ecclesiastical reforms were not without financial benefit. If the sheriff became the maid of all work of Norman government and administration in the shires it must be confessed that he was a well paid and powerful maid of all work and that his aggressions and exploitations became legendary. Yet in a curious way, as the royal agent acting through established courts, he also stood for the concept of a principle of territorial authority that prevented the worst feudal abuses from entering the English scene. King, sheriff and shire court stood for a more just order than that of the overweening lord exercising so-called feudal justice from a castle.

The power of the sheriffs was great and they acquired the role of king's right hand man in the localities. They often made their headquarters in the chief castle in the chief town of the shire, a living representative of the power of the new military regime. The effect on the towns themselves was considerable. Towns suffered at first because of the devastation caused by the destruction of houses to

---

34 *EHD ii, pp.* 431–2. Morris, pp. 53–74 provides a splendid analysis of shrieval perquisites of office and the following paragraph is based largely on his analysis.

make room for the new Norman castles. It has been estimated that about a ninth of the area of York was taken up by the clearings made for new fortifications and the situation elsewhere was often comparable.[35] As Norman peace became secure, and as castle-building and feudal military service gave protection to the administration, the towns assumed a special new importance. Church organization and administration were also centralized on the towns and by 1100 all the dioceses enjoyed an urban centre. The old structures survived within the towns as within the shires. Many private jurisdictions survived and many hundreds fell into private hands. The familiar traditional patterns persisted in shire court, hundred court and borough court to develop into one of the strongest pillars of English governmental as well as legal life. New men with new and increased responsibilities came to run with intensified vigour ancient established structures. In administration as in government Normans and continental trained scholars set themselves up as a competent, efficient ruling group. Men of the stamp of Geoffrey of Coutances, Gundulf of Rochester, Samson of Worcester or Ranulf Flambard (the chief *exactor* of the king's will at the time of William Rufus) took full use of their opportunities. Recent scholarship has emphasized three facets of the Norman enterprise in England, the colonizing element, the Norman gift for assimilation, and the dynamic force of the whole affair. In the administrative field all three aspects can plainly be recognized. New opportunities were open to Normans and to all French-speakers of energy in the conquered country though the rhythm of movement right through to the reign of Henry I and beyond is still matter for investigation and debate. Assimilation is a delicate business in administration, and it is clear that, as our knowledge of the antecedents of Domesday Book sharpens, we shall need a fresh statement of old questions concerning the reliance of William I on active survivors from the reign of Edward at quite a lowly level of administration and a fresh precision, too, in our approach to defining the moment when we can talk of a truly Anglo-Norman administration. The dynamism is evident from the earliest stages: wealth bought service and service created new opportunity to create more wealth. The working out of the Norman dynamic in the wider cosmopolitan world of the twelfth century is beyond our terms of reference, but it would be wrong not to end with a reminder that in administration as in other fields England in 1087 already exhibited that combination of old, deep-rooted administrative strength and new management that was to make the kingdom so powerful a unit in the affairs of the whole of feudal Europe.

35 J. *Tait, The Medieval English Borough* (Manchester, 1936), pp. 134−5; H.R. Loyn, *Anglo-Saxon England and the Norman Conquest*, p. 377. Recent archaeological investigation at York confirms the particular picture.

Bibliography

The following bibliography does not aim to be inclusive even of the most important studies, but sets out those books and articles which the author has found most useful in constructing this book. In two respects it is deliberately restrained. Comparatively few local studies have been included although it is freely recognized that much patient work that contributes ultimately to our understanding of administration both at royal and at local level, lies ready to use in the studies, notably of charter evidence, published in the pages of periodicals such as, for example, the *Wiltshire Archaeological and Natural History Magazine*. Critics may well note that there is a similar lack of titles in languages other than English. It is well understood that substantial advance may come in the next generation, particularly on the side of ecclesiastical administration, from scholars steeped in diplomatic studies of the Carolingian Age on the continent, but with one or two notable exceptions (for example the work of J.M. Wallace-Hadrill and James Campbell mentioned below) there are few yet who have achieved successful synthesis.

A Primary Sources

English Historical Documents, vol. i, c. 500–1042, ed.D. Whitelock (1st ed, London, 1955, 2nd ed 1979) provides a truly indispensable guide not only to the material itself in thoroughly dependable translation, but also to bibliography up to the time of publication of the second edition, i.e. 1979. Vol. ii, 1042–1189, ed. D.C. Douglas and G.W. Greenaway (1st ed, London, 1953, 2nd ed 1981) is also exceedingly valuable.

References in *EHD* give indication of the best texts to use.

Special attention is drawn to the following texts of outstanding importance:

1 *Chronicles and Narrative Histories*

Anglo-Saxon Chronicle. The Chronicle is best consulted in the edition of C. Plummer (based on an earlier edition by J. Earle). *Two of the Saxon Chronicles Parallel,* 2 vols. (Oxford 1892 and 99), reprinted with additional material by D. Whitelock, 1952. Good translations appear in *EHD* and separately in *The Anglo-Saxon Chronicle: a revised translation,* by D. Whitelock with D.C. Douglas and S.I. Tucker (London, 1961). G.N. Garmonsway's translation (London, 1955) is also reliable.

Bede The best edition of the *Historia Ecclesiastica* is the edition (with translation) by Bertram Colgrave and R.A.B. Mynors, *Bede's Ecclesiastical History of the English People* (Oxford, 1969). There is also much of great and enduring value in the fine edition of C. Plummer, *Baedae Historia Ecclesiastica gentis Anglorum: Venerabilis Baedae opera historica,* 2 vols. (Oxford, 1896).

Asser The standard edition is that of W.H. Stevenson, *Asser's Life of King Alfred,* new impression with article on recent work by D. Whitelock (Oxford, 1959).

2 *The Laws*

The great work of Felix Liebermann is indispensable: *Die Gesetze der Angelsachsen* (vol. 1, Text and German translation, 1903: vol. 2, Glossary and Index, Halle, 1912: vol. 3, Introduction to individual texts with critical notes, Halle, 1916), now available in a reprint (Tübingen, 1960). Useful editions with English translations are F.L. Attenborough, *The Laws of the Earliest English Kings* (Cambridge, 1922) and A.J. Robertson, *The Laws of the English Kings from Edmund to Henry I* (Cambridge, 1925). There is a good edition with translation of the *Leges Henrici Primi* by L.J. Downer (Oxford, 1972).

3 *Charters and Writs*

P.H. Sawyer, *Anglo-Saxon Charters: an annotated list and bibliography, RHS* Guides and Handbooks 8 (London, 1968) provides a first-class guide to charter material. The catalogues relating to separate areas published by the Leicester University Press also contain much useful and valuable commentary as well as primary material (see below under Secondary Sources, H.P.R. Finberg and C.R. Hart). A joint committee of the British Academy and the Royal Historical Society has initiated a new edition of all charters based on an archival approach: *Charters of Rochester,* ed. A. Campbell (London, 1973), *Charters of Burton Abbey* ed. P.H. Sawyer (London, 1979). The standard collections remain of great use and convenience: J.M. Kemble, *Codex Diplomaticus Aeve Saxonici,* 6 vols. (London, 1839–48) and W. de G. Birch, *Cartularium Saxonicum,* 3 vols. (London, 1885–93). The following works are especially valuable both for content and for exercise of diplomatic method:

The Crawford Collection of Early Charters and Documents, ed. A.S. Napier and W.H. Stevenson (Oxford, 1895).

F.E. Harmer, *Select English Historical Documents of the Ninth and Tenth Centuries* (Cambridge, 1914).
D. Whitelock, *Anglo-Saxon Wills* (Cambridge, 1930)
A.J. Robertson, *Anglo-Saxon Charters* (Cambridge, 1939)
F.E. Harmer, *Anglo-Saxon Writs* (Manchester, 1952)
D. Whitelock, (with Neil Ker and Lord Rennell), *The Will of Æthelgifu* (Roxburghe Club, Oxford, 1968)

For the period up to and over the Norman Conquest good guides are given in *Facsimiles of English Royal Writs to AD 1100,* ed. T.A.M. Bishop and P. Chaplais (Oxford, 1957) and the work of H.W.C. Davis, *Regesta Regum Anglo-Normannorum* vol. 1 (Oxford, 1913)

4 Councils and allied Documents

The basic collection for the earlier period is contained in the third volume of *Councils and Ecclesiastical Documents,* ed. A.W. Haddan and W. Stubbs (Oxford, 1871). For the later period reliance has had to be placed on older collections, notably that of D. Wilkins, *Concilia Magnae Britanniae et Hiberniae,* vol. i (London, 1737). A new collection from 871 to 1066 and from 1066–1204 has now appeared in *Councils and Synods with other Documents relating to the English Church,* ed. D. Whitelock, R. Brett, and C.N.L. Brooke (2 vols. Oxford, 1982).

5 Domesday Book

The authoritative edition was prepared by Abraham Farley and published in two volumes in 1783. Two further volumes, of indexes and supplementary texts, were added and published by the Record Commission (ed. Henry Ellis) in 1811 and 1816. Good translations with commentary appear for most English counties in the appropriate volumes of the Victoria County History.

B Secondary Sources

A revised version of Charles Gross, *The Sources and Literature of English History from the earliest times to about 1485* has been published (rev. E.B. Graves) under the title *A Bibliography of English History* to 1485 (Oxford, 1975), and constitutes an excellent basic guide. Good bibliographical advice is given in the appropriate volumes of *EHD*, not only in the bibliographies themselves, but in the notes to the individual documents. *The Annual Bulletin of Historical Literature* published by the Historical Association (London, annually) provides a convenient way of keeping in touch with the principal productions.

The following studies are of special value:

N. Banton, *Ealdormen and Earls in England from the Reign of King Alfred to the Reign of King Ethelred II* (unpublished thesis: Oxford, 1981)

F. Barlow, *The English Church, 1000–1066* (London, 1963, 2nd ed. 1979).

F. Barlow, *Edward the Confessor* (London, 1970).

G. Barraclough, 'The Anglo-Saxon Writ', *History* 39 (1954), pp. 193–215.

G.W.S. Barrow, *The Kingdom of the Scots* (London, 1973).

M. Biddle, *Winchester in the Early Middle Ages,* Winchester Studies 1 (Oxford, 1976).

T.A.M. Bishop and P. Chaplais (eds.), *Facsimiles of English Royal Writs to AD 1100* (Oxford, 1957).

P. Hunter Blair, *An Introduction to Anglo-Saxon England* (Cambridge, 1955, 2nd ed. 1978).

E.O. Blake (ed.), *Liber Eliensis,* Camden Third Series 92 (London, 1962).

M. Bloch, *Feudal Society* (Eng. trs., London, 1961).

M. Bloch, *The Royal Touch* (Eng. trs., London, 1973).

C.E. Blunt, 'The Anglo-Saxon Coinage and the Historian', *Medieval Archaeology* 4 (1960), pp. 1–15.

C.E. Blunt, 'The Coinage of Offa', *Anglo-Saxon Coins,* ed. R.H.M. Dolley (London, 1961), pp. 39–62.

C.E. Blunt, 'The Coinage of Athelstan, 924–939', *BNJ* 42 (1974), pp. 35–160.

R.H. Britnell, 'English Markets and Royal Administration Before 1200', *Econ. HR* 31 (1978), pp. 183–96.

C.N.L. Brooke, *The Saxon and Norman Kings* (London, 1963).

C.N.L. Brooke, asst. Gillian Keir, *London 800–1216 : the Shaping of a City* (London, 1975).

N.P. Brooks, 'The Development of Military Obligations in Eighth and Ninth-Century England', *England before the Conquest,* ed. Peter Clemoes and Kathleen Hughes (Cambridge, 1971), pp. 69–84.

N.P. Brooks, 'Anglo-Saxon Charters : the Work of the Last Twenty Years', *Anglo-Saxon England* 3 (1974), pp. 211–31.

N.P. Brooks, 'England in the Ninth Century: The Crucible of Defeat', *TRHS* 29 (1979), pp. 1–20.

R.A. Brown, *The Normans and the Norman Conquest* (London, 1969).

R.A. Brown (ed.), *Proceedings of the Battle Conference*, Ipswich, Bury St Edmunds, 1979 etc.)

R.L.S. Bruce-Mitford, *The Sutton Hoo Ship Burial* (vol. I, Cambridge, 1975, vol. II, Cambridge, 1979). Two further volumes are planned.

H.M. Cam, *Local Government in Francia and England* (London, 1912).

H.M. Cam, 'The Evolution of the medieval English Franchise', *Speculum* 32 (1957).

H.M. Cam, *Liberties and Communities in Medieval England* (Cambridge, 1966).

K. Cameron, *English Place-Names* (London, 1961).

A. Campbell, (ed.), *Charters of Rochester,* Anglo-Saxon Charters 1 (London, 1973).

J. Campbell, 'Observations on English Government from the Tenth to the Twelfth Century', *TRHS* 25 (1975), pp. 39–54.

J. Campbell (ed.), *The Anglo-Saxons* (London, 1982).

H.M. Chadwick, *Studies on Anglo-Saxon Institutions* (Cambridge, 1905).

W.A. Chaney, *The Cult of Kingship in Anglo-Saxon England* (Manchester, 1970).

P. Chaplais, 'The Authenticity of the Royal Anglo-Saxon Diplomas of Exeter', *BIHR* 39 (1966), pp. 1–34.

P. Chaplais, 'The Origin and Authenticity of the Royal Anglo-Saxon Diploma', *Journal of the Society of Archivists* 3 (1965–69), no 2. Also F. Ranger below.

P. Chaplais, 'The Anglo-Saxon Chancery, from the Diploma to the Writ' (*ibid.* no. 4). Also F. Ranger below.

P. Chaplais, 'Some Early Anglo-Saxon Diplomas on Single Sheets: Originals or Copies?' (*ibid.* no. 7). Also F. Ranger below.

P. Chaplais, 'Who introduced Charters into England? The case for Augustine' (*ibid.* no. 10). Also F. Ranger below.

P. Chaplais, 'The Letter from Bishop Wealdhere of London to Archbishop Brihtnoth of Canterbury: the Earliest Original 'Letter Close' Extant in the West', Parkes and Watson, *Medieval Scribes, Manuscripts and Libraries* (London, 1978).

C.R. Cheney, *Medieval Texts and Studies* (Oxford, 1973).

S.B. Chrimes, *An Introduction to the Administrative History of Medieval England*, 3rd ed. (Oxford, 1966).

M.T. Clanchy, *From Memory to Written Record, England 1066–1307* (London, 1979).

Peter Clemoes and Kathleen Hughes (eds.), *England before the Conquest* (Cambridge, 1971).

Helen Clover and Margaret Gibson (eds.), *The Letters of Lanfranc, Archbishop of Canterbury* (Oxford, 1979).

P. Crummy, 'The System of Measurement used in Town Planning from the Ninth to the Thirteenth Centuries', *Anglo-Saxon Studies in Archaeology and History 1* (*BAR* Brit. ser. 72 : Oxford, 1978) pp. 169–84.

Wendy Davies and Hayo Vierck, 'The contexts of the Tribal Hidage: Social Aggregates and Settlement Patterns, *Frühmittelalterliche Studien 8* (1974), pp. 223–93.

H.W.C. Davis, *Regesta Regum Anglo-Normannorum* 1 (Oxford, 1913).

R.H.C. Davis, 'The Norman Conquest', *History* 51 (1966), pp. 279–86.

R.H.C. Davis, *The Normans and their Myth* (London, 1976).

R.H.M. Dolley, 'Some Reflections on Hildebrand Type A of Aethelred II', *Antikvariskt Arkiv* 9 (1958), pp. 1–41.

R.H.M. Dolley (ed.), *Anglo-Saxon Coins* (London, 1961), including 'The Chronology of the Coins of Alfred the Great', pp. 77–95 (with C.E. Blunt) and 'The Reform of the English Coinage under Eadgar', pp. 136–68 (with D.M. Metcalf).

R.H.M. Dolley, *Anglo-Saxon Pennies* (London, 1964).

R.H.M. Dolley, *Viking Coins of The Danelaw and of Dublin* (London, 1965).

R.H.M. Dolley, *The Norman Conquest and the English Coinage* (London, 1966).

R.H.M. Dolley, 'The Coins', *Archaeology of Anglo-Saxon England*, ed. D.M. Wilson (London, 1976), pp. 249–72.

R.H.M. Dolley, Many contributions to *BNJ, Num. Chron.*, and to the Sylloge of Coins of the British Isles.

A. Dornier (ed.), *Mercian Studies* (Leicester, 1977).

D.C. Douglas, *The Social Structure of Medieval East Anglia* (Oxford, 1927).

D.C. Douglas, *Feudal Documents from the Abbey of Bury St Edmunds* (Brit. Acad. Records of Social and Economic History VIII, London, 1932).

D.C. Douglas, *William the Conqueror* (London, 1964).

D.C. Douglas, *The Norman Achievement* (London, 1969).

R. Drögereit, 'Gab es eine angelsächsische Königskanzlei?', *Archiv für Urkundenforschung* 13 (1935), pp. 335–436.

D.N. Dumville, 'The Anglian Collection of Royal Genealogies and Regal Lists', *Anglo-Saxon England* 5 (1976), pp. 23–50.

D.N. Dumville, 'The Aetheling : a Study in Anglo-Saxon Constitutional History', *Anglo-Saxon England* 8 (1979), pp. 1–33.

W. Endter (ed.), *König Alfreds des Grossen Bearbeitung der Soliloquien des Augustinus*, Bibl. der Ang.-Sächs. Prosa XI (Hamburg 1922).

Ethelweard, *The Chronicle of Ethelweard,* ed. A. Campbell (London, 1962).

H.P.R. Finberg, *Tavistock Abbey* (Cambridge, 1951).

H.P.R. Finberg, *Lucerna* (London, 1964).

H.P.R. Finberg, *The Early Charters of Wessex* (Leicester, 1964).

H.P.R. Finberg, *West Country Historical Studies* (Newton Abbot, 1969).

H.P.R. Finberg, *The Early Charters of the West Midlands,* 2nd ed. (Leicester, 1972).

H.P.R. Finberg, *The Formation of England* (London, 1974).

R.W. Finn, *The Domesday Inquest and the Making of Domesday Book* (London, 1961)

R.W. Finn, *The Liber Exoniensis* (London, 1964).

R.W. Finn, *The Eastern Counties* (London, 1967).

Florence of Worcester, *Chronicon ex Chronicis,* ed. B. Thorpe (London, 1848).

R. Flower, 'The Test of the Burghal Hidage', *London Medieval Studies* 1 (1937), pp. 60–4.

E.A. Freeman, *History of the Norman Conquest* (six vols. and index, London, 1867–79, etc.).

V.H. Galbraith, 'Monastic Foundation Charters of the Eleventh and Twelfth Centuries', *Cambridge Historical Journal* 4 (1934), pp. 205–22, 296–8.

V.H. Galbraith, *An Introduction to the Use of the Public Records* (Oxford, 1934).

V.H. Galbraith, *Studies in the Public Records* (London, 1948).

V.H. Galbraith, *The Making of Domesday Book* (Oxford, 1961).

V.H. Galbraith, *Domesday Book, its Place in Administrative History* (Oxford, 1974).

M. Gelling, 'The Chronology of English Place-Names', *BAR* Brit. Ser. 6 (1976) pp. 93–101.

M. Gelling, *The Early Charters of the Thames Valley* (Leicester, 1979).

M. Gibbs (ed.), *Early Charters of the Cathedral Church of St Paul, London* (Camden 3rd Series 48, London, 1939).

J. Gillingham, *The Kingdom of Germany in the High Middle Ages (Historical Association G77, 1971).*

A. Giry, *Manuel de diplomatique* (Paris, 1894).

A. Gransden, *Historical Writing in England c. 550 to c. 1307* (London, 1974).

A.W. Haddan and W. Stubbs (eds.), *Councils and Ecclesiastical Documents,* 3 vols. (Oxford, 1869–71).

H. Hall, *Studies in English Official Historical Documents* (Cambridge, 1908).

N.E.S.A. Hamilton (ed.), *Inquisitio Comitatus Cantabrigiensis* (London, 1876).

F.E. Harmer (ed.) *Select English Historical Documents of the Ninth and Tenth Centuries* (Cambridge, 1914).

F.E. Harmer, *Anglo-Saxon Writs* (Manchester, 1952).

K. Harrison, *The Framework of Anglo-Saxon History to AD 900* (Cambridge, 1976).

C.R. Hart, *The Early Charters of Eastern England* (Leicester, 1966).

C.R. Hart, *The Hidation of Northamptonshire* (Leicester, 1970).

C.R. Hart, 'The *Codex Wintoniensis* and the King's *Haligdom',* *Land Church, and People,* ed. J. Thirsk (Reading, 1970).

C.R. Hart, 'The Tribal Hidage', *TRHS* 21 (1971), pp. 133–57.

C.R. Hart, 'Danelaw Charters and the Glastonbury Scriptorium', *Downside Review* 90 (1972), pp. 125–32.

C.R. Hart, 'Athelstan "Half King" and his Family', *Anglo-Saxon England* 2 (1973), pp. 115–44.

C.R. Hart, *The Hidation of Cambridgeshire* (Leicester, 1974).

C.R. Hart, *The Early Charters of Northern England and the North Midlands* (Leicester, 1975).

S. Harvey, 'Royal Revenue and Domesday Terminology', *Econ. HR* 20 (1967), pp. 221–8.

S. Harvey, 'Domesday Book and Its Predecessors', *EHR* 86 (1971), pp. 753–73.

S. Harvey, 'Domesday Book and Anglo-Norman Governance', *TRHS* 25 (1975) pp. 175–93.

C.H. Haskins, *Norman Institutions* (New York, 1918, reprinted 1960).

H. Hearder and H.R. Loyn (eds.), *British Government and Administration* (Cardiff, 1974).

T.A. Heslop, 'English Seals from the Mid-Ninth Century to 1100', *J. Brit. Arch. Ass.* cxxxiii (1980), pp. 1–16.

D. Hill, 'The Burghal Hidage, the Establishment of a Text', *Medieval Archaeology* 13 (1969), pp. 84–92.

D. Hill and M. Jesson, *The Iron Age and its Hillforts* (Southampton, 1971).

D. Hill (ed.), *Ethelred the Unready, BAR* Brit. ser. 59 (Oxford, 1978).

W.S. Holdsworth, *A History of English Law,* vol. 1. (London, rev. edn 1956).

C.W. Hollister, *Anglo-Saxon Military Institutions on the Eve of the Norman Conquest* (Oxford, 1962).

C.W. Hollister, *The Military Organisation of Norman England* (Oxford, 1965).

C.W. Hollister, 'The Origins of the English Treasury', *EHR* 93 (1978), pp. 262–75.

A. Hughes, C.G. Crump and C. Johnson (eds.) *The Dialogue of the Exchequer* (Oxford, 1902).

N. Hurnard, 'The Anglo-Norman Franchises', *EHR* 64 (1949), pp. 289–327 and 433–60.

Eric John, 'War and Society in the Tenth Century: the Maldon Campaign', TRHS (1977), pp. 173–95.

J.E.A. Jolliffe, *Pre-feudal England: the Jutes* (Oxford, 1933, repr. 1962).

J.E.A. Jolliffe, *The Constitutional History of Medieval England* (Oxford, 1939).

K. Jost, *Wulfstanstudien* (Swiss Studies in English, vol. 23), (Berne, 1950).

K. Jost, *Die 'Institutes of Polity, Civil and Ecclesiastical'*, (Swiss Studies in English, vol. 47, Berne, 1959).

J.M. Kemble, *Codex Diplomaticus Aevi Saxonici*, 6 vols. (London, 1839–48).

N.R. Ker, 'Hemming's Cartulary : a Description of the two Worcester Cartularies in Cotton Tiberius A xiii, *Studies in Medieval History presented to Frederick Maurice Powicke*, ed. R.W. Hunt, W.A. Pantin, and R.W. Southern (Oxford, 1948), pp. 49–75.

N.R. Ker, *Catalogue of Manuscripts containing Anglo-Saxon* (Oxford, 1957).

F. Kern, *Kingship and Law in the Middle Ages* (trs. S.B. Chrimes : Oxford, 1939).

S.D. Keynes, *Studies on Anglo-Saxon Royal Diplomas*, 2 vols., unpublished Fellowship thesis, Trinity College, Cambridge (1976).

S.D. Keynes, *The Diplomas of King Aethelred 'the Unready', 978–1016* (Cambridge, 1980).

E. King, 'Domesday Studies', *History* 58 (1973), pp. 403–9.

D. Knowles, *The Monastic Order in England* (Cambridge 1950, 2nd ed. 1963).

L.M. Larson, *The King's Household in England before the Norman Conquest* (Madison, 1904).

W. Levison, *England and the Continent in the Eighth Century* (Oxford, 1946).

K.J. Leyser, 'Henry I and the Beginnings of the Saxon Empire', *EHR* 83 (1968), pp. 1–32.

K.J. Leyser, 'The German Aristocracy from the Ninth to the Twelfth Century', *Past and Present* 41 (1968), pp. 25–53.

K.J. Leyser, *Rule and Conflict in an Early Medieval Society : Ottonian Saxony* (London, 1979).

F. Liebermann, The National Assembly in the Anglo-Saxon Period (Halle, 1913).

H.R. Loyn, 'The Term *Ealdorman* in the Translations Prepared at the Time of King Alfred', *EHR* 68 (1953), pp. 513–25.

H.R. Loyn, 'Gesiths and Thegns in England from the Seventh to the Tenth

Century', *EHR* 70 (1955), pp. 529–49.

H.R. Loyn, *Anglo-Saxon England and the Norman Conquest* (London, 1962).

H.R. Loyn, *The Norman Conquest* (London, 3rd edn 1982).

H.R. Loyn, *Alfred the Great* (Oxford, 1967).

H.R. Loyn, *A Wulfstan Manuscript* (Copenhagen, 1971).

H.R. Loyn, 'Church and State in England in the Tenth and Eleventh Centuries', *Tenth-Century Studies,* ed. D. Parsons (Chichester, 1975) pp.94–102.

H.R. Loyn, *The Vikings in Britain* (London, 1977).

H.R. Loyn, 'England and Wales in the Tenth and Eleventh Centuries', *WHR* 10 (1981), pp. 283–301.

B.D. Lyon, 'The Money Fief under the English Kings', *EHR* 66, 1951, pp. 161–93.

B.D. Lyon, *A Constitutional and Legal History of Medieval England* (New York, 1960).

C.S.S. Lyon, 'Historical Problems of Anglo-Saxon Coinage' (presidential addresses) *BNJ* 36–38 (1967–69).

F.W. Maitland, *Domesday Book and Beyond* (Cambridge, 1897, revd ed. E. Miller, 1960).

F.W. Maitland, *Collected Papers,* ed. H.A.L. Fisher (Cambridge, 1911).

F.W. Maitland, *Selected Historical Essays,* ed. H.M. Cam (Cambridge, 1957).

J.F.A. Mason, *William I and the Sussex Rapes* (London, Hist. Ass., 1966),

R. McKitterick, *The Frankish Church and the Carolingian Reforms 789–895* (London, 1977).

A. Meaney, *A Gazetteer of Early Anglo-Saxon Burial Sites* (London, 1964).

D.M. Metcalf, 'The Ranking of Mints : Numismatic Evidence from the Reign of Ethelred II', *Ethelred the Unready : Papers from the Millenary Conference,* ed. D. Hill, *BAR* Brit. Ser. 59 (1978), pp. 159–212.

E. Miller, *The Abbey and Bishopric of Ely* (Cambridge, 1951).

W.A. Morris, *The Medieval English Sheriff to 1300* (Manchester, 1927).

A.S. Napier and W.H. Stevenson (eds.) *The Crawford Collection of Early Charters and Documents* (Oxford, 1895).

J.L. Nelson, 'The Problem of King Alfred's Royal Anointing', *J. Ecclesiastical History* 18 (1967), pp. 145–63.

J.L. Nelson, 'Inauguration Rituals', *Early Medieval Kingship,* ed. P.H. Sawyer and I.N. Wood (Leeds, 1977).

J.L. Nelson, 'Kingship, Law and Liturgy in the Political Thought of Hincmar of Rheims', *EHR* 92 (1977) pp. 241–79.

E. Okasha, *A Handlist of Anglo-Saxon Non-Runic Inscriptions* (Cambridge, 1971).

T.J. Oleson, *The Witenagemot in the Reign of Edward the Confessor* (Toronto, 1955).

M.B. Parkes and A.G. Watson (eds.), *Medieval Scribes, Manuscripts and Libraries : essays presented to N.R. Ker* (London, 1978).

J. Le Patourel, 'The Norman colonization of Britain', *I Normanni e la loro espansione in Europa,* (Spoleto, 1969).

J. Le Patourel, *The Norman Empire* (Oxford, 1976).

J. Le Patourel, 'The Norman Conquest 1066, 1106, 1154?', *Proceedings of the Battle Conference* (1978), ed. R.A. Brown, pp. 103–20.

T.F.T. Plucknett, *A Concise History of the Common Law* (London, 1956).

C. Plummer (ed.), *Two of the Saxon Chronicles Parallel,* 2 vols. (Oxford 1892–9), on the basis of an edition by J. Earle, reprinted with additional material by D. Whitelock 1952.

F. Pollock and F.W. Maitland, *The History of English Law before the Time of Edward I, 2* vols. (Cambridge, 1895 2nd edn 1968).

R.L. Poole, 'Seals and Documents', *Proc. Brit. Acad.* ix (1919), pp. 334–5.

O. Posse, *Die Siegel der deutschen Kaiser und Könige* (Two vols., Dresden 1909–13).

J.O. Prestwich, 'War and Finance in the Anglo-Norman State', *TRHS* (1954), pp. 18–44.

J.O. Prestwich, 'Anglo-Norman Feudalism and the Problem of Continuity', *Past and Present* (1963) 26 39–57.

P. Rahtz, 'The Saxon and Medieval Palace at Cheddar, Somerset – an Interim Report', *Medieval Archaeology,* 6–7 (1962–3), pp. 53–66.

F. Ranger (ed.), *Prisca Munimenta* (London, 1973); including four of P. Chaplais's most influential essays. (See Chaplais above).

H.G. Richardson and G.O. Sayles, *Law and Legislation from Æthelbert to Magna Carta* (Edinburgh, 1966).

A.J. Robertson (ed.), *Anglo-Saxon Charters* (Cambridge, 1939).

A Rogers (ed.), *The Making of Stamford* (Leicester, 1965).

H. Roseveare, *The English Treasury* (London, 1969).

J.H. Round, *Feudal England* (London, 1895. Reissued 1964).

W.B. Sanders, *Facsimiles of Anglo-Saxon Manuscripts,* 3 vols, Ordnance Survey (Southampton 1878–84).

P.H. Sawyer, *Anglo-Saxon Charters. An Annotated List and Bibliography* RHS (London, 1968).

P.H. Sawyer, 'Bharters of the Reform Movement: The Worcester Archive', *Tenth-Century Studies*, ed. D. Parsons (Chichester, 1975), pp. 84–93.

P.H. Sawyer (ed.), *English Medieval Settlement* (London, 1976, 2nd ed. 1979).

P.H. Sawyer and I.N. Wood (eds.), *Early Medieval Kingship* (Leeds, 1977).

P.H. Sawyer, *From Roman Britain to Norman England* (London, 1978).

P.H. Sawyer, *Charters of Burton Abbey* (London, 1979).

P.E. Schramm, *A History of the English Coronation*(Oxford, 1937).

Simeon of Durham, *Historia Regum,* ed. T. Arnold, Rolls Series (London, 1885).

K. Sisam, *Studies in the History of Old English Literature* (Oxford, 1953).

A.H. Smith, *English Place-Name Elements,* two vols., EPNS 25–6 (Cambridge, 1956).

A.P. Smyth, *Scandinavian York and Dublin, I and II* (Dublin, 1975 and 79).

P. Stafford, 'The Reign of Ethelred II, A Study in the Limitations on Royal Policy and Action', *Ethelred the Unready : Papers from the Millenary Conference,* ed. D. Hill, BAR Brit. Ser. 59 (1978), pp. 15–46.

P. Stafford, 'Historical Implications of the Regional Production of Dies under Æthelred II', *BNJ* (1978), pp. 35–50.

P. Stafford, 'The Farm of One Night and the Organization of King Edward's Estates in Domesday Book', *Econ.HR* 33 (1980), pp. 491–502.

P. Stafford, 'The Laws of Cnut and the History of Anglo-Saxon Royal Promises', *Anglo-Saxon England* 10 (1982), pp. 173–90.

D.M. Stenton and L.C. Loyd (eds.), *Sir Christopher Hatton's Book of Seals* (Oxford, 1950).

F.M. Stenton, *The Early History of the Abbey of Abingdon* (Reading, 1913).

F.M. Stenton, *The First Century of English Feudalism* (Oxford, 1932, 2nd edn 1961).

F.M. Stenton, *Anglo-Saxon England* (Oxford, 1943, 3rd ed 1971).

F.M. Stenton, *The Latin Charters of the Anglo-Saxon Period* (Oxford, 1955).

F.M. Stenton (ed.), *The Bayeux Tapestry* (London, 1957).

F.M. Stenton, *Preparatory to Anglo-Saxon England,* ed. D.M. Stenton (Oxford, 1970).

C. Stephenson, *Borough and Town* (Cambridge, Mass., 1933).

W.H. Stevenson, (ed.), *Asser's Life of King Alfred* (Oxford, 1904, rev. ed. D. Whitelock, 1959).

W. Stubbs (ed.), *Memorials of St Dunstan, Archbishop of Canterbury,* Rolls Series (London, 1874).

Dom T. Symons (ed.), *The Regularis Concordia* (London, 1953).

J. Tait, *The Medieval English Borough* (Manchester, 1936).

C.S. Taylor, 'The Origin of the Mercian Shires', *Gloucestershire Studies,* ed. H.P.R. Finberg (Leicester, 1957), pp. 17–45.

G. Tessier, *Diplomatique royale française* (Paris, 1962).

B. Thorpe, *The Homilies of the Anglo-Saxon Church,* two vols. (London, 1844–6).

B. Thorpe (ed.), *Florentii Wigorniensis Monachi Chronicon ex Chronicis,* 2 vols. (London, 1848–9).

B. Thorpe, *Diplomatarium Anglicum Aevi Saxonici* (London, 1865).

B. Tierney and P. Lineham (eds.), *Authority and Power* (Cambridge, 1980).

T.F. Tout, *Chapters in the Administrative History of Medieval England,* 6 vols. (Manchester, 1920–33).

W. Ullmann, *Principles of Government and Politics in the Middle Ages* (London, 1961).

W. Ullmann, *The Carolingian Renaissance and the Idea of Kingship* (London, 1969).

W. Ullmann, *Law and Politics in the Middle Ages*: *Introduction to the Sources of Medieval Political Ideas* (London, 1975).

H. Vollrath-Reichelt, Königsgedanke und Königtum bei den Angelsachsen bis zur Mitte des 9. Jahrhundert, *Kölner historische Abhandlungen* 19 (Cologne and Vienna, 1971).

J.M. Wallace-Hadrill, *The Long-Haired Kings and Other Studies in Frankish History* (London, 1962).

J.M. Wallace-Hadrill, *Early Germanic Kingship in England and on the Con-*

tinent (Oxford, 1971).

J.M. Wallace-Hadrill, *Early Medieval History* (Oxford, 1975).

A.B. White, *The Making of the English Constitution* 2nd ed. (New York, 1925).

D. Whitelock (ed.), *Anglo-Saxon Wills* (Cambridge, 1930).

D. Whitelock (ed.), *Sermo Lupi ad Anglos* (London, 1939, 3rd ed. 1963).

D. Whitelock (ed.), *English Historical Documents c. 500–1042* (London, 1955, 2nd ed. 1979).

D. Whitelock, 'The Dealings of the Kings of England with Northumbria in the Tenth and Eleventh Centuries', *The Anglo-Saxons,* ed. P. Clemoes (London, 1959), pp. 870–88.

D. Whitelock (ed.) (with D.C. Douglas and S.I. Tucker), *The Anglo-Saxon Chronicle,* a rev. trs. (London, 1961).

D. Whitelock (ed.) (with Neil Ker and Lord Rennell) *The Will of Æthelgifu* (Roxburghe Club, Oxford, 1968).

D. Whitelock, 'Some Charters in the Name of King Alfred', *Saints, Scholars and Heroes: Studies in Medieval Culture in Honour of Charles W. Jones,* ed. M.H. King and W.M. Stevens, two vols. (Minnesota, 1979) i, pp. 77–98.

Ann Williams, 'Some Notes and Considerations on Problems connected with the English Royal Succession, 860–1066', *Proceedings of the Battle Conference on Anglo-Norman Studies* I (Ipswich, 1979).

Ann Williams, *'Princeps Merciorum gentis,* the Family, Career and Connections of Ælfhere, Ealdorman of Mercia, 956–83', *Anglo-Saxon England 10* (1982), pp. 143–72.

D.M. Wilson (ed.), *The Archaeology of Anglo-Saxon England* (London, 1976).

P. Wormald, 'The Uses of Literacy in Anglo-Saxon England and its Neighbours', *TRHS* 27 (1977), pp. 95–114.

P. Wormald, Æthelred the Lawmaker', *Ethelred the Unready : papers from the Millenary Conference,* ed. D. Hill, *BAR,* Brit. Ser. 59 (1978), pp. 47–80.

B.A.E. Yorke, *Anglo-Saxon Kingship in Practice, 400–899* (unpublished thesis, Exeter, 1978).

Index

Abbotsbury 149, 153, 154
Abernethy 181
Abingdon 103, 107
Adamnan of Iona, biographer of
    St Columba 25
Æ *see also under* E (Ethelbert,
    Ethelred, Ethelwold *etc.*) *when
    those concerned are better
    known under that form. Also
    under* A *for* Alfred and
    Athelstan.
Ægelric, b. of Chichester 194
Ælfgar, earl 114, 115
Ælfgæt, sheriff 114
Ælfgifu, w. of Eadwig 91
Ælfheah, b. of Winchester 107
Ælfhere, ealdorman of Mercia 97,
    143
Ælfric, abbot of St Albans, later
    archb. of Canterbury 110
Ælfric, abbot of Eynsham and
    Cerne Abbas 84–7, 100
Ælfric, ealdorman of Hampshire
    97
Ælfwald, thegn 89, 111
Ælfwine, grandson of Ealhelm 89
Ælfwine, *scriptor* to Ethelred 109
Ælle, k. of Northumbria 15
Ælle, k. of S. Saxons 6, 24, 25
Æthelflæd, d. of Alfred, w. of
    Ethelred, ealdorman of Mercia
    62, 76, 135, 141
Æthelgeard 140
Æthelgifu, will of 160
Æthelmær, thegn 98

Æthelnoth, ealdorman of Somerset
    75
Æthelsige, s. of Athelstan Half-
    King 132
Æthelsige the Red 140
Æthelweard, ealdorman of the
    'Western Provinces' 97, 132
Æthelwig, abbot of Evesham 181,
    185
Æthelwine, ealdorman of E.
    Anglia 97, 132, 143
Æthelwold, s. of Athelstan Half-
    King 132
Æthelwulf, ealdorman of Berkshire
    76
Æthelwold, s. of k. Ethelred I 90
Agnus Dei 123
Aidan, b. of Lindisfarne 47
Aix-la-Chapelle 27
Alcuin of York 16, 17, 27, 59
alderman 151–2
Alfred, k. of Wessex 8, 10, 31,
    Ch. 3, 81, 84, 90, 93, 115, 131,
    133, 135, 149, 150, 152, 164, 168
Alfred, s. of k. Ethelred 91
Alhred, k. of Northumbria 19
alms 66, 75, 154; plough-alms 160
Amesbury 95, 103
Anastasius, emperor 20
Andover 103, 104
Angevins, courts 94
Angles 6, 25
Anglesey 25, 39
Anglo-Saxons 20, 169
Anglo-Saxon Chronicle 5, 10, 13,

17, 24, 56, 59, 63, 75, 84, 103,
    104, 121, 132, 135, 136, 164,
    167, 189, 190
Anjou 83
Anselm, St, archb. of Canterbury
    183
Apsley 112
archbishops 56–8, 89, 106, 181–2,
    185–6, 189; *see also* Canterbury,
    York, Augustine *etc.*
archives 107
armour 164, 167, 168
Arthur, k. 6
assay 118
Asser, b. of Sherborne 19, 24, 62,
    63, 66, 68, 69, 72–4, 76, 158
Asthall 22
Aston Bampton 109
Athelney 62, 73, 75
Athelstan, b. of Hereford 139, 140
Athelstan Half-King, ealdorman
    125, 132
Athelstan, k, 90. 96, 97, 102, 106,
    122, 135, 137, 142, 146, 147, 158
Athelstan, s. of k. Æthelwulf 29
Athelstan, s. of k. Ethelred 97
Augustine, St, archb. of
    Canterbury 6, 8, 43; Abbey of,
    see Canterbury
Augustine, St, b. of Hippo 69;
    Soliloquies 68, 115
Axminster 103
Aylesford 103

Badon, Mount, battle of 6
baileywick 145
Bamburgh 53
Banwell 55
Barbury 5
baronage 127, 166, 180, 182, 187,
    191; 'honorial' 182
Bath 71, 81, 84, 85, 92, 103, 123,
    189; see of (and Wells) 159
Battle, abbot of 183
Bayeux 178; tapestry 17, 167; *see
    also* Odo
Bede 8, 12, 15, 20, 21, 24, 25, 26,
    28, 38, 39, 40, 43, 47, 50, 52,

59, 69; *Ecclesiastical History* 8,
    38
Bedford 62, 135; shire 112, 119,
    137, 159
Bedwyn 95, 149, 153, 154
Benedictines 84; abbeys 84, 118,
    129, 159, 178; Reformation 96,
    107, 109, 155, 161; *Regularis
    Concordia* 84
Benty Grange 22
Beorhtric, k. of Wessex 26
Beornred, k. of Mercia 16
Beornwulf, k. of Mercia 28
Beowulf 16, 17, 21, 34, 47
Berkhamstead 103
Berkshire 7, 76, 112, 119, 137, 158
Bernicia 7, 16, 23
Beverstone 103
Bewcastle 58
Bible, The 13, 14, 64, 65, 83, 85,
    101
bishops 45, 73, 88, 97, 100, 101,
    102, 106, 111, 113, 130, 139,
    143, 146, 154ff., 159, 160, 171,
    186, 189, 195; bishoprics 110
    (episcopal sees), 114, 149, 195;
    coadjutor b. 160; Norman 181–
    2; *see also* archbishops,
    Winchester, *etc.*
Bjorn 128
bloodprice 45, 47, 53, 147; *see also*
    wergeld
Boethius 69, 87
Boniface, St, archb. of Mainz 47
bookland 66, 107, 113, 155, 180
borh 46, 48, 53, 65, 127, 147
borough 71, 124, 135ff., 143,
    148ff., 193; burgage 151, 152,
    153; revenues 149; *see also* court
Bretwalda 24, 25, 28
bridges 32, 33, 34, 111, 155, 164,
    165
Brighthampton 109
Brihtwulf, ealdorman of Essex 75
Bristol 55, 148, 182
Brixworth 57, 58
Broomfield 22
Bryning, sheriff 140

Buckingham 71, 135, 188; shire 8, 22, 119, 159, 188
Burchard of Worms 83, 87
Burghal Hidage 70-2
burh 33, 34, 71, 122, 149, 150; *see* borough
burial 92, 93, 144, 154, 159; ship 19-22
Burpham 71
Bury St Edmunds 129, 159, 163, 189; abbot of 181
Buttington 75
Byrhtnoth, ealdorman of Essex 89, 120, 132

Cadbury 124
Cædmon 52
Calne 95, 103, 104
Cambridge 135, 148, 149, 153; shire 129, 144, 190, 191, 193
Canterbury 41, 55, 59 (school), 122, 125; diocese 10, 58, 75, 149, 158, 160; archbishops 56, 89, 90, 110, 111, 181, 182, 185, 188, 195; Christ Church 40, 149, 161, 189; St Augustine's 108, 149, 181; *see also* Augustine, Theodore *etc.*
Capet, Hugh 82, 90; Capetians 82, 83, 90
carucage 119, 120, 165
cassati 39
castles 196, 197; *see also* fortifications
Ceadda, b. of York 56
Ceawlin, k. of Wessex 24, 25
Celts 7, 27, 160; Celtic customs 119
Cenwalh, k. of Wessex 15
Cenwulf, k. of Mercia 10, 16, 18, 32
Ceolmund, ealdorman of Kent 75
Ceolwulf I, k. of Mercia 10, 16
Ceolwulf II, k. of Mercia 61
ceorl 51, 167
Cerdic, k. of Wessex 15, 84, 85, 90, 92
chamberlain 118

Chancellor 108, 117, 185, 186
chancery 82, 114, 117, 118
chapter, cathedral 155; monastic 155, 161
Charlemagne 41, 63, 82, 98, 187
charters 26-7, 30, 32, 38-41, 67, 75-6, 83, 89, 96-8, 102, 106-18, 129-30, 133, 155, 162, 170, 180, 186; coronation 85, 194
Cheddar 96, 103, 104
Chelsea 103
Chertsey 53
Cheshire 10, 62
Chester 62, 76, 81, 85, 96, 123, 125, 135, 144, 148, 153
Cheveley 191
Cheviots 7
Chew 55
Chichester 71, 122, 152; b. of 194
Chilcombe 121
Chilterns 8, 13, 22, 32
Chippenham 61, 95, 103
chirographs 113
Christianity 1, 9, 13, 14, 18, 22, 25, 44, 63, 64, 74; Christian society 88, 89, 135; *see also* conversion
Church, the 14, 25, 27, 44, 52, 56ff., 63, 72, 74, 85, 86, 89, 106, 154ff., 171, 186, 195; and state 82, 89, 91, 104, 105; festivals 104, 183; reform of 178, 181, 196, 197; *see also* clergy
churchscot 160
Cilternsæte (an) 23
Cinque Ports 121, 148, 169
circuits (Domesday commissioners) 187, 189, 190
Cirencester 62, 103
Cissbury 5
Clarendon 181
clas church 55, 56, 160
clergy 102, 155, 160, 187; abbots 181, 194, 195; archdeacons, deacons, deans 161
Clofeshoh 57, 59
Clovis 23

Cnut, k. of England 81, 82, 86, 87, 89, 91, 92, 95, 101, 106, 113, 116, 121, 123, 126, 129, 132, 139, 149, 166, 168, 179; laws 64, 126, 127, 143, 146, 149, 155, 157, 166
coinage (coins) 20, 40-1, 118ff., 122-6, 130, 148, 170-1, 192-4
Colchester 135
Coldingham 53
Columba, St 25
comes 32
comitatus 138-40
commissioners (Domesday) 187, 189, 191-2
compensation 4, 15, 44-8, 51-4, 64, 72, 86, 153; *see also* bloodprice, wergeld
compurgation 139, 157
Congresbury 55
consecration 22-3, 47, 85, 104
Constantinople 20, 177
conversion 6, 25, 30, 43-4, 53, 56ff., 62; *see also* Christianity
Cookham 103
Coombe 22
Cornwall 28, 113, 137, 158-9
coronation 23, 81, 84-6, 90-3, 123, 180, 193-4
cottars 189
councils, church 27, 33 (Gumley), 56-9; royal (*see also* witan) 10, 18, 47, 65, 67, 72, 75 (Droitwich), 82, 92, 96, 100-6, 108, 146, 183, 187
counterfeiting 127, 194
Countisbury 62
courts 41-2, 48-9, 51-4, 63, 109, 112-13, 127, 151, 169, 171; bishop's 157-8; borough 142, 148-52, 197; feudal 183, 196; folk 54, 69, 72, 88, 138; hundred 129, 137, 140-4, 147, 150-1, 157, 162-3, 171, 191; local 4, 68, 192; private 128-30, 161-3; public 52, 157, 163; royal 22, 32, 39, 41-2, 47, 66-7, 73, 83, 91, 94ff., 109, 119, 126ff., 138, 154,

176, 179, 183-6, 194, 196-7; shire 68, 72, 76ff., 115, 127, 131, 138-40, 142, 145, 148, 157-8, 188-90, 195-7
Crediton 149, 156, 158
cremation 21-2
Cricklade 34, 55, 70, 71
Cuddesdon 22
Cumbria 85
curia regis 194
currency 40-1, 60, 67, 148, 193-4
Cyneberht, ealdorman 26
Cynethryth, q. of Mercia, w. of Offa 41
Cynewulf, k. of Wessex 18, 26

Danegeld 120-1, 125, 127, 138
Danelaw 62, 90, 119, 125, 127, 144-5, 159
Danes 12, 28-9, 55, 60, 61ff., 67, 73-4, 99, 119-21, 132-5, 162-3, 166-7; royal dynasty 21, 81, 120-1
Deben, r. 19
Dee, r. 81, 85
deemsters 144
defence 6, 27-8, 31-4, 40, 66, 70-1, 104, 121, 130, 136, 149, 151-2, 155, 163-9; naval 66, 99, 121, 148, 163-4, 166, 168-9
Deira 7, 16, 51, 56
demesne, royal 40, 187, 189
Denewulf, b. of Winchester 158
Dengie 8
Denmark 116; *see also* Danes
deposition 18, 19
Derby 76, 136, 148; shire 22, 119; *see also* Peak District
desertion (from army) 163-4
designation 17, 18, 97
Devon 56, 59, 62, 119, 137, 158-9
dies (die-cutting) 124-5, 193
dinar 41
diploma 111-13; *see also* charters
Domesday Book 55, 95, 119, 120, 125, 137-9, 165, 170, 176, 180, 181; Inquest and Survey 187ff.; commissioners 187-92

Dorchester (Dorset) 103, 122, 133
Dorchester (Oxon.) 103, 160; b. of
    159; see of 137
Dorset 56, 76, 154, 158
Dover 169
Droitwich, council 75
dues 51, 75, 77, 112, 118, 125,
    130, 146–7, 192; customs 54;
    church 157; feudal 196; royal
    139, 189
Dunfermline 91
Dunstan, St, archb. of Canterbury
    84, 91, 92, 96, 104, 105, 107,
    111, 155
Dunwich, see of 56, 57
Durham 54, 178; castle 183; see of
    St Cuthbert 159, 183, 185
dux 27, 75
dynasties 23, 27–9, 44, 47, 48, 60,
    63, 81, 82, 89, 92, 98, 132

Eadred, k. of Wessex 89, 93, 98,
    107, 109, 135
Eadric, k. of Kent, laws 42, 45
Eadric Streona, ealdorman of
    Mercia 97, 133
Eadric, shire-reeve 195
Eadwig, k. 89, 90, 91–3
ealdorman 25, 27, 47ff., 65–6, 69–
    70, 73–7, 96–7, 99, 100, 102,
    111–12, 124, 130, 132, 135–9,
    143, 145, 150, 165, 171; *see also*
    earls
Ealdred, b. of Worcester, archb.
    of York 158
Ealing 7
earls 150, 157, 165–6, 171;
    rebellion of 182, 183; Saxon 196;
    see also ealdorman
East Anglia 7, 8, 10, 16, 21, 26,
    28, 30, 36, 41, 51, 57, 61, 62,
    67, 84, 96, 97, 131, 135–7, 141,
    148, 159, 166, 186, 195; E.
    Angles 8, 21, 28, 29; dynasty 20,
    26, 28
East Saxons 13, 28, 29
Ebsbury 5
Ecgfrith, k. of Mercia, s. of Offa

10, 16, 22, 27, 47
Eddius Stephanus 38, 54
Edgar, k. 81–2, 84, 88–93, 99,
    101, 102, 106, 108, 109, 111,
    123, 125, 133, 140, 142, 148,
    155, 168, 169; coronation 84,
    91–2
Edgar the Atheling 91, 97
Edington 62, 103
Edith, q., w. of Edward Confessor
    17
Edith, q., w. of Henry I 92
Edmund Ironside 89, 91–3, 97,
    113, 167
Edmund, k. 90, 92–3, 96–7,
    135–6, 140
education 9, 14, 63, 66, 69, 72,
    195; schools 66
Edward Atheling, s. of Edmund
    Ironside 91, 97
Edward the Confessor, k. of
    England 18, 81–2, 91–2, 95–6,
    103, 110, 114–16, 118, 121, 123,
    126, 133, 136, 148, 152, 166,
    168, 170, 176, 183, 185, 189, 194;
    Leges Edwardi Confessoris 145
Edward the Elder, k. of Wessex
    67, 75–6, 90, 93, 107, 120, 123,
    135, 137, 141–2, 158
Edward the Martyr, k. 91, 92
Edwin, abbot of Westminster 114
Edwin, k. of Northumbria 15, 19–
    20, 25, 47
Edwin, s. of Enniaun 139, 140
Egbert, archb. of York 59
Egbert, k. of Kent 40, 41
Egbert, k. of Wessex 10, 16, 24–5,
    28–9, 31, 56, 60, 90
Egbert, s. of Ethelred the Unready
    97
election 101
Elmham 57, 58, 186
Ely 53, 84, 91, 108–10, 129, 144,
    163; abbey of 189, 191, 194; Isle
    of 137
Emma of Normandy, q. 92, 94–5
Eorpwald 18
Eowa 16

Eric Bloodaxe 159
Escomb 58
Essex 6–8, 10, 18, 22, 26, 89, 135, 137, 144, 159, 188, 193; *see also* East Saxons
Ethelbald, k. of Mercia 9, 24, 25, 29
Ethelbert, k. of Kent 8, 10, 15, 24–5, 29, 38, 43, 47, 65; laws 42–4, 51
Ethelbert, St, k. of E. Anglia 26, 28
Ethelhelm, ealdorman of Wiltshire 75
Ethelred, ealdorman of Mercia 62, 76
Ethelred, k. of Mercia 9
Ethelred I, k. of Wessex 29, 31
Ethelred, s. of Moll, k. of Northumbria 19
Ethelred II, the Unready, k. 81, 86–7, 91–3, 95, 97, 101, 109, 115, 122–5, 132, 135, 138, 143–4, 149, 151, 155, 163, 168, 170; laws 143, 159, 192
Ethelwold, St, b. of Winchester 84, 107, 111
Ethelwold, s. of K. Ethelred of Wessex 90
Ethelwulf, k. of Wessex (f. of Alfred) 13, 16, 19, 24, 28–9, 59, 98, 107
Evesham, abbey of 194; abbot of 181, 182, 185, 189
Exbury 5
Exchequer 94, 118, 192–3
exculpation, right of 147
Exeter 71, 103, 122, 125, 141, 146, 148, 154, 158, 182, 186, 189

Faversham 55, 103
fealty 127, 195
fees, knights' 180
Felix, clerk 107
Fenlands 9, 84, 96, 148, 159, 181
fiefs 119, 180, 182; French 83; money-fiefs 183; quotas 181
finance 118–28, 137, 147

fines 32, 48–52, 65, 70, 72, 118, 127, 157, 163–4, 176 (*murdrum*), 196
FitzWimarc, Robert 17
Five Boroughs 89, 135–7, 144, 148
Flanders 83, 177
fleet 99, 168–9
Florence of Worcester 85, 99, 121, 167–8
flymenafyrmth 114, 127
folkright 42–3, 67, 141–2, 171
food-rents 95, 119
Fordwich 149, 169
forests 127–8, 176, 196
forfeit(ure) 46, 48, 53, 65, 163
fortifications 32–4, 66, 71, 73, 76, 111, 127, 135–6, 155, 163–4, 180, 196–7
France 82–3, 85, 90, 169; Frenchmen 190, 191
Frankia 7, 82; Franks 26, 43
frankpledge 147, 196
freemen 4, 18, 31–2, 43, 45, 47ff., 65, 71, 77, 101, 126, 128, 138, 142, 147, 160, 163–4, 167, 176, 180, 189
Frisia 50, 61
Frome 140
fyrd 32, 48, 133, 164; *fyrdwite* 163–5; 'select' fyrd 165

geld 41,119–22, 125, 130, 137–9, 168, 187, 190, 192, 196; *see also* Danegeld, *heregeld*
genealogies 6, 13, 19, 23, 84
Geoffrey, b. of Coutances 179, 185, 194, 197
Germany 82–3, 94, 169; Germans 6–7, 12, 13, 24
gesiths 48ff.
Gildas 6
Gilla 7
Glastonbury 93, 107, 108
Gloucester 5, 10, 93, 103, 104, 135; shire 114, 136
Godric of Stoke 140
Godwin, earl of Wessex 103, 122, 128, 168

Gorm the Old, k. of the Danes 81
Gosfrith, port reeve of London
    177
Grately 146
Gregory the Great, pope 57, 69;
    Cura Pastoralis 68, 84, 115
guilds 149, 151–3; see also peace-
    guilds
Gumley, council of 33
Gummingas 7
Gundulph, b. of Rochester 197
Guthrum, k. 62, 75
Gyrwe 23

Hæsta 7, 13
Haimo (dapifer) 195
Hampshire 5, 18, 59, 112, 116,
    121, 127, 133, 137, 158, 195
Hardicnut, k. 81, 91, 122, 168
Harold II, s. of Godwin, k. of
    England 17, 81, 92, 96, 114–15,
    133, 176; sons of 182
Harrow 7
Harthacnut, k. see Hardicnut
Hastings 7, 13, 26, 71, 82, 122,
    169, 183; Battle of 91, 176, 195
Heabert, k. of Kent 41
Heahmund, b. of Sherborne 72
Henbury 39
Henry I, k. of England 17, 138,
    185, 194
Henry II, k. of England 138, 194
heptarchy 6, 23–4, 48
Hereford 28, 34, 57, 125, 135, 139,
    150, 153, 159, 168; b. of 139,
    155; Gospel bk. 139, 140;
    Minster 140; see of 137; shire
    10, 140
heregeld 121, 168
Herfast, b. of Elmham 185
heriot 166
Hertford 135; Council of 57; shire
    119, 137, 159, 193
Hexham 54, 57
hide 36, 38–41, 67, 71, 100, 111,
    119–22, 137, 141, 158, 164, 167–
    8, 189; County Hidage 120;
    double hide 119; Five-hide units

165, 167; see also Tribal Hidage
Hlothere, k. of Kent 42, 45
housecarl 96, 122, 128, 166
household, royal 96–7, Ch. 3
    passim, 185, 186
Hugh, earl of Chester 188
Hugh of Port-en-Bessin 195
Humber, r. 6, 24, 25, 28, 56, 96,
    124, 136, 159
hundred 54, 114, 119–20, 129, 131,
    137–8, 140ff., 176, 190–1, 196–
    7; men 186; double hundred 145;
    Hundred Ordinance 142
hunting 96, 176
Huntingdon 119, 135; shire 159
hustings 150, 151
Hwicce 10, 23, 27, 57, 89, 135, 159
Hythe 169

Ida, k. of Bernicia 16
Imma, thegn 50
immunities 33, 111
imperium 26; imperatores 28
imprisonment 72, 77
Ine, k. of Wessex 10, 16, 32, 46,
    65, 163; laws 4, 42, 48, 52, 54
infangenetheof 114, 129, 162
inheritance 15, 18, 140, 166, 177;
    partible 23
inquest, sworn 191, 192
Inquisicio Eliensis 189, 191
insignia, royal 22, 116; see
    coronation
Institutes of Polity 86, 88
investiture 22, 23, 90
Investiture Contest 83, 84, 94
Iona 39
Ireland 7, 61; Irish 33
Italy 3, 41, 177–8

Jænberht, archb. of Canterbury
    41
Jarrow 9
John of Worcester 167
judges 88, 187, 194, 196
Judith, w. of Ethelwulf 24
jurisdiction 42, 54–5, 149–52, 189;
    episcopal 157–8; private 161ff.;

see justice, sake and soke
jury, 192; of presentment 144;
juror 191, 194
justice 68, 85–7, 140–7, 196;
administration of 67, 69, 104–6,
126–30, 144–5, 196; ecclesiastical
143, 156–8
justiciar 185

Kennet, r. 55
Kent 6–8, 10, 12, 28–9, 31, 34, 36,
51, 55, 65, 75, 116, 119, 133,
137, 144–5, 149, 153, 158, 164;
kings of 4, 16, 22, 25–6, 28, 45;
laws 42-5
Kineton 89, 111
King's Enham 103
kingship 4–6, 12, 14, 15, 19, 23–4,
27–8, 31, 62–3, Ch. 4, 94, 185;
see also monarchy
Kingston-upon-Thames 85, 90, 92,
103
kinship 4–5, 7, 15, 16, 23, 38, 46,
61, 91; kindred 18, 46, 49–51,
66, 77; royal kindred 13–18, 23,
85, 90, 97
Kirtlington 96, 103

lænland 180
Lambourne 192
land, episcopal 33, 155ff., 194;
folkland 180; grants 38–40, 59,
102, 107, 109–10, 129; royal
135, 149, 180, 189, 193; tenure
43, 151–2, 180, 181, 187–8;
transmission of 26, 38, 40, 110,
112–13, 143; use 55, 149, 165,
187; see also charters
landbooks 108–9, 114
Lanfranc, archb. of Canterbury
89, 179, 181–3, 185–6, 194
language 8, 52, 180; Latin 99, 111,
113, 122, 132, 186–7, 190;
Scandinavian 144; vernacular 43,
48, 63, 83, 98, 105, 111, 113,
116, 186–7, 190, 192, 195
lathes 54–5, 145, 148
law 3, 41ff., 48, 51, 62, 64, 67, 69,

82, 127, 139, 141, 155, 164, 170,
176, 192, 194; biblical 64; canon
157; codes 30, 33, 50, 63–5, 83,
86, 88ff., 102, 144–6; forest 176,
196; of 'North People' 167; of
Northumbrian Priests 161; see
also folkright
Lea, r. 62
leet 119
legates, papal 23, 27, 59
Leges Henrici Primi 127–8
Leicester 58, 136, 148, 159; shire
119
Leofflæd, w. of Thurkil the White
139, 140
Leofgar, b. of Hereford 155
Leofric, earl 122, 166
Leofwine, ealdorman 139
Leofwine of Frome 140
Leofwine, s. of Wulfsige 139
Lew 109
Lewes 71, 122
Liber Eliensis 108
Liber Winton 153
Lichfield 7, 27, 58, 159; see of 137
Lincoln 96, 102, 125, 136, 148,
152–3; shire 119, 136
Lindisfarne 9, 58
Lindsey 7, 9, 16, 23, 58–9
literacy 43–4, 53, 69, 106ff., 110,
118, 155, 187, 190, 195
Liudhard, b. 43
Loire, r. 3
London 10, 12, 26, 41, 45, 50, 56,
58, 62–3, 76, 91–5, 102–4, 121–
3, 125, 137, 146, 148–53, 177,
179, 193; see of 159, 177; Tower
of 186
lordship 5, 30, 54, 133, 162–3,
171, 183
Lydford 34, 71
Lyfing, archb. of Canterbury 110
Lyminge 53, 55
Lympne, r. 73

Magna Carta 85
Magonsætan (Magonsæte) 10, 23,
28, 57, 135, 159

Maine 178, 182
Maldon, Battle of 120, 132, 167
Malmesbury 71, 93, 103
Man, Isle of 25, 39, 145
manentes 39
Matilda 17
manors 149, 151, 160, 188, 189;
    royal 118, 141
mansæ 39
mansiones 39
manumission 52
Margaret, w. of Malcolm
    Canmore, k. of Scots 91
marriage 4, 26, 51, 131, 139
Maugersbury 5
Maurice (chancellor), b. of
    London 186
Maximus, pope 67
mercenaries 182
Mercia 8–10, 30, 32–6, 39–41, 46–
    7, 50, 57, 61–2, 76–7, 89–92,
    127, 135, 138, 141, 159, 166;
    dynasty 6, 15, 24–6, 41, 47
Mersey, r. 119, 124, 136
Middle Angles 7, 9, 23
Middlesex 7, 119, 137, 159
migration 5, 7, 12, 31
Milton 55
mint 41, 118, 122ff., 145, 148,
    151–3, 171, 193
missionaries 33, 38, 43, 56, 82;
    missions 107
monasteries (monastic houses) 38,
    40, 56, 66, 73, 91, 107–8, 110,
    154, 159–60, 181; monastic
    revival 110, 129; *see also*
    Benedictines
monetagium 193, 194
moneyer 118, 122ff., 150, 151, 193
moot, folk 151; ward-moots 151;
    see courts
Mowbray 185
Mul, br. of k. Cædwalla 46
mund 127, 147, 164
murder 46, 128 (homicide), 157
murdrum 176

Nicholas II, pope 158

Norfolk 57, 136, 188
Norman Conquest 89, 94, 108,
    115, 120, 126, 153, 159, 161,
    164, 169, 175ff., Ch. 7
Normandy 81, 83, 91, 193;
    Normans 106, 150
Northampton 7, 120, 135; shire 57,
    119, 129, 137; Geld Roll 120
Northumbria 7–9, 15, 16, 18, 25–
    6, 40, 46, 50, 56, 61, 67, 75, 77,
    89, 119, 131, 135–6, 147
Norwegians 136
Norwich 125, 148, 153
Nottingham 102, 136, 148; shire
    119

oaths, oath-taking 45, 48, 51, 62,
    72, 85, 101, 126, 142–3, 147,
    157, 176, 190–2, 194
Oda, archb. of Canterbury 90
Odda, ealdorman of Devon 62, 75
Odo, b. of Bayeux 179, 182–3,
    185, 194
Odo, b. of Winchester 118
Odo, goldsmith 193
Offa, k. 9, 10, 22, 26, 27–8, 34,
    39–40, 47, 60, 65; Offa's Dyke
    26, 27
Olney 103
ora 193
ordeal 139, 144, 157
Ordulf, thegn 98
Orkney 145
Orleans 83
Orosius 69
Osbern, b. of Exeter 186
Osburh, m. of Alfred 98
Oshere 23
Oslac, ealdorman of Northumbria
    143
Oslac, grandfather of k. Alfred 98
Osmund (chancellor), b. of
    Salisbury 186
Ostrogoths 13
Oswald, St, b. of Worcester 84,
    111, 160
Oswald, St, k. of Northumbria 15,
    23, 25, 47

Oswaldslaw 163
Oswin, k. of Deira 47
Oswy, k. of Northumbria 9, 15, 25, 47
Otto the Great 82
Ouse, r. 62
outlawry 105–6, 127–8, 138, 142, 151
Oxford 62, 71, 103, 135, 148, 153, 188; shire 7, 22, 109, 119, 159

Paris 83
parish 181; system 58–60
peace-guilds 142, 146; special 143
Peada 23, 39
Peak District 8
penalties 42, 45, 48, 51, 72, 105, 125, 142–3, 145, 157, 161, 163–4; *see also* fines, *fyrdwite*, punishment
penance 157
Penda of Mercia 9, 15, 16, 23, 25, 39
Penge 8
Pennines 6
Peppin 82
Peterborough 84, 129, 163, 181, 189; Soke of 129, 137, 163
Peter's Pence 195
Philip VI of France 90
Picts 9, 25, 55
Pilheard 32
Pinnenden Heath 194
place-names 7–8, 53
pleas, dominical 127; of hundreds, boroughs 196; land 185, 187, 194; royal 127–8
population 151–3
Portchester 71
Portskewett 96
priests 98, 102, 109–10, 131, 152, 157, 160–1, 188, 191
principes 25
Pucklechurch 90
punishment 46, 105; corporal 5, 42, 45, 52–3, 143, 162; *see also* penalties, fines
Pybba 16

Rænbald, priest 188
Ramsbury, see of 137, 158
Ramsey 84, 181
Ranig, ealdoman 139
Ranulf Flambard, b. of Durham 185–6, 197
rapes of Sussex 145, 148
Redwald (Rædwald), k. of East Anglia 8, 15, 18, 20, 25
reeve (*gerefa*) 40, 45, 48, 52, 66, 69, 74, 77, 88, 99, 131, 133, 135, 139, 141, 144–7, 152, 171, 186, 191–2; royal 66, 133, 144–5, 152; shire 133, 135, 139, 171, 195; town 45
Regenbald, clerk to Edward Confessor 185
reguli 23, 27
relevamentum 166
relics 109
renders, annual 32, 40, 74, 112; food 39, 95; *see also* taxation
Rendlesham 20
revenue 66, 125, 189, 193, 196; *see also* dues, renders, taxation *etc.*
Rhine, r. 7
Ribble, r. 119
Richard fitzNigel, b. of London 192
Richard, reeve at Cheveley 191
ridings 136, 145, 148
rights, bishop's 160; borough right 150–1; burial 160; coinage 126, 149; franchisal 162–3; of freemen 147; gallows 162; heriot 166–7; land 110, 113, 139–40, 150, 171, 176, 180, 189, 192; manorial 54–5, 129–30; royal 127–30, 135, 138, 153, 174, 176, 180; *see also* folkright, jurisdiction, justice, law
Ripon, bishops 56, 57
Robert Bloet, chancellor 186
Robert of Mortain 188
Rochester 27, 55–6, 58, 75, 122, 149, 158, 189; b. of 74, 197
Roger, b. of Salisbury 185
Roger, earl of Hereford 185

Rome 24, 154; Church of 57, 66, 75; Empire 3, 52; Papacy 157–8, 195
Romney 169; marsh 71
Rouen 179
Rutland 119, 137
Ruthwell 58

St Albans 110
St Germans 158
St Paul's, cathedral 93, 151
sake and soke 114, 129, 150, 162, 171; see also soke
Salisbury, (Coombe Bissett) 22
salt 149
Samson of Worcester 197
sanctuary 45, 72, 109, 159
Sandwich 149, 169
satraps 12
Scandinavians 5, 10, 33, 60–1, 120, 126, 165, 168
sceattas 41
scholarship 84; see also literacy, education
scot 114; church-scot 45
Scotland 7, 53, 55, 91, 178, 181; Scottish Isles 61
Scots 25, 85, 92
scrinarius 109
scriptorium 107, 109, 117
scutage 183
seals, Great 117, 179; royal 115–17, 179, 186
Seaxneat 13
secretariat 106ff., 116, 130, 186–7, 190
Sedulius 87
seisin 143
Selsey 58, 158
Severn, r. 10, 27, 30, 103, 104, 122
service 40, 48, 139; knight's 180ff.; military 32ff., 48–9, 71, 99, 111, 112, 127, 163ff., 180ff., 197; see also fief
settlement, of land 6–8, 54, 133, 149, 159, 177–8, 181, 185; urban 71
Shaftesbury 71, 122

Sherborne 58, 72, 93, 158
sheriff 114, 133, 138–40, 147, 163, 186, 191, 194–6
Sherston 167
shipsoke 168
shire 53–6, 60, 67, 70, 75, 77, 101, 114, 117, 120, 131ff., 145, 147, 149, 153, 158–9, 165, 171, 176, 188–9, 194–7; moot 115, 117; see also courts
Shrewsbury 125, 135
Shropshire 10
Sicily 177, 178
Sigebert, k. of E. Anglia 18, 21
Sigeric, archb. of Canterbury 120
silver 67, 73, 95, 118, 121, 123, 125–6, 193; coins 125–6, 193; penny 123, 193; see also coinage, currency, wealth
Sittingbourne 116
Siward, earl 122, 133, 166
slander 127
slavery, slaves 5, 42, 49, 51ff., 69, 73, 189
Snape 22
soke 114, 129, 150, 152, 162, 171; soke-land 54; sokemen 189
Solent, the 103
Somerset 55–6, 59, 112, 158–9, 182, 195
Somerton 55, 103, 133
Southampton 6, 41, 71, 103, 122
South Saxons 13, 28–9
Southwark 71
Spain 3, 177
Stafford 62, 135
Stamford 136, 137, 148
Stamford Bridge, Battle of 168
Stigand, archb. of Canterbury 17
Stoke 140
Sturry 53
subreguli 23, 27
succession 15-19, 23, 48, 81, 85, 90ff., 97, 177
Sudbury 119
Suffolk 19, 22, 57, 129, 136, 188, 193
Surrey 8, 28–9, 53, 76, 119, 137,

158
Sussex 5, 7, 8, 28, 34, 38, 76, 133,
    137, 145, 158
Sutton Hoo 19–22
Sweyn, s. of earl Godwin 128
Swithwulf, b. of Rochester 74
synod 18, 52, 56, 58, 64, 102, 195;
    see also Whitby

Tamar, r. 10
Tamworth 7, 34
Taplow 22
Taunton 192
Tavistock 181
taxation, 41, 66-7, 77, 87, 114,
    118ff., 130, 144, 189–90
team 114, 129, 162
Teinfrith, 'church-wright' 114
tenants-in-chief 180–2, 187–90, 194
tenure *see* land
terra unius familiæ 36
Thames, r. 7, 10, 21, 28–9, 31, 55,
    58, 62, 71, 75, 91, 103–4, 135,
    158–9
Thanet, Isle of 12
theft 7, 44–5, 48, 106, 127, 141,
    146–7, 157, 165; cattle-theft
    142–3, 146–7; thieves 86, 129,
    162–3
thegn 19, 32, 40, 46, 47ff., 59,
    66–9, 73–4, 97–102, 111, 114,
    123, 135, 139–40, 143–5, 148,
    151, 153, 157, 162, 165–7, 171,
    188, 192
Theoderic, goldsmith 117
Theodore of Tarsus, archb. of
    Canterbury 38, 52, 56–8
Thetford 136, 148
Thinghoe 119
third penny 133, 149–50
Thorpe-le-Soke 163
Thunderfield 146
Thurkil the White 139–40
Tilshead 95
tithes 59, 160
tithing 140ff., 165, 176, 196
Tofi of Somerset 195
Tofi the Proud 140

toll 114, 129, 162–3
tort 143
Tostig, s. of Godwin 133
tourn, sheriff's 147
township 146, 148–51; *see also* vill
trade 7, 41, 45, 143, 148–52, 162;
    traders 66
treason 66, 127
treasure trove 127
treasury 41, 118ff., 193
Trent, r. 7, 9
Tribal Hidage 7, 34ff., 53
tributarii 39
tribute 25, 34, 120, 141
trinoda necessitas 33–4
tufa 19

unction 85–6
urbanization 71, 96, 103, 195
    (bishoprics), 197; *see also*
    township *and* settlement
Urki, Danish housecarl 154
Urse of Abetot 195

Vange 8
vengeance 4, 17, 46, 49–50, 52, 77,
    128, 153
vernacular *see* language
vicomtes 196
Vikings 9, 34, 55, 75, 85, 159
vill 118, 143, 146–7, 151, 171, 176,
    190
villeins 189, 191
Visigoths 13
Vita Eadwardi 17

Wærferth, b. of Worcester 68, 115
Waleran, s. of Ranulf 193
Wales 7, 63, 160, 178; border areas
    147, 165; Welsh(men) 52, 76, 85,
    155, 168
Wallingford 71, 116, 152
Walter Gifford 188
Waltham 140
Wantage 76, 103–4, 144
wapentake 54, 120, 137, 142–5,
    148, 163, 171, 176, 192
ward 145

Wardour 67
Wareham 34, 71, 122
Warminster 95
warranty, vouching to 162
Warwick 70, 135; shire 62, 89,
    111, 114
Wash 69, 136
Watchet 71
Watling Street 62, 93, 138, 159
Weald 73
Wearmouth 9
Wedmore 75
Weeke 116
Wellington 140
Wells 158-9
Wendover 188-9
Weohstan, ealdorman 56
wergeld 4, 15, 45-52, 105, 147,
    164, 166-7
Wessex 4, 7-8, 10-12, 15, 24, 28-
    9, 31-2, 34, 36, 45, 48, 51, 54-
    6, 60, 62-3, 67, 70, 75-6, 89,
    103-4, 127, 132-3, 135, 137-8,
    141, 148
Westbury 39
Westminster 92, 103, 110, 114,
    178, 186; *Westminster
    Domesday* 114
West Saxons 12, 26, 34, 36, 56, 67,
    76, 92, 120, 125, 135; dynasty
    12, 24, 89-92
Whitby, Synod 9, 56
Whithorn 58
Wiglaf 28
Wilfrid, St, b. of Ripon and York
    56-7
William, b. of London 177
William Fitzosbern, earl of
    Hereford 177, 179, 183, 185
William I, L., Duke of Normandy
    18, 81-2, 89, 92, 94, 103-4, 116,
    120, 170, 175ff.
William II, k., Rufus 177, 183-5,
    197
William of Malmesbury 75, 178
William of Warenne 188
wills 67, 83, 96, 98, 107-9, 131,
    139, 164, 171
Wilton 55, 71, 133

Wiltshire 5, 22, 55-6, 59, 67, 75,
    95, 112, 119, 133, 137, 158, 164,
    167, 195
Wimborne Minster 93
Winchcombe 103, 136
Winchester 71, 93-6, 103-4, 107,
    110, 118, 122, 125, 127, 148-53;
    bishops 56, 58, 84, 111, 192; Old
    Minster 161; see of 121, 137, 158
Wine, b. of London 56
witan (witenagemot) 18, 52, 66, 72,
    96-8, 100-6, 108-12, 130
witenagemot *see witan*
witness 69-70, 108, 111, 132, 140-
    3, 149, 157, 163; lists 96-8, 112
Woden 13
wool 149
Worcester 30, 39, 58, 99, 111-12,
    114-15, 129, 135, 149, 163, 195;
    bishop of 68, 84-5, 104, 111-12,
    114-15, 158; see of 137, 158-9,
    160-1, 194; shire 114, 119, 122,
    137
Wrekin 8, 13
Wrington, Vale of 55
writ 68, 130, 170; royal 112-18,
    127, 170, 177, 179, 181, 186,
    195; of summons 181-2
Wroughton 28
Wroxeter 62
Wuffingas 20
Wulfhere, s. of Penda 9
Wulfred, archb. of Canterbury 160
Wulfred of Hampshire 74
Wulfstan, archb. of York 86-9,
    101, 157-8
Wulfstan, b. of Worcester 114-15
Wycombe 32
Wye 55
Wye, r. 96
Wynsige, shipman 140

yardland 189
York 96, 125, 136, 144, 148, 150-
    3, 159, 179, 197; archbishops 57,
    59, 86, 89, 153, 181, 195;
    bishops 57; see of 158-60; shire
    119, 136, 144-5; *see also*
    Wulfstan *etc.*